DEMOCRACY WITH A GUN

DEMOCRACY WITH A GUN

America and the Policy of Force

Fumio Matsuo

Translated by David Reese

Stone Bridge Press • *Berkeley, California*

Published by
Stone Bridge Press
P. O. Box 8208
Berkeley, CA 94707
TEL 510-524-8732 • sbp@stonebridge.com • www.stonebridge.com

The word order of Japanese names follows Western usage, family name last.

Text © 2007 Fumio Matsuo.

Originally published in Japanese in 2004 as *Juu o Motsu Minshushugi* by Shogakukan Publishing, Tokyo.

First edition 2007.

Jacket design by Linda Ronan.

Printed in the United States of America.

2012   2011   2010   2009 2008 2007   10 9 8 7 6 5 4 3 2 1

LIBRARY OF CONGRESS CATALOGING-IN-PUBLICATION DATA
Matsuo, Fumio, 1933–
   [Ju o motsu minshu shugi. English]
   Democracy with a gun: America and the policy of force / Fumio Matsuo; translated by David Reese.
       p. cm.
   Includes bibliographical references and index.
   ISBN 978-1-933330-46-4
   1. United States—Politics and government. 2. United States—Foreign relations.
3. Democracy—United States. I. Reese, David, 1958– II. Title.

E183.M2813 2007
320.973—dc22
2007030456

Contents

To My American Readers

As I pen this passage, I recall a night sixty-one years ago, July 19, 1945, and I am filled with deep emotion. At the time I was a student in the sixth grade in Fukui, a city of around one hundred thousand people in the western part of the main Japanese island of Honshu. It was there that I met the "enemy," my life having been spared by a defective bomb during nighttime indiscriminate incendiary raids conducted by 127 B-29 bombers. About one month later, Japan was defeated by the United States. Since then, I have insistently asked two questions: "Why did Japan fight the United States?" and "What kind of place is this country called America?"

This book, *Democracy with a Gun: America and the Policy of Force*, is an English rendition of my book, *Juu o Motsu Minshushugi: Amerika to iu Kuni no Naritachi*. In it, I consider, study, and discuss "this country called America" back to its founding days. It is a product of my more than forty years of journalistic coverage of the United States in a career that began at the foreign news desk of Kyodo News in Tokyo where I monitored Voice of America's live radio broadcast of the balloting at the 1960 Democratic National Convention in Los Angeles. This book also reflects the career of a journalist who carried in his bosom the dream of becoming a foreign correspondent in the United States of America. In that sense I appreciate the good fortune of being able to bring this book, the fruit of my many years of preoccupation with the United States, directly to American readers.

I think Americans who read this book will be startled by a Japanese person discussing the *Mayflower Compact*, analyzing the actions of the

Founding Fathers, and explaining the Second Amendment's place in history. Some readers may also object to the labeling of the United States as a "democracy with a gun."

In response to such reactions, however, I would ask for the reader's understanding of this quote from the author's preface to *Democracy in America* by the French writer Alexis de Tocqueville, known to many as the forefather of foreign analysts of America:

> It is not, then, merely to satisfy a curiosity, however legitimate, that I have examined America; my wish has been to find there instruction by which we may ourselves profit.

Mine is no match for the brilliant sensibility of this twenty-six-year-old French aristocrat who offers a sharp yet fair analysis of American democracy under President Andrew Jackson though having spent a mere nine months traveling in the United States in 1831.

I only wish for American readers to understand that the work of "finding there instruction by which we may ourselves profit" through an examination of America is even more important for Japan in the twenty-first century than it was for France in the early nineteenth century. The modernization of Japan, which began with Commodore Matthew Perry's historic visit in 1853, has been a success. However, since the Meiji Period, modern Japan has imported and reproduced America's materialistic society superficially, but has not understood the essence of America and its democracy. In some respects, these two countries are like ships passing in the night. The most unfortunate evidence of this lack of understanding was the outbreak of war with the United States with the 1941 attack on Pearl Harbor. Nevertheless, the result of the subsequent U.S. occupation of Japan after the end of World War II was that democracy successfully took root in Japan.

The friendly relations that exist between Japan and the United States today are political, economic, military, and social, even spreading into sports, as symbolized by the success of Hideki Matsui, Ichiro Suzuki, and Daisuke Matsuzaka in Major League baseball. There may be no closer bilateral relationship to be found in the history of the world, particularly between two nations with such completely different cultures, histories, and social values.

In the United States, sushi has become a common sight even in college campus cafeterias, baseball fans nationwide are conversant about Red Sox sensation Matsuzaka, and bookstores are selling Japanese *manga*. Yet despite the physical appearance of Japanese elements in American pop culture, do Americans really understand the Japanese psyche or what it means to be Japanese? This question I leave to my American colleagues across the ocean; I will not try to answer it within these pages.

At the same time, in Japan, McDonald's restaurants, Starbuck's Coffee, and Clint Eastwood movies are everywhere to be seen. Yet as is the case in the United States, does the appearance of American elements in Japanese pop culture automatically lead to an understanding of the American psyche? Despite this overwhelming physical presence, are not the Japanese really still perpetuating a metaphysical state in which America is "so close and yet so far," just as we did prior to the start of World War II? As a Japanese myself, I feel that the burden of understanding the mindset of our American friends rests solely on us. These are the things I have been considering.

Aren't the crossed paths and misunderstandings between the United States and Japan, which gave birth to the unfortunate war, still continuing to this day? This book is the product of the apprehensions I hold as one of the last of a generation who personally experienced the misery of that war and the use of merciless force by America's "democracy with a gun."

To avoid a repeat of past failures in different form, to alleviate by even just a little this mutual misunderstanding, and to contribute to friendly relations between the United States and Japan for the sake of peace in Asia and the world, I wish to take up anew the formidable task of fully grasping the United States from its origins.

Once again, I find inspiration in de Tocqueville, who wrote in his preface:

> I do not know whether I have succeeded in making known what
> I saw in America, but I am certain that such has been my sincere
> desire.

In conveying this intent, I await the frank comments of my American readers.

For my American readers, I need to point out that I have not added any new material to this book in principle since the original version was written in December 2003, but I have adjusted some parts of the translation so as to adopt a more updated voice. Although much has happened since then, particularly with regard to the reelection of President Bush and developments in the Iraq war, I feel that the points presented within have been illustrated adequately enough to support the title and subtitle of this book.

Still, there has been one significant event since then that I feel obliged to mention. In April 2005, I had the distinct honor of meeting retired Air Force Lieutenant Colonel Richard Cole and his family at their home in suburban San Antonio, Texas. As I wrote in the following prologue, Lieutenant Colonel Cole was the first American I ever encountered. I caught a glimpse of his hawkish nose from my school yard as he co-piloted the lead B-25 of the Doolittle Raiders who, at very low altitude, bombed Tokyo and other cities for the first time, only four months after the Pearl Harbor attack.

We achieved our dramatic reunion sixty-three years later by means of an introduction by a mutual friend who saw Lieutenant Colonel Cole's name in the prologue of this book. When we met the first thing he asked was whether or not I had gotten injured during the American bombing. Mr. Cole later drove me to the Admiral Nimitz Memorial War Museum in Fredericksburg, Texas, where I saw an actual B-25 on display. He also invited me to Mystic, Connecticut, for the annual reunion of Doolittle's Raiders that year, where I was asked to deliver a speech at the closing banquet.

Mr. Cole is now over ninety years old, yet we continue to communicate as friends by telephone from time to time. So, while throughout this book I continually emphasize concerns over "crossed paths" that have led to possible misunderstandings between Japan and the United States, I personally feel that I have achieved a level of very happy empathy with Americans, ironically through the first "enemy" I ever encountered.

All things considered, the completion of this book was made possible thanks to the good will and encouragement of many American friends. First among them were the many good neighbors who helped my wife and me when we first set foot on American soil on December 16, 1964. During my ten-year stay as a foreign correspondent posted to New York and Washington, D.C., our first two daughters were born.

I regret that I am unable to list the names of everyone to whom I wish to express my deep appreciation. In their place, I wish to express my gratitude to two deceased individuals who provided me as a journalist with significant raw indicators for my U.S. reporting.

The first is Harvard Professor David Riesman, who, from the heart of East Coast liberalism in 1967, predicted to me in an interview the rise of the "new conservatives," even citing the name of the future President Reagan. The second is Francis Valeo, the former secretary of the Senate who passed away in April 2006 at the age of ninety. While serving as the long-time executive assistant to Democratic Senate majority leader Mike Mansfield, Mr. Valeo was the first to predict to me, immediately following the New Hampshire primary in February 1968, the Nixon victory later that year. Many sections of this book are the result of what these gentlemen and others shared with me about major trends in U.S. politics.

I wish to express my sincere and heartfelt appreciation to David Reese, a bright American living in Japan who, in striving to build a bridge between Japanese and American cultures, took up the challenging and difficult task of translating my book into English. I also would like to express my deep gratitude and appreciation to Urban Lehner, Bob Neff, and Claude Erbsen, three distinguished journalist friends who helped polish and put the finishing touches on Mr. Reese's translation.

I also wish to thank Toyota Motor North America, Inc., which provided the grant that made possible the publication of an English version of a book by a Japanese author about the United States, one of only few such instances in the history of U.S.-Japanese cultural exchanges.

Finally, I wish to express my deepest gratitude to Mr. Peter Goodman, Stone Bridge Press publisher, who possesses an authentic understanding of Japan, to Ari Messer and Nina Wegner for their help with proofing, and to the brilliant editor Mr. David Cole, who took up the immense challenge of clarifying this translation for American readers.

Fumio Matsuo
Tokyo, July 2007

An Encounter as "Enemies"

Face-to-Face with Doolittle's Raiders

My relationship with the United States begins with World War II, not as a combatant but as an unarmed civilian boy encountering American military aircraft attacking the Japanese mainland. During those attacks my family and I came under an indiscriminate nighttime incendiary bomb raid. Thanks to a defective cluster bomb, we survived, though many others were not so fortunate.

When I sat down to write about America, a nation which has opened a Pandora's Box through its invasion of Iraq, but a country upon which Japan cannot turn its back, I found that I had to start by describing my own childhood experiences. In addition, the writing of this account unexpectedly became a search for the true face of America.

I was born in 1933, the eighth year in the reign of Emperor Hirohito. I was eight years old and a second grader in elementary school (one of the institutions redesignated as a "national school" during World War II) at the start of the war with the United States in December 1941. When we suffered defeat in August 1945, I was a twelve years old and in the sixth grade. We were a generation of "little patriots," educated in a militarism that taught us to sing, "Come out, Nimitz, MacArthur!" and to shout slogans excoriating the American and British "devils."

We listened intently as our teachers asked, "Why aren't American soldiers as strong as Japanese soldiers? It's because their seat-style toilets cause their backs to be underdeveloped," and observed, "There will be a lot of rubber delivered from the South Pacific, so all Japanese roads will soon be laid with rubber."

Sitting next to me in class was a young adult student about ten years older than me who was kind enough to teach me math. He had come to Japan from Mongolia to learn Japanese as part of a program to educate and develop the future leaders of the Greater East Asia Co-Prosperity Sphere. In art class, above a map of the United States and Japan was a picture I had drawn for which I won a prize. It showed teams of American and Japanese children in a tug of war. Both my father and grandfather had been career military officers in the former Japanese Imperial Army. As a descendant of samurai, I was quite conscious of this ancestral tradition and I spent my days thinking only of passing the entrance exams for army prep school.

This was also the time when I saw the face of an American for the first time, in a face-to-face encounter with a pilot of the Doolittle Raiders. This encounter happened at a time when Doolittle's Raiders were shaking the Japanese military leadership with surprise air attacks on the mainland with Tokyo as the focal point, igniting a chain reaction that eventually led to the Japanese defeat at Midway.

It was on the afternoon of April 4, 1942, when the smell of victory was still strong in the air following the surprise attack on Pearl Harbor, I had gone out into the schoolyard of Toyama Elementary School. The school was adjacent to the downtown side of the Yamanote commuter loop line near Shin-Okubo Station in central Tokyo. Each day I had walked on my way to school through a neighborhood now known as the large ethnic minority community of Hyakunincho, now part of Tokyo's expansive Shinjuku district. At the time this area was located in a quiet residential neighborhood not far from the huge Toyamagahara Army Training Ground on the other side of the tracks of the Yamanote Line. The are was known as the site of the former residential quarters of the Teppogumi, the 100 elite marksmen in the service of Edo Castle during the reign of the Tokugawa Shogunate.

I had just entered third grade, and it was right after Saturday class had ended at noon for the day. Suddenly, I heard a loud engine noise in the sky from the direction of the Hozen Business High School's Kaijo School to the east and a huge twin-engine airplane, of a kind I had never seen before, appeared with the tip of its tail sticking straight up. Before I knew it, the plane had vanished into the west toward Shinjuku having flown across the top of my eyesight from left to right.

It skimmed along barely above ground level, so low that it just missed hitting the two-story school building. The windproof glass that encased the cockpit allowed me to clearly see the face of the Caucasian crewmember seated inside the right of the aircraft. He wore a dark brown leather flight suit, and his white face and large nose remain burned in my memory. The aircraft fuselage was khaki in color with a blue star on the hull.

I knew this was an American aircraft because after the plane had passed, there was a black barrage of what was probably antiaircraft fire in the eastern sky. Shortly after that, air raid sirens sounded from all directions. Yet, even then, I did not feel the fear of an enemy air raid rising within me but rather a great feeling of exhilaration at having encountered the enormous airplane. To be honest, it was not until later that I became frightened. Returning home I reported the event to my mother who promptly and strongly retorted with a stern look, "Don't speak of this to anyone!" I can still remember the nightmare I had that evening as though it were yesterday.

There is, fortunately, independent evidence to support the notion that the aircraft I saw was the lead aircraft of Doolittle's Raiders on their first attack on Tokyo. In his book *Tokyo no Senso* [The War at Tokyo] published in July 2001, the famous Japanese author Akira Yoshimura writes that on that same day at approximately the same time, as he was flying a kite by the clotheslines on the roof of his home in Nippori, he saw a twin-engine aircraft passing so low in front of his eyes that he "was afraid the kite might become entangled and hurriedly wound in the string." Mr. Yoshimura states that this aircraft was one of the Doolittle Raider B-25s and that the two pilots were wearing orange scarves about their necks. The gist of Yoshimura's testimony is confirmed by military journalist Kazutoshi Hando, who conducted a detailed research of documents from the American side and announced his findings in an article titled "The Aircraft of the First Tokyo Air Raid of April 18th: *The War at Tokyo*, A Historical Investigative Report" in the May 2002 edition of the *Bungei Shunju Monthly*.

According to Mr. Hando, among the sixteen B-25s of the Doolittle Raiders that were scrambled and launched from the aircraft carrier USS *Hornet*, six had flown over Tokyo, including the lead aircraft. Yoshimura has reproduced each plane's flight route on a map, and has determined that the plane that flew by his house was the very same lead aircraft. The path of the lead aircraft is plotted from below Mr. Yoshimura's home in Nippori toward the direction of Nakano, with the neighborhood of my own Toyama National School falling unmistakably along that route. Furthermore, according to Mr. Hando's laborious work, the Caucasian crewmember with the large nose I had spotted was First Lieutenant Richard Cole, the copilot sitting in the right-hand seat. Sadly, I could not see the flight leader in the pilot's seat, Lieutenant Colonel James Doolittle. But above all else, his orange-colored scarf is etched forever in my memory.

Saved by a "Defective Breadbasket"

When I reflect back to that time, my way of life was still comparatively care-free. However, when I entered the fourth grade, the cheerfulness that was boiling in me as a patriotic boy all but disappeared. I was evacuated to my ancestral home in Fukui City, about 300 miles west of Tokyo along the shore of the Sea of Japan. I spent each passing day laboring, even while in school. I gathered up fallen grain from rice paddies and steamed grasshoppers in drum cans, leaving them to dry in the schoolyard before grinding them to powder for use as a meal supplement. Our schoolteachers told us to think of the American bombings in terms of notes on the musical scales so we could distinguish the different types of engine sounds. They also made us practice gymnastics so we could become boy soldiers.

During the third quarter of my fifth-grade year from December 1944 to March 1945, I had gone to celebrate the New Year at Zentsuji City in Kagawa Prefecture on the island of Shikoku across the Inland Sea from the main Japanese island of Honshu. This is where my father was stationed as an Imperial Army colonel and division chief of staff. While there, we came under fire from Grumman F6F Hellcat fighters launched from a U.S. carrier, and we suffered in the days that followed. As an elementary school student I was still not entitled to wear gaiters (lower leg cloth wrappings). Those were reserved for the older junior high students who held a higher social status as the result of having begun military training. These older students also were given the honor of being assigned to cut down pine trees, which we "little patriots" without gaiters hauled down the mountain into town for their pine oil. Not only the junior high students undergoing military training, but we, the "non-combatants," were strafed by machine-gun fire.

When March came, my father moved with his unit to Kochi Prefecture facing the Pacific Ocean in preparation for an American invasion of the main-land. My family visited Konpira Shrine to pray for family safety and Japanese victory and spent the night in the town of Kotohira. That night there was a farewell ceremony for my father heading off to battle, commemorating the medieval Japanese warrior Masashige Kusunoki and his son Masatsura for their faithful service to the emperor, as recorded in the old historical leg-end *Sakurai no Wakare* [Parting at Sakurai]. The next day, when my mother, younger brother, and I had arrived in Takamatsu on our way back to Fukui, the Uko ferry, which connected Takamatsu on the island of Shikoku to Uno on the main island of Honshu, had stopped running due to what appeared to have been a Grumman F6F Hellcat fighter strike. After being made to wait overnight at the waterfront at Takamatsu Port, we finally made our way to Honshu. The cities of Kobe and Osaka, which our train passed through, had become a scorched plain in the space of only four months.

On the night of July 19, 1945, twenty-seven days before the end of the war, Fukui City came under night attack by 127 B-29s. The *History of the Fukui Air Raids*, published in 1987 by volunteers from the Fukui City Hall War Damage Historian Office archives, records that the attack that lasted for about two hours and began about 10:55 p.m. on the night of July 19. Over an area measuring 4.8 kilometers north-south and 3.2 kilometers east-west in Fukui City, 9,466 incendiary bombs of two types and five high-explosive bombs were dropped on a population of 99,940 people. In the end 93.2 percent of the population suffered casualties, 96 percent of the area was destroyed, 1,784 people were killed, and 6,039 suffered injuries. The city had been annihilated.

I came under the bombing at my home, 55 Teyosekami-cho in eastern Fukui City. In the midst of the explosions, which lit up the night sky like mid-day, twelve of us—including my mother, younger brother, sister, and cousins—crossed the Arakawa River Bridge in front of the house and ran for the rice paddies facing Mount Yoshinogadake in the eastern part of the Echizen Plain. The houses lined up along both sides of the bridge's traffic lanes and parapets were burning red. Even now, the vividly glowing spec-tacle of those red-ocher wooden panels within the orange-colored flames is burned in my memory.

When we plopped ourselves down in a sweet-potato field at the dead end of a farm road, we heard the loud sound of something that had fallen from above. A few seconds later, the muddy water from the rice paddies poured like a hard rain upon the handmade anti-air-raid hoods that we wore. It was at this moment that my life was spared. I still recall my mother gripping my right hand so hard that it hurt. By chance, the thirty-eight napalm incendiary rounds packed into an M69 cluster bomb did not disperse 300 meters above ground as intended but dropped into the rice paddy in front of us, producing only a huge splash of muddy water.

For some unknown reason, this kind of cluster bomb had been dubbed the "Molotov Breadbasket" in Tokyo. In recent years, when I have told Americans that I am here today on account of this defective "breadbasket," I have been greeted with looks that are half amused and half serious. But in those moments more than sixty years ago, what I witnessed was no joke. The B-29s were truly relentless. Time after time they circled overhead, blithely exposing their silvery gray shapes, which, I later reflected, resembled large sharks.

After the explosions subsided and daylight began to creep back into the night sky, I caught my first glimpse of human carnage as I made my way back into the city. Mangled corpses lay sprawled out next to the shot-up remains of manure stalls along the farm road, which may have appeared as pillboxes from above. Back in the city, countless charred bodies lay blackened on the streets and in building entranceways. I saw one with his right arm stretching upward as if to grasp the sky. In central Fukui, the floating corpses of men and women covered the moat around Fukui Castle.

As I stood aghast and in shock at the sight of my house, completely destroyed, the only trace two remaining gateposts, a lone B-29 quietly approached, flying low. This aircraft, on a reconnaissance mission to assess battle damage, was clearly visible to everyone. No one tried to run for cover. We simply gazed up at it. Everybody knew that there was nothing left to bomb.

The next day we were able to recuperate at the Senpukuzan Hokyoji temple of the Soto Buddhist sect, located in a deep ravine by Ono City near the border of Gifu Prefecture. We chose this renowned temple—established in A.D. 1229 by the Chinese priest Jakuen Zenji who came to Japan from China where he had spent his days as a follower of the sect's founder, Dogen Zenji—because its chief priest also served at my family temple in Fukui. We spent our time there utterly deprived of food and drink, with only the clothes on our backs to wear.

Despite all this, and in order for me to be able to pass the entrance exams for junior high and army prep school, my mother made me go not to a rural branch school, but to a school in Ono City. There I stayed in a room at the small convent at Bodaiji Temple. My father sent me a postcard that read, "Charge through your junior high school admission with the same confidence that you charged through those American air raids." During this period, I used to walk home on the weekends along 12 kilometers of mountain roads to spend time at my mother's side. Finally, the day of Japan's surrender, August 15, arrived.

Why Did We Fight the United States?

Before I knew it, the world had come to an end for the little patriot that I was. The classrooms that had been adorned with the Japanese flag were now decorated with statues of the Virgin Mary. I asked my teacher, "Why?" and I can still recall the troubled look on his face. I returned to Fukui City in November, and in March 1946 attended my elementary school graduation ceremony in the main hall of the temple that still stood on the outskirts of town. But just before I was to enter prefectural junior high school, my father, who had been demobilized and sent home, made a firm decision to move the family to Tokyo. We were uprooted into the midst of postwar society under the U.S. military occupation.

In April 2003, as I watched the televised images of American occupation soldiers and crowds in Baghdad bringing down the statue of Saddam Hussein, I recalled the complex emotions I felt in those days at being on the side of "the liberated." Still, for me, the encounter with the American "enemy" during the Pacific War, particularly the shock of my experiences with the B-29 bombings, has always remained. It also left its mark: "What kind of country is the U.S.?" "Why did we fight a war?" "Why did we lose?" These questions stuck firmly in the consciousness of this young lad from the militarist nation long after those days were over. When I was aspiring to find work as a journalist, I dreamed of being assigned to the United States and taking up the challenge of finding the answers to these questions.

Eventually my dream came true. In 1956 I joined Kyodo News, and after spending four years in Osaka as a reporter for the local news section, I was assigned to the Foreign News Desk at the head office in Tokyo where I started work covering the 1960 American presidential election. That was the same year as the first televised debates between Kennedy and Nixon. During the Los Angeles Democratic National Convention, I was given the task of monitoring Voice of America (VOA) radio, the only real-time source of U.S. information in those days, frantically jotting down and tallying the number of votes from each state for the nomination of Kennedy and Johnson. I have continued to follow the U.S. in the succeeding four and one-half decades.

I first set foot on American soil as Kyodo's New York staff correspondent in December 1964, right after Japan had enjoyed the twin successes of the Tokyo Olympics and the launch of the bullet trains. Even so, the differences between the American and Japanese standards of living were still very great. In Harlem, which I visited shortly thereafter to cover the assassination of Malcolm X, I was amazed to find that all the homes had running hot water. One dollar bought 360 yen in those days.

In February 1965, under the Johnson administration that had picked up the reins following the Kennedy assassination, and in the midst of the pride resulting from the success of the Great Society, America took an incautious step and fell into the trap of military escalation in Vietnam. Antiwar demonstrations, the Black Power Movement, and anti-establishment movements arose simultaneously. The presidential election year of 1968 saw continuous rebellion, violence, and chaos, culminating in the assassinations of Martin Luther King, Jr., and Robert F. Kennedy, and the clashes surrounding the Democratic National Convention in Chicago.

This was the year when the counterculture movement that began with the appearance of the hippies reached its zenith. In the middle of all this, the liberal faction of the Democratic Party led by Kennedy, then Johnson, self-destructed, and Nixon, advocating a return to law and order, won the White House. I was able to cover this drama as a Washington correspondent, and I am still counting the blessings of this good fortune.

In May 1968 I was dispatched to Paris to report on the Vietnam peace negotiations that Johnson had finally been able to accept. There I also saw the beginning of the historical May revolution by French students. While on the beat in downtown Paris, which had become paralyzed by general strikes and the stoppage of the Metro, I found myself covering this event as well. The famous student occupation of the Odeon Theater occurred right before my eyes. On another day, at the scene of a clash between students and police in front of the offices of the French Communist Party newspaper *L'Humanité*, I found myself in the middle of a tear gas attack by the French police. While I was covering my eyes with my handkerchief, I started to realize that this attack was much lighter than the one I endured only a month before in Washington when National Guard troops fired on a black demonstration protesting the King assassination. The tear gas attack I endured that April day was so intense that I felt like my eyes would pop out of my head. I could feel the difference in my skin between the Paris altercation, a mere scuffle between Caucasians, and the extreme intensity of the black-versus-white confrontation in the United States. I can recall these deep, dark feelings as though I had experienced them only yesterday.

From 1972 until the fall of Saigon in April 1975, I was on location in Indochina covering the final days of the Vietnam War into which the United States had deployed an enormous force of more than five hundred thousand, suffering more than fifty thousand deaths. Then, in the early 1980s, I returned to the United States again as Washington Bureau Chief, and covered the process by which the foundation for the American victory in the Cold War was built, with Ronald Reagan, on a platform of tax reductions and military buildup, challenging the "evil empire" of the Soviet Union with slogans of a "strong America." During the eighteen years from late 1984 to 2002, I headed a cooperative enterprise with the U.S. information industry and came in contact with the true face of Wall Street. There has not been a single year since 1984 that I have not visited this nation. My involvement with the United States, which began with a baptism of bombing as an "enemy" in 1945 when I was twelve years old, is a part of my life even today.

A Nation Close and Yet So Far

In these times, I repeatedly ask myself the questions "Do we know less about America the more we learn about it?" and "Is this not a country so close and yet so far?" These are questions that also linger when I reflect on my own experience as a journalist in this land.

Among the nations of the world today, there is no country closer to Japan than the United States. Thanks to the success of Hideki Matsui and Ichiro Suzuki, American major league baseball has become a part of the Japanese living room. In politics, economics, military affairs, society, culture, sports, and anywhere else you look, our relationship with the United States is evident. Whether or not the Japanese are aware of this, the United States casts an ever-growing shadow into all corners of Japanese daily life. It is perhaps safe to say that the deep bilateral relationship between these two nations, with vastly different histories and cultures and separated by a time difference of fourteen hours (thirteen during daylight saving time), is the first such relationship in the history of the world.

But this relationship and the ability of the Japanese to precisely grasp the true character of the United States are two different things. In contrast to the intimacy that exists on the surface of U.S.-Japan relations, the two nations continue to be "ships passing in the night."

Though Japan seized many opportunities to modernize granted by its opening by American naval vessels in the middle of the nineteenth century, it spent little time studying the United States itself. In the mid-twentieth century, Japan waged war on America but was defeated and occupied. Afterward America played a major role in the development of Japan's infrastructure as an economic power through the promulgation of the peacetime constitution during the occupation. Even now, the U.S. demands "reform" of present-day Japan. The image of passing ships in the night truly reflects the state of U.S.-Japanese relations both past and present. Isn't the fact that the war in the Pacific had to be fought proof of this above all else? For this reason, we must study this country called America once more.

The year 2006 marked 153 years since the ships under the command of U.S. East India Fleet Commander Commodore Matthew Perry arrived at Uraga. It has been 152 years since the Tokugawa Shogunate signed the Treaty of Peace and Amity under pressure, opening the ports of Shimoda and Hakodate. Sixty-one years after waging and losing a three-year, eight-month war, as we struggle to interpret our Japanese constitution born under American occupation, we must again try to examine the true face of that nation across the Pacific.

In May 2002, I returned to my original occupation and once more pursued my work as a journalist in order to answer these challenging questions.

Accordingly, this book is a record of the never-ending struggle of a man of the last generation who witnessed firsthand the war with America, and who still struggles to understand the implications of his childhood experiences.

ONE

A Decoration for General LeMay

My Encounter with the LeMay Attack

My account begins with the air raid on Fukui City. On my desk is the *Tactical Bombing Report* from the 58th Bomb Wing, 21st Bomber Command, 20th Air Force, U.S. Army Air Corps, recording the sorties launched from Tinian West Airfield that day. I obtained a copy of this report in January 2003 from the National Archives in College Park, Maryland, near Washington, D.C.

At first reading, it is readily apparent that while we had been scrambling for our lives, for the Americans the raid had been simply another tactical operation. The report states that the four cities targeted for fire bombing on July 19—Fukui, Hitachi, Choshi, and Okazaki—were among 180 small-to-medium-size industrial cities selected, in addition to large population centers, with the objective of destroying Japan's will to fight. In accordance with the operational standard for nighttime incendiary bombing, it was determined that a successful air attack on Fukui City would destroy industries, disrupt railroad networks, and degrade Japan's ability to restore its combat power, since the city contained within an urban area ninety-five industrial facilities that manufactured such products as aircraft parts, electrical components, engines, and various types of metal goods and fibers.

A former classmate from Ono City told me that military aircraft parts were in fact being manufactured at the fiber factories that made up the primary industry in the area surrounding Fukui City. These were hauled by horse and cart through the mountainous region of Gifu Prefecture toward Nagoya.

Nevertheless, having been a twelve-year-old sixth-grade student living in the city of Fukui, I know that the significance of the city as a bombing target as stated in the *Tactical Bombin Report* was exaggerated. The daily life of civilians was one of severe food shortages and power failures while far from any industrial activity. Moreover, there were neither fighter nor antiaircraft units, nor any military troops to speak of. Even the report states that previous aerial photographs had indicated that no antiaircraft capability existed. In addition, the five antiaircraft sites encountered upon ingress and egress from Fukui—Tsuruga, Takefu, Tateishi Cape, Kakamigahara, and Tajimi—were assessed as either "poor," "inaccurate," "short," or "medium." In fact, only one American casualty was reported out of the 1,513 crewmembers on the 127 B-29s that participated in the raids.

In short, the bombing was as simple as kissing a baby's hand. It was indiscriminate bombing and nighttime scorching of 100 percent civilian cities under the cover of complete U.S. air superiority. The operation didn't include the participation of fighter escorts, and instead of reforming into flight formations when the bombing was completed, the 127 aircraft simply returned to their base on their own. The success of the raid, which dropped no less than 953.4 tons of bombs, was summarized by one simple word, "normal."

The report is signed by Curtis LeMay, commander, 21st Bomber Command, the man recognized as the brains of the operation, a signature that will remain with me forever.

Curtis LeMay, the name of a general long gone and forgotten, but with the new preemptive strike strategy now being executed in Iraq by the United States under the Bush administration, I have come to think about him anew, and I believe that it is time to reexamine his career.

This is important because I think the scorched-earth operation that General LeMay drew up and executed can be regarded as the origin of the Bush Doctrine. Of course, times and circumstances and people change over the years, and any analysis must be undertaken coolly. Still, the LeMay operations may very well lie at the root of this policy. For me, who suffered and survived the indiscriminate nighttime B-29 incendiary bombings under LeMay's command, it becomes an unavoidable task. I have come to feel that this might be an encounter with the true face of America.

A Rapid Rise to the Top

Curtis LeMay was born in 1906 and died in 1990 at the age of eighty-four. He hailed from Columbus, Ohio, the eldest son of a French father who emigrated to the United States and a British mother. His father was a railroad construction worker who moved the family from Ohio to Montana, California, Pennsylvania, and then back again to Ohio. The family was poor but close and lived by the father's motto, "If you take something on, you should finish it. Don't do a sloppy job."

Young Curtis was raised as an upright boy who first fought and then made good friends with the people he knew. He dreamed early on of becoming a pilot. It is said that, as a young boy, he once saw Henry H. "Hap" Arnold fly—the same man who, later, as commander of the U.S. Army Air Corps, supported LeMay's rise as an officer.[1]

LeMay graduated from Ohio State University with a degree in civil engineering while working his way through school part-time at a foundry. After completing Reserve Officer Training Corps (ROTC) training, he became a fighter pilot in what was then the Army Air Corps. This was decades before the creation of the Air Force as a separate entity. Nevertheless, LeMay concluded that bombers would become more significant in future conflicts, so he began to pilot those aircraft. In the years before World War II, he was already well on his way to becoming a crack pilot, demonstrating his talents in celestial navigation by flying a B-17, the first four-engine large bomber, to a rendezvous with a luxury liner more than 700 miles from land.

After the U.S. entry into World War II, LeMay was first stationed in the European Theater where he devised new tactics after it became apparent that precision bombing from tight high-altitude formations was not producing results.[2] While there he devised a new bombing tactic employing a loose flight formation, known as the Combat Box, that enabled aircraft to enhance the bombers' defenses effectively while shifting altitude, a move that significantly increased bombing accuracy during long-range flights. Almost overnight, LeMay became known as a "brave commander who feared neither German antiaircraft barrages nor fighter attacks."

In August 1944, LeMay was transferred to the Pacific Theater where he was appointed to lead the 20th Bomber Command. His assignment was to bring the fight to the Japanese occupied territories in Asia and China and to the Japanese mainland utilizing the B 29s that had just been deployed at

Chengdu, China. He had been personally selected for this duty by Army Air Corps Commander Hap Arnold.

Starting with its first bombing of the Yawata Iron and Steel Company in Kitakyushu in June of that year, the 20th Bomber Command had raided such targets as the Palembang oilfield in Indonesia and the Showa Iron and Steel Works in Manchuria. By August, however, when fourteen of the sixty-two B-29s that participated in the second Yawata raid were shot down by Japanese fighters, an especially displeased General Arnold relieved no less than two commanders and appointed LeMay to the task. LeMay was promoted to major general at the youthful age of 38. In four short years he had advanced from the rank of lieutenant colonel to that of general, a pace of promotion extraordinary even in wartime.

Upon arriving for duty, General LeMay immediately seized the reins and began himself to bombard the Japanese occupied territories. In December, he directed the incendiary bombing of Hankou, China, which was under Japanese Imperial Army occupation, and the entire area burned for three days. During this time, he received his next advancement. At this point, General Arnold put LeMay in charge of the 21st Bomber Command, a Guam-based unit that had been newly established in November 1994 with the sole mission of conducting air raids against mainland Japan but had performed poorly. The new unit absorbed the B-29s of the 20th Bomber Command, thus unifying the command of all B-29 bombing operations against the Japanese mainland under General LeMay.

At this point, a brief discussion of General Arnold's career is in order. A graduate of the U.S. Military Academy at West Point, Henry H. Arnold was among the officer elite. Upon graduation he joined the Army Air Corps, which had its beginnings with the purchase of one airplane from the Wright brothers in 1907, and received pilot training directly from the Wright brothers. He was, literally, a pioneer aviator.

Upon assuming the post of Army Air Corps commander in 1938, General Arnold nurtured the growth of U.S. airpower, which had been lagging behind that of Europe since the end of World War I. He persuaded President Roosevelt and the industrial complex to elevate the development of airpower to the highest level of national importance. Following the establishment of the newly independent Air Force after World War II, he became known as the father of the U.S. Air Force. In September 1940, over a year prior to the Japanese attack on Pearl Harbor, General Arnold led the army to sign a contract with Boeing Corporation to develop the B-29. The plane is still regarded as a masterpiece in aviation history.

While deployment of the B-29 in Europe had lagged, in January 1945, the powerful air strike capability of the B-29 was effectively employed to destroy the entire socioeconomic base of Japan. Employing the same shock-and-awe effect used in the Iraq War, the U.S. bombing campaign degraded the Japanese will to fight and accomplished the "great deed" of bringing Japan to surrender without the need for assault landings. It was the success of these air strikes that enabled General Arnold to realize his lifelong dream of an air force independent of the army or navy.

General Arnold was indeed a master at his craft. He maneuvered carefully to remove the 20th Air Force, and his pet B-29s, from the command of Douglas MacArthur, who regarded airpower merely as a means of supporting ground warfare. He then successfully influenced Army Chief of Staff George Marshall, a long-time personal friend of General Arnold and whose rivalries with MacArthur were well known, to resubordinate the 20th Air Force under the Joint Chiefs of Staff, which at the time was nominally chaired by President Roosevelt. As Japan's defeat was becoming a certainty, a drama of thick political maneuvering was developing within the U.S. military that included the dropping of atomic bombs on Hiroshima and Nagasaki in August. [3]

Nighttime Indiscriminate Incendiary Bombing

General LeMay completely lived up to General Arnold's expectations by devising the tactic of nighttime incendiary bombing that destroyed entire cities, including the residential areas of noncombatant civilians. The logic for this strategy was based on four points.

1. During the day, flight formations conducted precision bombings at altitudes of 20,000 to 30,000 feet using the Norden optical bombsight. However, strong westerly winds over the Japanese mainland caused the aircraft to deviate from their flight routes, degrading the effectiveness of the missions and forcing aircraft to descend to low altitudes of 5,000 to 9,000 feet. Afterward planes returned to base individually to save fuel and extend their range by not assembling into formation.

2. Defensive gunnery equipment had been removed from planes as were the gunners to keep aircraft weight as light as possible. This permitted the maximum number of bombs to be carried, up to six tons of ordnance. Incendiary bombs were employed abundantly in light of the large number of wooden structures in Japan.

3. Japan's fighters and antiaircraft guns lacked radar equipment, and thus could not effectively intercept the bombers. In addition, raids were shifted to nighttime, which made it difficult for fire fighting units to function. Daylight would break when the bombers returned to base, facilitating emergency landings and crewmember rescues.

4. Not only large cities like Tokyo, but small and mid-size cities of twenty to forty thousand people were listed as targets and scorched one by one, destroying the Japanese people's will to fight. At the same time, ports were bombed nationwide, creating a state of blockade.

In short, this new nighttime incendiary bombing tactic was clearly recognized from the beginning as having involved noncombatant civilians as targets. Even when the traditional strategic bombing to which General LeMay's predecessors adhered resulted in casualties among the general civilian population, the most important targets of high-altitude daytime precision bombing were limited ultimately to military facilities and munitions factories.

As for General LeMay's change of tactics, there are varying opinions. It was, perhaps, the result of his experiences with the successful incendiary bombings of Hankou while at Chengdu, or it may have been influenced by the indiscriminate and completely destructive bombings initiated against the ancient German city of Dresden on February 13, 1945 by the Royal Air Force under Air Marshal and Commander-in-Chief of Bomber Command Arthur Harris, sometimes called "Britain's LeMay." It has also been suggested that, his dauntless command ability notwithstanding, the real reason for the powerful impression General LeMay made was because of his haughty cigar-smoking attitude and "frenzied character." However, I think it should be understood that the nighttime indiscriminate incendiary bombing that LeMay devised was part of the larger U.S. combat strategy against Japan.

In October 1943, an organization under the National Defense Research Committee (NDRC), which President Roosevelt established in 1940 prior to World War II, was testing the recently developed M69 incendiary bomb at Salt Lake, Utah. Photographs recorded the temperature of combustion before and ten, fifteen, and twenty minutes after M69s were dropped onto sixteen buildings constructed with the same room arrangements, building materials, furniture, paint, and everyday items used in civilian homes in Tokyo and Berlin during that period. The results verified the superior effectiveness of these bombs against Japanese homes. These results were transmitted all the way up to General Arnold.

The M69 itself was developed under the direction of Robert Russell, a scientist, vice president of Standard Oil Company, and a leading member of the NDRC. This was the first time that the powerful agent napalm was employed. The M69 was a small, lightweight, hexagonal pipe-like cluster bomb measuring twenty inches long, three inches wide, and weighing about 6.17 pounds. Each ordnance dropped contained two chambers of nineteen bombs, for a total of thirty-eight bombs, which spread out into rose-like patterns at an altitude of 985 feet. Upon shock of impact, the napalm ignited, flared up, and scattered 2,400-degree flames 100 feet in all directions, resulting in complete combustion and enveloping in flames all flammable objects in the area. When bombs fell to earth, the powerful flames depleted the surrounding areas of oxygen, claiming people's lives by suffocation. The technology made fire extinguishing very difficult, and people exposed to even a little of the napalm spray received burns that could not be treated.

As I look back, I realize I was like a cat with nine lives that night in Fukui City.

Furthermore, among the American private sector industries associated with the NDRC, there had been one fire insurance company with experience operating in Japan prior to the war. Responding to the question of whether the inner-city areas of Japan were vulnerable to fire attack, the company quickly offered data that is said to have strongly convinced the government and military that incendiary bombs would be useful in bringing about an end to the war.

The actions of the United States at the time are explained in full detail in a book by the American historian Ronald Schaffer, which resonates with the theme that the U.S. attacks on Japan were indiscriminate slaughter lacking in morals, carried out in the name of justice. According to Schaffer, in the spring of 1939, instructor Major C. Thomas had already given a lecture at the Army Air Corps Tactical School stating that incendiary bombs would bring fearful destruction to the cities of Japan, as had been shown by the fires that accompanied the Great Kanto Earthquake of 1923.[4]

The Biggest Firecracker

The report delivered to General Arnold detailing the results of the incendiary bombing tests and proposing a scorched-earth strategy was written while the United States was at peace with Japan. The report concluded that the use of powerful incendiary bombs would be enormously costly to the infrastructure and morale of a nation where 90 percent of the buildings were made of wood. Such bombs would annihilate Japanese cities, and destroy its military facilities and industries. Moreover, it noted that military installations and munitions factories were not only adjacent to residential areas, but parts-manufacturing plants were intermingled among civilian homes.

At the time, the United States officially declared that it was not conducting indiscriminate urban raids. First, President Franklin Roosevelt himself issued a statement condemning the Soviet bombings of Finland in November 1939, stating that the bombing and machine-gunning of unarmed citizens was nothing short of brutal. Secretary of State Cordell Hull also blamed the Japanese Imperial Army for its indiscriminate bombings of China, and Secretary of the Army Henry Stimson—in spite of the United States having added 276 B-17s and B-24s as a third wave to Britain's indiscriminate bombings of Dresden—issued a statement denying that citizens of enemy nations had been entrapped in the bombing. Even General Arnold, just before the massive Tokyo air raids in March, issued an official statement affirming that the mission of the Army Air Corps was the precision bombing of military targets, adding that the use of incendiary bombs on cities was contrary to the traditional national doctrine of limited bombings of military targets.

As policy, this position fell apart in the end, however, because the Army Air Corps leadership under General Arnold was aiming to influence the independence of a postwar Air Force. As such, they were competing for influence with the army under MacArthur, who made the recapture of the Philippines and the preparations for amphibious landings on Okinawa a reality, and the navy under Admiral Chester Nimitz, who successfully led the marines in capturing Pelileu Island in the Palau Island group and Iwo Jima. For Arnold to win this power struggle, it was imperative to drive Japan to surrender through the use of air raids alone. The voices that decried the brutal attacks on unarmed civilians subsided amid growing speculations that an amphibious assault on the Japanese mainland would cost a million American casualties.

General Arnold had legitimized LeMay's new tactics in February 1944, and the entire execution of these tactics was left to the discretion of LeMay as the on-site commander. There was absolutely no hesitation on the part of General LeMay.

"You're going to deliver the biggest firecracker the Japanese have ever seen," General LeMay told his crews when the 325 B-29s carrying a total payload of about 2,000 tons headed for Tokyo on March 10, 1945. This marked the start of the scorched-earth operation. *New Yorker* reporter St. Clair McKelway, who was posted as a public relations officer in the LeMay headquarters on Guam, relayed this statement after the war, according to a very painstaking and comprehensive article on LeMay by Richard Rhodes in the June 19, 1995 issue of the *New Yorker*, titled "Annals of the Cold War—The General and World War III."[5]

Waiting anxiously for the bombers to return, LeMay was also heard to say, "In a war, you've got to try to keep at least one punch ahead of the other guy all the time. A war is a very tough kind of proposition. If you don't get the enemy, he gets you. I think we've figured out a punch he's not expecting this time."

To be sure, the punch exceeded Japan's expectations. A 10.4 square mile area of downtown Tokyo blazed continuously for six hours, and an announcement from the Tokyo Metropolitan Police Department, which has been criticized as too conservative, put the casualty figure at 83,793 dead. Among those, more than half died of suffocation. Another 40,918 were injured. It was a massacre under the name of nighttime indiscriminate incendiary bombing. Regarding this "firecracker," the United States Strategic Bombing Survey later concluded that there was no other example in human history in which so many people had perished in flames.

In my own family, my uncle, aunt, and newborn cousin fell victim. It was reported that the smell of death entered the aircraft whenever a B-29 crew opened its hatch to drop an incendiary bomb.[6] Some 260,771 buildings were destroyed by fire, and 18 percent of Tokyo's industrial capacity was extinguished in one night. Each aircraft dropped 1,520 cluster bombs, each containing thirty-eight M-69s, at 500-foot intervals. It was a thorough operation. Fourteen B-29s were shot down by Japanese antiaircraft guns, and forty-two incurred some damage. But there had been no damage suffered from Japanese fighters.

McNamara's Confession

In recognition of this slaughter, General LeMay received a congratulatory telegram from General Arnold stating, "This mission shows your crews have got the guts for anything." Years later, when a cadet at the Air Force Academy asked him how much "moral considerations" had affected his decisions, LeMay responded frankly, "I suppose if I had lost the war, I would have been tried as a war criminal. Fortunately, we were on the winning side."

In 2003 another man uttered those same words, Robert McNamara, Secretary of Defense under the Kennedy and Johnson administrations and one of those responsible for the failed military intervention in Vietnam. I learned of this after starting to write this book.

The eighty-seven-year-old McNamara spoke of his World War II activities in director Errol Morris's documentary film *The Fog of War: Eleven Lessons from the Life of Robert S. McNamara*, which was screened at the 56th Annual Cannes Film Festival in May 2003 and at the New York Film Festival in October of that same year.

In *The Fog Of War* McNamara states that he worked in LeMay's Guam headquarters toward the end of the Pacific War, engaging in the calculations that facilitated the fire bombings of sixty-seven Japanese cities. He recalled a conversation with LeMay in which LeMay said, "If we'd lost the war, we'd all have been prosecuted as war criminals."

"And I think he's right," McNamara further observed. "He—and, I'd say, I—were behaving as war criminals." He later added, "Killing 50 to 90 percent of the people in sixty-seven Japanese cities and then bombing them with two nuclear bombs is not proportional in the minds of some people to the objectives we were trying to achieve."[7]

In 1940, one year prior to the attack on Pearl Harbor, Mr. McNamara, under the strong influence of General Arnold, encouraged the Harvard University School of Business to initiate a new course in munitions production and procurement, for which he served as assistant professor and distinguished himself by developing a new statistics-based management system. This was the first of many occasions when his considerable intellect was mobilized in the service of wartime objectives. During World War II, McNamara held the rank of lieutenant colonel in the U.S. Army and employed program analysis and operations analysis to ensure the completion of both mass production and crew training for the B-29s. David Halberstam's book, *The Best and the Brightest*, gives a vivid account of McNamara at that time, a man who stepped in effectively and immediately helped complete the enormous task of delivering bombs to the Japanese mainland.[8]

Until now, the record has always stated that McNamara worked at 20th Air Force under the supervision of General Arnold. However, the unusual fact that McNamara had been working for General LeMay in the subordinate 21st Bomber Command, the operational unit directly involved in the Japanese scorched-earth operation, has only recently come to light. McNamara himself had never spoken of this before. In his memoirs published in 1995, McNamara dropped a self-critical bombshell by calling the Vietnam War a mistake, and later paid a visit to Hanoi to further explain his confession in talks with former Vietnamese leaders.

It is said that the objective of director Morris's prolonged interview was to arrive at the true nature of McNamara's conversion. However, at the start of the interview, Morris was reportedly surprised by McNamara's sudden emotional confession of his own participation in the incendiary bombings of Japan. I also interviewed Mr. McNamara after he resigned as president of the World Bank in 1983. He spoke only of his misgivings over the Vietnam War policy and said nothing of his involvement in the war with Japan.

In boosting the Army Air Corps from a force of only 295 pilots in 1940 to ninety-six thousand pilots one year after Pearl Harbor, McNamara showed his prodigious talents. After the war, he joined with other young, bright, ambitious colleagues in the reconstruction of the Ford Motor Company. At the age of forty-four, just after becoming company president, he was chosen from among many candidates to serve as secretary of defense in the Kennedy administration.

Thus, as seen in the incendiary bomb tests conducted for General Arnold before the war, the brightest intellects in America had joined forces to support General LeMay's nighttime indiscriminate incendiary bombings.

As Mr. McNamara confessed, these bombings began on March 10 with the large cities of Tokyo, Nagoya, Osaka, Kobe, Yokohama, and Kawasaki, were continued on June 17 with the four cities of Kagoshima, Omuta, Hamamatsu, and Yokkaichi, then an additional sixty-one small-to-medium-size cities including Kumagaya and Isesaki. This campaign continued until August 14, one day prior to Japan's surrender. My own Fukui City was one of four cities in the tenth wave. The cities and the dates they came under attack are repeated here for posterity.

June 17: Kagoshima, Omuta, Hamamatsu, Yokkaichi
June 19: Toyohashi, Fukuoka, Shizuoka
June 28: Okazaki, Sasebo, Moji, Nobeoka
July 1: Kure, Kumamoto, Ube, Shimonoseki
July 3: Takamatsu, Kochi, Himeji, Tokushima
July 6: Chiba, Akashi, Shimizu, Kofu
July 9: Sendai, Sakai, Wakayama, Gifu
July 12: Utsunomiya, Ichinomiya, Tsuruga, Uwajima
July 16: Numazu, Oita, Kuwana, Hiramatsu
July 19: Fukui, Hitachi, Choshi, Okazaki
July 26: Matsuyama, Tokuyama, Omuta
July 28: Tsu, Aomori, Ichinomiya, Uji-Yamada, Ogaki, Uwajima
August 1: Hachioji, Toyama, Nagaoka, Mito
August 5: Saga, Maebashi, Nishinomiya, Mikage (present-day
Higashinada Ward in Kobe City), Imanuma
August 8: Yawata, Fukuyama
August 14: Kumagaya, Isesaki

These combat missions comprised 32,612 sorties flown by 1,056 aircraft stationed at two bases on Guam, two on Tinian, one on Saipan, and, from August, bases on Okinawa. A total of 147,000 tons were dropped on sixty-seven cities. These included 94,000 tons of incendiary bombs and 53,000 tons of general purpose bombs. In addition, 12,000 tons of mines were dropped in port and harbor areas.

The brilliant results of the LeMay bombings encouraged the Naval Air Corps as well, producing the secondary effect of strengthened indiscriminate air strikes by carrier aircraft against such cities as Nagano. The navy, too, wanted to maintain postwar influence.

Bombers over Atomic Bombs

Uncannily, there was one city group that had been removed from the LeMay bombing target list. These were the five cities of Hiroshima, Nagasaki, Ogura, Niigata, and Kyoto. These sites had been proposed as targets for the dropping of the atomic bomb, which President Roosevelt, who would die in April 1945, had decided to employ during talks with British Prime Minister Churchill at Hyde Park on September 19 of the previous year.

This target selection was performed by a top-secret team linked directly to the White House and included Secretary of the Army Stimson, Army Chief of Staff Marshall, Army Air Corps Commander Arnold, and Manhattan Project Director Leslie Groves. General Groves had persisted in recommending Kyoto as the first target because its topographical features were best suited to test the atomic bomb's performance. In contrast, Secretary Stimson, who had already begun shaping the post-victory image of the United States for the Japanese people, pushed and successfully convinced President Truman into rejecting such a notion. [9]

General LeMay had been left out from this effort. However, certain information came to his attention that the specially formed 509th Composite Group under his command, and later commanded by Lieutenant Colonel Paul Tibbets, the famous pilot of the Enola Gay, systematically continued specialized training in large bomb release and that a special facility had been constructed on Tinian Island. Reportedly, LeMay had received a detailed report from Arnold in June in which Arnold said that, although he didn't know how powerful it was, a bomb using nuclear energy was under development.

According to Robert Norris, a nuclear issues expert and biographer of Manhattan Project Director Groves, it didn't matter much to General LeMay whether a wartime enemy was killed by conventional weapons or nuclear weapons, and his position on the Manhattan Project was to simply stand by and wait for the results. [10] On August 1, General LeMay was promoted to commander of the newly established Strategic Air Command (SAC), under which the 21st Bomber Command was subordinated. Colonel Tibbets assumed direct command of the 509th, and it was left to LeMay's successor, General Nathan Twining, to report the dropping of the atomic bomb on Hiroshima.

In his autobiography, written in cooperation with Pulitzer Prize winning author MacKinlay Kantor and published after he retired from active service,

General LeMay describes his feelings about the appearance of the atomic bomb in words which, I think, represent his true sentiments:

> These bombs . . . brought a strange pervading fear which does not seem to have affected mankind previously, from any other source. This unmitigated terror has no justice, no basis in fact. Nothing new about death, nothing new about deaths caused militarily. We scorched and boiled and baked to death more people in Tokyo on that night of March 9–10 than went up in vapor at Hiroshima and Nagasaki combined.[11]

Following Japan's surrender, General LeMay flew nonstop by B-29 to the United States (Hokkaido to Chicago to Washington) to demonstrate postwar air power. During a press conference afterward, he stated harshly that the new atomic bomb was the worst thing that had happened and that "the war would have been over in two weeks without the use of the atomic bomb or the Russian entry into the war."

It has been said that General LeMay and his colleagues fully intended to organize seventy-two air wings independent of the army and navy, build a network of air force bases around the world, and employ air power as the core of global security. For them, the bombers were more important than the atomic bombs.

Behavior Bordering on Rebellion

One ironic fact is that after the war, General LeMay—who step-by-step was promoted to the posts of commander of United States Air Forces Europe, where he commanded the Berlin Airlift, SAC commander, and Air Force chief of staff—became part of the faction advocating the use of nuclear weapons, and he devised strategies for that purpose. With his actions as a planner of nuclear tactics, the true intentions of the man who developed the B-29 nighttime indiscriminate incendiary bombings become clear.

For me, the DNA of America, which unhesitatingly employs its present unstoppable military might, may be visible in the tracks left by this General LeMay. Therefore, I think it is necessary to follow these tracks in order to understand American strategic thinking.

In November 1945, three months after Japan's surrender, General

LeMay remarked in a speech to the Ohio Society of New York that the next war would be an air war fought with fantastic new weapons, "rockets, radar, jet propulsion, television-guided missiles, speeds faster than sound, and atomic power. . . . There must be no ceiling, no boundaries, no limitations to our air power development." Continuing, he declared that this war, "once it is launched, [cannot] be completely stopped." Accordingly, U.S. airpower would have to be developed to the point where it could immediately recover from an attack and retaliate, thereby preventing an attack in the first place. It was not long thereafter that the concept of deterrence became a watchword of American defense.

However, four years later, in 1949, when it became known that the Soviet Union possessed the atomic bomb, LeMay, who had been assigned as SAC commander the previous year, clarified the position that that the United States should not hesitate to launch a first or preemptive strike in order to maintain nuclear superiority over the Soviet Union and to ensure that SAC's nuclear arsenal would not become a "wasting asset."

For almost a half century until the conclusion of the Cold War, the principle of maintaining peaceful coexistence though the mutual deterrence of nuclear power became the axis of U.S.-Soviet relations. Actions bordering on rebellion surfaced against the authority of four presidents—Truman, Eisenhower, Kennedy, and Johnson—as LeMay, using his discretion as on-site commander, repeatedly attempted to recreate the successes of his scorched-earth bombings of Japan.

The first such incident occurred in 1949. A plan for nation killing was drawn up by which the United States would drop all of the 133 atomic bombs in its possession onto seventy Soviet cities, delivering 2.7 million deaths and four million casualties over a period of three weeks. This plan was promptly squashed by President Truman. In spring 1953, after commander Doolittle, the hero of the first Tokyo Air Raid, which I had witnessed, retired from the Air Force at the rank of lieutenant general, he served as chairman of a committee on Soviet strategy that proposed giving the Soviet Union the choice of abandoning its nuclear weapons in two years or facing a preemptive nuclear strike. LeMay's influence was clearly at work here.

President Eisenhower rejected this notion and instead issued a special update on basic national security policy statement that said, "The United States and its allies must reject the concept of preventive war or acts intended to provoke war."

Still, General LeMay did not give up. He continually sent reconnaissance planes over Soviet territory and continued provoking the Soviets. According to the minutes of a briefing held at SAC headquarters on March 15, 1953, LeMay explained triumphantly to those assembled that while the Soviet Union might need a month to deliver its arsenal of 150 atomic bombs, the United States could drop as many as 750 bombs in a few hours by employing its famous "Sunday Punch," or preemptive simultaneous nuclear assault, driving the Soviet Union into total destruction.[12]

By 1957 the responsibility for atomic weapon storage had been transferred from the Atomic Energy Commission to SAC, and the authority to push the nuclear war button lay in General LeMay's hands. In the final analysis, the question of whether or not this authority would be exercised boiled down to a question of loyalty to the president. The general's blunt remarks about the president are recorded by history: "If I see that the Russians are amassing their planes for an attack, I'm going to knock the shit out of them before they take off the ground. . . . It's my job to make it possible for the president to change his policy."

Earlier, during the Korean War that began in 1950, General LeMay, in his capacity as SAC commander, intended to slaughter about two million people, or 20 percent of North Korea's population, by exercising indiscriminate bombing over North Korea's cities, large agricultural dams, and farming regions, according to the Richard Rhodes article. This fact has barely been reported. The number of deaths was far higher than the five hundred thousand killed in the scorched-earth operations against Japan.[13]

It is also known that LeMay proposed dropping atomic weapons on eastern China and the southeastern Soviet Union in the event that the Korean armistice fell apart. To LeMay, the United States was not raising its ante high enough in either the Korean or Vietnam Wars. It was his consistently held view, in the last years of his career, that atomic bombs should be used to bring an immediate end to a war.

LeMay was opposed to the Johnson-McNamara policy of limited strikes in the Vietnam War, remarking, "We are swatting flies in the South when we should be going after the manure pile in Hanoi. . . . We're going to bomb them back into the Stone Age." He pressed on with total bombings of North Vietnam's ports and dams. In *The Best and the Brightest*, LeMay is quoted as saying, "Here we are at the height of our power. The most powerful nation in the world. And yet we're afraid to use that power, we lack the will."

Toward the Brink of Nuclear War

Taking note of the Tokyo wartime radio broadcasts directed toward U.S. forces near the end of the war with Japan characterizing him as a "bloodthirsty manic" and a "wanton killer," and of the attacks that he led, General LeMay recalled in his autobiography, "I think it's more immoral to use *less* force than necessary, than it is to use *more*. If you use less force, you kill off more of humanity in the long run, because you are merely protracting the struggle. We have the same situation all over again, both in Korea and in Vietnam."

This sums up his insistence on using all the power at his nation's disposal.

However, after being appointed Air Force Chief of Staff during the Kennedy administration, his direct confrontations with the White House over the Cuban Missile Crisis of October 1962 led to his finally being reassigned. President Kennedy's confrontation with Chairman Khrushchev led to the withdrawal of Soviet missiles deployed to Cuba, but General Thomas Power, LeMay's successor as SAC commander, had strongly advised Kennedy during the crisis to immediately bomb Cuba's military facilities. General Power had been a unit commander during the Tokyo Air Raid of March 10, 1945. He was even more trigger happy than LeMay, and even within air force circles was regarded as something of a sadist.

In his book *Thirteen Days*, Robert Kennedy, President Kennedy's younger brother and attorney general, describes a conversation between President Kennedy and LeMay:

> When the President questioned what the response of the Russians might be, General LeMay assured him there would be no reaction. President Kennedy was skeptical. "They, no more than we, can let these things go by without doing something. They can't, after all their statements, permit us to take out their missiles, kill a lot of Russians, and then do nothing. If they don't take action in Cuba, they certainly will in Berlin."

National Security Advisor McGeorge Bundy reportedly had briefed President Kennedy immediately after his inauguration that some of those in uniform posed a danger of starting a nuclear war.

In 1987, Robert McNamara recalled that during the time he served as secretary of defense, President Kennedy had invited the Joint Chiefs of Staff to the White House after the blockade strategy was successful and the crisis mitigated. Kennedy expressed his appreciation. Furious that the LeMay-Power proposal had been rejected, LeMay shocked the guests by saying, "We lost! We ought to just go in there and knock 'em off!"

The fact is, at that time, Chief of Staff LeMay and SAC Commander Power used the situation to raise, by executive order, the force-wide posture from the normal Defensive Condition (DEFCON) 5 to DEFCON 3 and, by Joint Chiefs of Staff (JCS) direction, the posture of SAC to DEFCON 2, just one step below the state-of-war DEFCON 1.

The thinking was that placing 672 B-52s and B-47s and 381 aerial refueling tankers on twenty-four-hour aerial standby alert would be an efficient strategy. U.S. military history tells us that circumstances just prior to and following the declaration of DEFCON 2 raised the possibility of the start of total nuclear war with the Soviet Union.

One of the B-52 pilots on aerial alert at the time has testified that they were ordered to provocatively encroach upon Soviet territory closer than usual, and, if war broke out, Leningrad (present-day St. Petersburg) was to be immediately attacked. A B-52 could carry a maximum of four nuclear bombs, and it was said that the top number of nuclear bombs that could be employed in combat possibly totaled 1,627.[14]

These confrontations between President Kennedy and the military in the White House have been skillfully recreated in director Roger Donaldson's 2000 film *13 Days* starring Kevin Costner and based upon Robert Kennedy's book.

Without a doubt, the world at that time stood upon the brink of nuclear war.

The War LeMay Wanted

The reason I have written so much about LeMay, who has already passed into history, is because his principles of total military strength and preemptive punch are so contemporary. The "Bush Doctrine" by which the United States plunged into Iraq with preemptive military force is quite conceivably a throwback to the basic mindset of General LeMay, transfigured and transformed beyond his wildest dreams.

This is the result of the removal of the Cold War framework under which four U.S. presidents from Truman to Johnson had said "No" to the war LeMay wanted. I believe that all the major developments in American military policy since that time can be traced to the results of the end of the Cold War.

In other words, there is now no principle of peaceful coexistence, or to go a step further, no balance of fear through deterrence as the mutually assured destruction of nuclear power has all but disappeared with America's victory in the Cold War. On March 4, 1992, two B-52s flew over Moscow, a goodwill flight that LeMay and his contemporaries could never have dreamed possible and an event that illustrates the passing of the fears of previous decades.

This may also be an era in which the complete American victory that General LeMay had sought by preemptive strike has already been realized, and I think it is important to go beyond a debate of the pros and cons and digest this reality.

The United States, at the peak of its unilateral power, used the preemptive strike option prohibited during the Cold War and launched the toppling of Saddam Hussein. It has proclaimed itself an "empire of liberty" committed to the creation of a new post–Cold War world order, with an entirely changed Middle East beginning with the democratization of Iraq. It is in this manner that a Pandora's Box has been opened. As one of the still-surviving Japanese who had been on the receiving end of the nighttime indiscriminate incendiary bombings, it's quick and easy for me to invoke the image of LeMay when attempting to understand America. I, who once was such a target, can feel the continuation of LeMay's policies in Bush with chills in my bones.

Two days before the start of the Iraq War, President Bush declared,

In the twentieth century some chose to appease murderous dictators whose threats were allowed to grow into genocide and global war. In this century when evil men plot chemical, biological and nuclear terror, a policy of appeasement could bring destruction of a kind never before seen on this earth. Terrorists and terrorist states do not reveal these threats with fair notice in formal declarations. And responding to such enemies only after they have struck first is not self-defense, it is suicide. The security of the world requires disarming Saddam Hussein now.

Two days before the start of the Iraq War, Vice President Cheney—who holds close ties to neoconservative (neocon), or rather neo-imperialist, individuals and groups that used their influence on the Bush administration with regard to the war—declared in a television interview that if the United States had coped with the tragedy of 9/11 using the standards of the twentieth century, it would be clearly exposed to an attack from Iraq.

Such logic is reminiscent of, or, indeed, the same as that which was used in General LeMay's Vietnam "flyswatter" declaration. I believe that both statements unquestionably originate from the same roots.

"The National Security Strategy of the United States of America," a report President Bush delivered to Congress in September 2002, announced officially the necessity for preemptive strikes of the kind that General LeMay repeatedly sought. The report states:

> The United States possesses unprecedented—and unequaled— strength and influence in the world. Sustained by faith in the principles of liberty, and the value of a free society, this position comes with unparalleled responsibilities, obligations, and opportunity. . . .
>
> While the United States will constantly strive to enlist the support of the international community, we will not hesitate to act alone, if necessary, to exercise our right of self-defense by acting preemptively against such terrorists, to prevent them from doing harm against our people and our country. . . .
>
> While we recognize that our best defense is a good offense, we are also strengthening America's homeland security to protect against and deter attack.
>
> This Administration has proposed the largest government reorganization since the Truman Administration created the National Security Council and the Department of Defense. Centered on a new Department of Homeland Security and including a new unified military command and a fundamental reordering of the FBI, our comprehensive plan to secure the homeland encompasses every level of government and the cooperation of the public and private sector.
>
> Given the goals of rogue states and terrorists, the United

States can no longer solely rely on a reactive posture as we have in the past. . . . We cannot let our enemies strike first.

The greater the threat, the greater is the risk of inaction— and the more compelling the case for taking anticipatory action to defend ourselves. . . . To forestall or prevent such hostile acts by our adversaries, the United States will, if necessary, act preemptively.

I believe that the use of military force against Iraq based on this Bush Doctrine could be termed a new version of "LeMay's War."

I saw General Lemay "up close and personal" on just one occasion. This took place in October 1968 when former Alabama Governor George Wallace, an advocate of discrimination against blacks, was nominated as the American Independent Party's candidate for president. LeMay had been chosen as his vice-presidential running-mate and had come to campaign in Alexandria, Virginia, in the Washington suburbs. I intended to cover this campaign, later recorded as a watershed of American politics, because of early indications that the Wallace-LeMay ticket might win enough votes to throw an already close presidential election into the House of Representatives. This procedure is specified in the American Constitution in the event that no candidate receives a majority in the Electoral College.

General LeMay's opinionated theories on the Cuban Missile Crisis earned him quite a bit of fame at the time, leading George Wallace to select him as his vice presidential candidate. Stanley Kubrick's controversial 1964 film *Dr. Strangelove or: How I Learned to Stop Worrying and Love the Bomb* featured Sterling Hayden playing a character said to have been modeled after LeMay, a disheveled, plainly deranged general chomping on a cigar.

Not surprisingly, and true to his reputation, LeMay lashed out sharply at both President Johnson and the war, hammering on the theme that the United States could not win in Vietnam because it wasn't employing 100 percent of its power. But with the exception of his distinctively imposing eyes, I still recall the disappointment that I felt on beholding this short, pale man who seemed so ordinary.

The Disparity with Dresden

On February 13, 1995, I flew to Washington on business as the head of a business information service involving a joint venture between Kyodo News, Dow Jones, the Associated Press, and Telerate, and also a partnership with Russia's newly formed Interfax News Service.

That morning the news leaped out at me from the television in my Washington hotel room. It was the fiftieth anniversary of the indiscriminate bombing of Dresden in eastern Germany.

In February 1945, the Soviet Army had crossed the border, and in order to deal the finishing blow to dark gray Nazi Germany, RAF Air Marshal "Bomber" Harris, planned a destructive operation against nonmilitary cities. The number one target was Dresden, famous for its rows of beautiful Baroque houses. In addition, the city was overflowing with refugees.

Over a two-day period, February 13–14, three waves of British and American bombers delivered 7,049 tons of incendiary bombs. The first wave consisted of 244 RAF Lancaster bombers, the second wave of 529 Lancasters, and the third wave of 276 U.S. Army Air Corps 8th Air Force B-17s and B-24s for a total of 1,619 participating U.S. and British aircraft. According to an announcement by Dresden City Hall, at that time part of communist East Germany, thirty-five thousand people fell victim to these attacks.

A fiftieth anniversary Requiem Mass was performed in commemoration of this event, and I was amazed at its magnificence. In attendance were German President Roman Herzog, Chancellor Helmut Kohl, and Federal Armed Forces Inspector General Nauman. From the United Kingdom came the Duke of Kent representing Queen Elizabeth and former Chief of the Defense staff Peter Inge. The lineup of faces from the United States included America's top military member, Chairman of the Joint Chiefs of Staff General John Shalikashvili decked out in full four-star uniform. Also featured was an interview with an American Air Force pilot who had taken part in the war and said, "The bombing was excessive."

The immediate thought that flowed from my heart was that, if only such a lineup of Japanese and American faces would have been assembled for a fiftieth anniversary commemoration of the March 10 Tokyo Air Raid, the result would be a ceremony that would be cause for a true repose of souls and reconciliation. The next day, all the American newspapers carried articles and photographs of the Dresden reconciliation, and the *Wall Street Journal* went so far as to reprint at the top of its opinion page a contribution by *London Times* correspondent Simon Jenkins titled "Dresden: Time to Say We're Sorry."

In Germany the Dresden bombing was considered "Germany's Hiroshima," and it seems that long arguments have since continued promulgating theories of justification for both the German and British-American sides. These arguments involve the RAF's emotional retaliation for Germany's raids on British cities in the war's early stages and for Stalin's balking at postwar reconstruction. Former Prime Minister Winston Churchill also reportedly criticized the raid.

In 1992 when the Queen Mother held an unveiling ceremony for a statue of General Harris in front of the Great Britain's Ministry of Defense in London, a number of German leaders, beginning with Prime Minister Kohl, protested the event. Perhaps such a display of great differences was called for.

Even so, I find it difficult to reconcile the commemoration of Dresden with that of the Tokyo air raids, Hiroshima, and Nagasaki. Many more victims were sacrificed in these events and the descendents still suffer.

After I returned home to Japan, U.S. Ambassador to Japan Walter Mondale attended the anniversary observance of the Tokyo air raids on March 10 and said he was "sorry," representing the first-ever expression of U.S. regret. However, I have found myself lost in the thought that this does not sufficiently distinguish the two, because although the Dresden bombing and what it represented have come to a conclusion, the bombing of Tokyo has not. The U.S.-Japan relationship continues to remain far from stable compared to that achieved between Germany and the United States as symbolized by the Dresden ceremony of reconciliation.

The most unforgettable thing for me in the whole ceremony was the first section of President Herzog's speech, carried the next day by the *Washington Post*. Later I was able to obtain the official English translation from the German government, which reads as follows:

> As we recall this event today, as so often before, clarification is needed. No one present in this room intends to indict anyone or expects anyone to show remorse or indulge in self-accusation. No one wants to offset the wrongs committed by the Germans in the Nazi state against anything else. If that had been the intention, the people of Dresden would not, once again, have extended such a warm welcome to our British and American guests. We are here first and foremost to mourn, to lament the dead—an expression of human emotion dating back to the beginnings of civilization.

The United States and Japan have not yet adopted Herzog's logic of no "offset of wrongs" by conducting similar memorial service to honor the souls killed in the air raid over Tokyo and other cities, and Hiroshima and Nagasaki where atomic bombs dropped. I still recall as though it were yesterday the weighty question of why such a speech could not be delivered by a postwar Japanese leader.

In the same year, I was discouraged to hear of the plan to cancel the exhibit of the Enola Gay at the Smithsonian Air and Space Museum in Washington. The cancellation was due not so much to the display itself, but rather to strong objections from the American Legion and Air Force Association, which had forced the Smithsonian director to withdraw placards describing the one hundred forty thousand deaths at Hiroshima and the seventy thousand at Nagasaki, and to resign from his position over the controversy. A senior Reagan administration official with whom I spoke at the time remarked, "It's regrettable, because this was the best chance to remove the atomic bomb thorn from U.S.-Japanese relations. The Smithsonian should have considered the proposal a little more carefully."

Hiroshima and Nagasaki are not things of the past for Americans, either. Eight years have passed since I began thinking that, unlike the reconciliation between Germany, Britain, and the United States, Japan and the United States are not holding any simultaneous "ceremonies" to seek closure to the memories of the LeMay bombings like those of Dresden.

Our association now with the sole victor of the Cold War, the United States, is that of an ally, and I absolutely think that Japan, which has deployed its Self-Defense Forces to Iraq in its own national interest, needs recognize the disparity between Dresden and Japan. As a survivor of the LeMay bombing, this disparity and lack of reconciliation is one of the reasons that inspired me to embark on this journey to discuss the true America. I touch on the disparity with Dresden once again in the epilogue to this work.

One further fact of note: on December 4, 1964, the Japanese Cabinet decided to present the First Order of the Grand Cordon of the Rising Sun to U.S. Air Force Chief of Staff General Curtis LeMay. Japan Air Self-Defense Force Chief of Staff General Shigeru Ura presented the decoration on December 6 at Iruma Air Base. LeMay received this award for his achievements in nurturing the JASDF.

TWO

The DNA of the Use of Force

The Banner of the Second Amendment

From what I myself have observed with my own eyes as a target, the composition of what I call the "DNA of the use of force" makes itself apparent in ever-belligerent General LeMay's belief in the use of military force. That belief is continued in the Bush Doctrine, the United States' pride in its position in the world, and the world's acceptance of the concepts of freedom and equal democracy. On the flip side of the glory of American democracy, the unquestionable face of the use of military force reveals itself.

A proclivity to use force is common to all mankind, not just Americans. But as I will argue in this book, the use of force was an integral part of America's founding, part of its genetic makeup, as it were. The use of force is part of America's DNA.

What makes America's DNA so important to understand is America's emergence as the world's sole democratic superpower. For Japanese like me, who have both survived World War II and enjoyed a vital relationship with America and Americans throughout the latter half of the twentieth century, it is especially important. On some level I can't help but think that General LeMay's indiscriminate bombing is part of America's heritage as a nation founded on the use of force.

I believe this is a reality that must be faced head-on, not as a criticism of the United States, but as a precise, fair examination of the prototype of democracy. And for this, we must go back into the history of this country called America, back to the very founding of the nation itself.

This is the challenge I have undertaken. To begin with, allow me to introduce an excerpt from a speech.

> We're often cast as the villain. That is not our role in American society, and we will not be forced to play it.
>
> Our mission is to remain, as our vice president said, a steady beacon of strength and support for the Second Amendment even if it has no other friend on this planet. We cannot, we must not, let tragedy lay waste to the most rare and hard-won human right in history. A nation cannot gain safety by giving up freedom. This truth is older than our country. Those who would give up essential liberty to purchase a little temporary safety deserve neither liberty nor safety. Ben Franklin said that.
>
> Now, if you like your freedoms of speech and of religion, freedom from search and seizure, freedom of the press, and of privacy, to assemble, and to redress grievances, then you'd better give them that eternal bodyguard called the Second Amendment.
>
> The individual right to bear arms is freedom's insurance policy. Not just for your children, but for infinite generations to come.
>
> . . . Our essential reason for being is this: as long as there is a Second Amendment, evil can never conquer us, tyranny in any form can never find footing within a society of law-abiding, armed, ethical people. The majesty of the Second Amendment that our founders so divinely captured and crafted into your birthright guarantees that no government despot, no renegade faction of armed forces, no roving gangs of criminals, no breakdown of law and order, no massive anarchy, no force of evil or crime or oppression from within or from without can ever rob you of the liberties that define your Americanism.

These words were spoken by Charlton Heston, the veteran actor and former president of the National Rifle Association (NRA, established in

1871), the largest anti-gun-control lobby in the United States, in a keynote speech during the NRA's annual meeting in Denver, Colorado, in May 1999.

The tragedy to which he refers is the Columbine High School shooting carried out by two students in nearby Littleton. Twelve students and one teacher were killed, and twenty-three people were injured. The two perpetrators took their own lives during the incident.

The tenacity of the NRA was proven vividly in this statement, made even as the entire nation was still reeling from the shock of this event. The statement attracted wide attention for its praise of the Second Amendment of the United States Constitution as a right "that our founders so divinely captured and crafted into your birthright" and for its fierce declaration of the ideology of the anti-gun-control movement.

I saw these words only in print until recently when I saw Charlton Heston speak them on-screen. This was in news footage of his address during the opening sequence of the documentary film *Bowling for Columbine* by director Michael Moore. This film, which keenly captured the atmosphere of the de facto uncontrolled gun sector of American society, won the 2003 Academy Award for Best Documentary Feature and was screened in Japan as well.

The scene in which Heston, known for his portrayal of Moses in *The Ten Commandments*, defiantly declares, "The mayor of Denver sent me a message: 'Don't come here.' . . . We are a 128-year-old fixture of mainstream America. . . . So we have the same right as all other citizens to be here," resonated throughout the theater.

Heston formally resigned from the post of president at the NRA convention in April 2003 after his physician announced in August 2002 that he was showing symptoms of Alzheimer's disease. His successor was Kayne Robinson, former Des Moines assistant chief of police and chairman of the Iowa Republican Party, who had supported Heston for five years as NRA vice president. In his opening words upon assuming office, Robinson declared that he would continue along Heston's path of preserving the Second Amendment.

An Amendment Unchanged for More Than 210 Years

So what exactly is this Second Amendment? One of ten amendments to the Constitution of the United States that were enacted as the Bill of Rights in

1791, three years after the Constitution's ratification, it is placed directly after the renowned First Amendment, which guarantees the rights of freedom of religion, speech, press, assembly, and petition.

The text of the Second Amendment reads:

> A well regulated Militia, being necessary to the security of a free State, the right of the people to keep and bear Arms, shall not be infringed.

The gun-control and anti-gun-control factions are presently at odds over the interpretation of this clause. It may be safe to say that American public opinion is divided on this issue, a fact not evident to the Japanese.

According to one school of thought, this amendment guarantees each state the right to recognize a citizen's right to bear arms when that citizen serves as a member of the former militia or the present-day National Guard, so the problem of gun control does not become a constitutional issue, but rather one of the preservation of public security. By contrast, another school of thought contends that in view of the increasing tyranny of the centralized federal government, it is the indispensable right of individuals to preserve civic freedom and the very lifeline of American democracy. Such confrontation between the theories of state rights and individual rights is carried into the entirety of U.S. politics and society even today.

As matters presently stand in America, the anti-gun-control faction is currently in a position of superiority. After Columbine, the gun-ban bill proposed by President Clinton and the Democratic Party passed in the Senate but was firmly rejected in the Republican-controlled House of Representatives, never seeing the light of day. The succeeding Bush administration, under pressure from the NRA, shelved the bill completely, and there lies the root of the problem.

The U.S. Constitution has been amended twenty-seven times. Article 5 stipulates that the Constitution can be amended with a two-thirds vote of both houses of Congress and ratification by two-thirds of the nation's state legislatures, and provides that such an amendment can be later repealed by the same process, a safety valve adopted in the earliest days of the American nation. A simple example is the famous Eighteenth Amendment of 1919 prohibiting intoxicating liquors, which was later repealed by the Twenty-First Amendment in 1933.

Multiracial power, which I regard as being the asset that supports the unrivaled power of the United States, can manifest itself only through the workings of the amendment process of the Constitution.

The Constitution was enacted in 1788 and begins with the phrase, "We the people of the United States . . ." At that time "We the people" did not include black slaves or Native Americans. However, this discrimination was later corrected and remains so to this day. Both the facts of American willingness to discriminate, and the nation's later willingness to correct discrimination, must be recognized.

Pursuing its just cause against the Confederacy during the Civil War, the Union took President Lincoln's Emancipation Proclamation of 1863 and enacted the Thirteenth Amendment abolishing slavery in 1865. The Fourteenth Amendment in 1868 recognized all persons under its jurisdiction as citizens whether by birth in the United States or by naturalization. The Fifteenth Amendment of 1870 declared, "The right of citizens . . . to vote shall not be denied or abridged . . . on account of race, color, or previous condition of servitude." Furthermore, the denial of the right to vote in presidential and other elections due to nonpayment of poll tax and other taxes was lifted by the Twenty-Fourth Amendment of 1964. Such events illustrate the effectiveness of corrective action through amendment.

Regarding this point, Ms. Barbara Jordan, who was elected as the first African American Representative from Texas, delivered the following now-famous line in a speech in 1974:

> When the document was completed on the seventeenth of September 1787, I was not included in that 'We the people.' . . . But through the process of amendment, interpretation, and court decision, I have finally been included in 'We the people.' . . . My faith in the Constitution is whole, it is complete, it is total.

Native Americans have yet to reach this point socially. But the true picture of American multiracial power will be analyzed in chapter 7.

The point here is that the Second Amendment has passed through this "process of amendment, interpretation, and court decision," as Ms. Jordan states, and has remained with us as it is. It is necessary to understand this circumstance.

If the power of the gun-control faction were strong enough, and the opinions of the public majority and many members of Congress were taken into consideration, it would be feasible to repeal the Second Amendment on the grounds that it has provided an excuse for violent, gun-related crime. But the Amendment has survived unchanged for more than 210 years, proving its own historical predominance and that of the anti-gun-control factions. Therefore, any study of the Second Amendment must take into consideration the use of force contained in America's DNA.

Americans Oblivious of Gandhi

Let's return once more to *Bowling for Columbine*. Because I felt a certain racial bias of the white intelligentsia in the directorial style of Michael Moore, I did not find the film very persuasive.

However, there was one scene to which I must tip my hat. Moore asked James Nichols, one of the persons arrested but not prosecuted for the April 1995 Oklahoma City Federal Building terrorist bombing that killed 168 people, "Well, why not use Gandhi's way? He didn't have any guns and he beat the British Empire."

Nichols merely shook his head and responded, "Well, I'm not familiar with that." Nichols is the brother of Terry Nichols, who had received life imprisonment as an accomplice of the already executed Timothy McVeigh. After this reply, James Nichols described to Moore how he and younger brother Terry had been raised with guns on a Michigan farm, and had grown up making and playing with homemade explosives and napalm. As in the Heston speech, Nichols says that the right to bear arms is every American's right, and then proceeds to escort Moore into his bedroom, where he displays the .44 Magnum that he sleeps with under his pillow each night.

The NRA makes its influence felt on Americans because so many of them are oblivious to the lessons taught by Mahatma Gandhi, the leader of the movement that achieved independence for India through nonviolent disobedience, and because they believe in bearing arms as a right of American democracy. I believe this exposes the true face of contemporary America and shows why Heston's statements have such a strong influence.

But that isn't all. The scene in Moore's film raises a more essential problem, the existence of armed paramilitary groups—active primarily in the western and midwestern states—and their common ideological roots with the NRA under the Second Amendment.

McVeigh was born in New York State. He joined the army after graduating high school, fought in the Persian Gulf War and was promoted to sergeant. However, after leaving the army at age twenty-three, he began to make hostile statements against the federal government and wore a T-shirt emblazoned with the Latin phrase *sic semper tyrannis* (thus always to tyrants). This is not only the state motto of Virginia but also the phrase shouted by John Wilkes Booth immediately after he assassinated Abraham Lincoln. He met the Nichols brothers, known at the time for the same rightist talk and conduct, and the three of them lived together and exploded small bombs on the Nichols farm. They later formed ties with private paramilitary groups like the infamous Michigan Militia.

During this time, in April 1993, the FBI had attacked the Branch Davidian cult, which had confined itself in a compound in Waco, Texas, with tear gas and tanks. In consequence, eighty cult members, including twenty-four children, died by fire. The NRA joined with Congressional Republican conservatives to vehemently criticize Clinton administration Attorney General Janet Reno, the Bureau of Alcohol, Tobacco and Firearms (ATF), and the FBI, which together had commanded the Waco operation and whom they felt were responsible for the tragic events that ensued.[1] Vehemently opposed to this action, McVeigh launched a terrorist bomb attack using homemade explosives and timed it to coincide with the two-year anniversary of the Waco incident. Americans, oblivious to Gandhi's lessons, were forming their own terrorist reserve armies and, indeed, had been doing so for quite some time.

Since September 11, 2001, the United States has become engaged in a war against Islamic terrorism, and for the country that toppled the Hussein regime in Iraq in the name of homeland defense, the act of a white terrorist at home is an old wound not to be reopened. At the same time, Heston's interpretation of the Second Amendment as a right that "no government despot can ever rob" has inflicted a fresh, if indirect, wound. The authorities have reportedly strengthened their controls following the Oklahoma incident in an effort to annihilate such groups, which have their roots in the Ku Klux Klan (KKK). However, the groups have not disappeared.

In my attempt to trace America's DNA of the use of force, this one piece of media made me realize after many years how powerful images can be. I left the theater feeling sorry for the United States.

While in the theater I bought a pamphlet and was surprised to learn that the social scientist Shinji Miyadai had written, "The black humor of this work will probably evoke memories of Kubrick's *Dr. Strangelove* for many." It seems that the movie said to be modeled after General LeMay was only the first chapter of a larger story.

In *Dr. Strangelove*, there is a scene in which the cigar-chomping parody of General LeMay, embodied as commander of Burpelson Air Force Base, diverts a formation of B-52s carrying 1,400-megaton nuclear bombs toward the Soviet Union. In his private room, which had been cut off from the White House and the Pentagon, he tried to sermonize to British officers at the base that "the duty of the United States is to exterminate communism." There may be some continuity between this caricature, the Moses-like proclamations of Charlton Heston, and the Gandhi-ignorant Americans portrayed in *Bowling for Columbine*.

Moore's film has not been the only American film using Columbine as its subject matter. At the 56th Annual Cannes Film Festival in May 2003, Gus Van Sant's *Elephant* shattered all previous conceptions of the incident and captured both the top-rated Golden Palm and Best Director Awards. Perhaps those gathered at Cannes realized that they, too, needed to understand the United States starting from its roots.

Ambiguity in Textbook Interpretations

The place of the Second Amendment in America is too complex to present in cartoonish terms. Principles and real intentions are interwoven and twisted among one another. The following quote presents an example.

> Since early time, Americans have debated the exact meaning of the Second Amendment. Some experts believe that it guarantees individuals a basic right to bear arms. Others argue that it simply guarantees the individual states the right to maintain a militia. Gun control is one of the most complex and controversial constitutional issues facing Americans today.

This passage about the Second Amendment is contained in a high school history textbook titled *The American Nation* (Prentice Hall, 2003). It amply illustrates that even the writers of this nation's textbooks have thrown up their hands over the confrontation and confusion.

A major factor is that the U.S. Supreme Court has in fact suspended its function of confronting this question. Daito Bunka University International Relations Assistant Professor Yukio Tomii—who summarized the laborious work *Republicanism, Militias, and Gun Control: How to Read the Second Amendment* (February 2002, Showado) in Japan, where little full-fledged research into the amendment has been conducted—comments that there are very few judicial precedents in America's federal courts regarding the interpretation of the amendment.

Only three cases have been elevated to the Supreme Court and established as primary judicial precedents. These are: *U.S. v. Cruikshank* (1876), *Presser v. Illinois* (1886), and *U.S. v. Miller* (just before World War II in 1939). Furthermore, each of these three decisions is undeniably characterized by an overall open-ended ambiguity toward state rights.

Let's consider the example of the most recent case, *U.S. v. Miller*, the impact of which is still being felt today. The decisions in the two cases that preceded it contain almost the same logic.

In the *Miller* case, the defendant had been arrested for violation of the National Firearms Act, which had been enacted in 1934 as a guaranty of tax revenue during Prohibition. Miller had transported a 12-gauge Stevens shotgun from Oklahoma to Arkansas without a permit. His defense began the case by insisting that the law itself violated the Second Amendment.[2] Since this argument was accepted in the lower court, the Supreme Court accepted a "discretionary appeal" and rendered a direct judgment.

The result was an inarticulate decision that did not clearly conclude the debate over state rights versus individual rights. George Washington University Professor Robert Cottrol, known for his opinion that African Americans have been disregarded in interpretations of the Second Amendment, has also said that it was a decision that could justify the positions of both the gun-control groups and opposition groups. The court did not render an overall decision about the entire Second Amendment. It ruled that the law in question interfered with state rights to form militias, but left open—without specifically affirming—the possibility that individual citizens possess the right to bear arms.

Looking at the issue from a general perspective, it is possible to conclude that a citizen's right to arms is permissible only when that citizen becomes a member of a state militia, that is, the present-day National Guard. However, anti-gun-control groups, including the NRA, have taken the stand that the decision refers to the rights of all citizens and not just National Guardsmen. Thus, gun lobbies like the NRA can flaunt the Second Amendment as their banner for anti–gun control.[3]

The Supreme Court Avoids the Issue

In the years since the highly ambiguous *Miller* decision of 1939, the U.S. Supreme Court has not established a new judicial precedent, nor has it clearly rendered a black-and-white interpretation of the Second Amendment. Occasionally, a decision recognizing a citizen's right to bear arms by reason of the Second Amendment springs up, and anti-gun-control groups like the NRA are stirred into action, as in the March 1999 case of the *U.S. v Emerson* in the United States Court for the Northern District of Texas. However, in the *Emerson* case, the Supreme Court received a "discretionary appeal" from the U.S. Fifth Circuit Court of Appeals, but rejected it on June 10, 2002, marking the seventh time since the *Miller* decision that the Supreme Court had refused to accept an appeal. Accordingly, the *Miller* ruling still stands as a time-tested precedent.

It's possible that there is another, less readily apparent reason for the Supreme Court's standoff posture: the heat it generates among African Americans. As Professor Yukio Tomii points out, the issue of gun control as a civic right had never been discussed in connection with the Second Amendment in the United States until the black slaves were liberated after the Civil War of 1861–65.

The first Supreme Court ruling came with the *U.S. v. Cruikshank* interpretation of the Second Amendment as existing to prevent Congress from infringing on state rights. This came immediately after African Americans were accorded equal rights as citizens by the Thirteenth, Fourteenth, and Fifteenth Amendments following President Lincoln's Emancipation Proclamation. For the whites, a kind of panic ensued with the rapid abolition of racial discrimination. Consequently, armed terrorism against blacks, as represented by the organization of the KKK, commenced immediately after the slave system was abolished in 1865.

Another reaction is said to have come from the expectation that African

Americans would be excluded as citizens from the right to bear arms as a result of interpreting the Second Amendment, not as a question of human rights, but as one of state rights. The *Cruikshank* ruling used the Second Amendment to appeal the arrest of whites for the unjust KKK slaughtering of over a hundred blacks in Louisiana. Two later incidents, including the *Miller* case, also involved African Americans. This was also around 1892 when a new policy of racial discrimination, known as Jim Crow, was implemented in the South. The consideration of human rights along with state rights is easily seen in the Supreme Court's position.

African Americans also gained awareness of the Second Amendment. In the late 1960s, with tensions between blacks and whites reaching their zenith, I covered Malcolm X as he argued that all blacks had the right to bear arms for self defense under the Second Amendment, the same position now supported by the NRA. Although Malcolm X was assassinated in 1965, his posthumous influence peaked in 1967 with the founding of the Black Panther Party (BPP), the most militant Black Power movement produced under his ideological inspiration. Armed with pistols, shotguns, and rifles, this group demonstrated in front of the California state legislature during deliberations of a proposed gun-control act. Party leader Huey Newton commented that whatever anti-gun law passed, blacks would continue to arm themselves, and any attempt to disarm them would ultimately fail.

In California and elsewhere, armed demonstrations were lawful so long as weapons were not concealed, and because the police could not interfere, outlandish demonstrations were permitted. Of note, just as he had frequently expressed his support for the late Reverend Martin Luther King, Jr., former NRA President Heston opposed anti-black and anti-minority behavior on human rights principles. He also sought to peel African Americans away from the gun-control advocacy groups of the Democratic Party. The deep-rooted nature of this problem lies where the Second Amendment asserts the right to arms for both whites and blacks.

The theoretical conspiracy theories of the militias produced the terrorist bombing of the Oklahoma City federal building. This, in turn, demonstrates that interpretations of the Second Amendment have clearly become entangled in numerous confrontations and hidden agendas in American society. Against this background, the Supreme Court hesitates to arbitrate clearly. One may say that it is one of the spells cast on the nation from its founding.

The NRA-Supported Bush Administration

With the freeze in political rulings regarding the Second Amendment by the Supreme Court that has continued since 1939, it may be said that the anti-gun-control groups have managed to keep their efforts alive as a result of the *Miller* decision. But in reality, the NRA, with more than three million members, has abundant funds, and its power has grown increasingly. After the inauguration of the Republican Bush administration and the 9/11 terrorist attack, gun purchases rose sharply throughout the United States. Gun-control factions that were active during the Clinton era have been all but silenced. In June 2003, a spokesman for the anti-NRA gun-control lobby Coalition to Stop Gun Violence said that the Democratic Party had abandoned its responsibility to speak out on the issue of gun control, that the Democrats had decided to cease issuing slogans promoting gun control from the 2002 midterm elections because it wouldn't get them votes, and that those who advocated a policy of promoting gun control had deserted the party.

Indeed, among the primary candidates who had announced their candidacy to run for the Democratic presidential nomination in 2004, none had supported a gun-control platform. Former Vermont governor Howard Dean, the only anti–Iraq War candidate and a man with a knack for raising funds through the Internet, did raise the gun problem as an issue, slipping his pronouncements right past the NRA.

Former Attorney General John Ashcroft is anti–gun control as a matter of course and clearly supports the NRA 100 percent. Ashcroft informed all federal public prosecutors in November 2001 that the public position of the Justice Department was that the Second Amendment recognized the right of citizens and not just members of the National Guard to bear arms. Since his days in the Senate and as governor of Missouri, Ashcroft has been known for not just his opposition to gun control but also for opposing abortion, supporting capital punishment, and toeing the conservative line. While his professed views reflect the overwhelming predominance of the NRA in the politics of his state, not all Republican leaders have followed his example. After many years as an NRA member, the elder George Bush resigned from that organization after becoming dissatisfied with the its attitude following the Oklahoma City bombing. His son, however, has maintained his membership.

During the Clinton era, the National Association for the Advancement of Colored People (NAACP) started a petition in about thirty major cities, including Chicago, Atlanta, and New Orleans, where gun-control groups have a strong hold on many of the municipal assemblies, requesting compensation from gun manufacturers in the same style as in the tobacco lawsuits. The petition contended that crime is encouraged by overproduction of guns. In response, in April 2003 the House of Representatives passed a bill prohibiting lawsuits against gun vendors. It is expected that the bill will be passed in the Republican-majority Senate. If the bill becomes law, all of these pending petitions will be nullified.

At any rate, the determination of the anti-gun-control groups, beginning with the NRA, is relentless. The Brady Bill, named for Press Secretary James Brady, who was seriously injured during the attempted assassination of President Reagan in 1981, was enacted in November 1993 under the Clinton administration. The bill imposes the obligation on a gun merchant to conduct a background check to see if a potential purchaser of a handgun has a criminal history. The following year, in 1994, a new federal domestic anti-crime bill that restricted powerful lethal weapons like the AK-47 narrowly passed through Congress. However, this was the last legislation on gun control. No more gun control measures have been taken since 1994, at least on at the federal level. As for Ashcroft, he proposed that gun-purchase records archived for ninety days in the National Instant Criminal Background Check System (NICS), the heart of the Brady Bill, be destroyed after twenty-four hours.[4]

A slip in the NRA's defenses recently materialized in the District of Columbia, the cradle of the federal government, where the most restrictive gun control of all local self-governing bodies in the United States has been in effect since 1976. In July 2003, Orrin Hatch, the Republican Chairman of the Senate Judiciary Committee, introduced the D.C. Personal Protection Act into the Senate, allowing the possession and carrying of firearms into homes and workplaces, stating, "The prohibition of firearms in the District of Columbia is as ineffective and deplorable as it is unconstitutional." The city's Democratic leaders and citizens fought back strongly, stopping the first real NRA offensive in over ten years dead in its tracks.

More Guns, Less Crime

Today it seems evident that American public opinion, for the most part, supports the notion that it is difficult to establish a correlation between access to guns and an increase in crime. The book *More Guns, Less Crime: Under-*

standing Crime and Gun Control Laws by Yale University Law School Senior Research Scholar John Lott is a typical treatise of the time.[5]

Lott is also a scholar of economics, and using detailed statistics and interviews with criminals, his analysis concludes that:

1. The number of armed burglaries in the United States, where ordinary citizens are allowed to possess guns, is 13 percent lower than that in Britain and Canada;

2. The frequency of crimes in crime-ridden cities is unexpectedly and sharply decreasing as a result of legalizing concealed weapons; and

3. The legalization of concealed weapons has resulted in the rate of victimization of gun-carrying women decreasing three to four times compared with that of men.

Accordingly, the anti-gun-control position that it is better to maintain peace through education in the proper use of guns has spread further while the number of small arms in the U.S. market has grown to more than 230 million. (About one-third are handguns.) In order to cope with the reality of an increase of three to four million guns each year, there has been an emergence of the attitude that educating citizens on the proper use of guns is more effective than clamping down with a vain toughening of regulations.

Cato Institute analyst David Kopel, known for his book analyzing the gun-control situation in every country of the world, including Japan (*The Samurai, the Mountie, and the Cowboy: Should America Adopt the Gun Controls of Other Democracies?*),[6] takes a neutral position toward the NRA.

Kopel, who owns and carries a gun in accordance with the law, believes in the "educational process" used for necessary minimum self-defense. He argues that the only realistic option for the United States is to nurture a culture of responsible gun possession.

Kopel notes that during the development of the frontier in the western United States, order was built by cowboys who practiced such "responsible gun ownership." Further, he claims that some major cities in the present-day United States are in the same situation as the frontier of the past.

The NRA supports this educational process, including the Brady Bill's NICS system. The certificate of completion of the NRA-sponsored gun-training classes, which until recently the Pentagon supported by providing firing ranges, ammunition, and transportation for participants, serves as a publicly recognized license for carrying a gun. Thus, the system of permitting the carrying of concealed weapons, which was advocated very strongly by Mr. Lott for its social effectiveness, has spread across half of the nation's states, beginning with Florida in 1987, and obtaining the NRA certificate of completion became a condition for such permission. In this situation the NRA has played the role of a de facto public organization.[7]

According to the FBI's Annual Report on Crime for 2000, the number of murder cases and the number of those cases in which firearms were used certainly had dropped, as shown in the following table:

FIREARMS USED IN U.S. MURDER CASES

	1996	1997	1998	1999	2000
Murder Cases	16,967	15,837	14,276	13,011	12,943
Handguns	9,266	8,441	7,430	6,658	6,686
Rifles	561	638	548	400	396
Shotguns	685	643	633	531	468
Other	20	35	16	92	51

Since 9/11, the American flag has been displayed everywhere, and the nation's cohabitation with firearms has deepened throughout society.

Allow me to illustrate this point with one particular episode. In July 2003, during my fourth visit to the United States, while researching and writing this book, I came across a television news story about a jumbo jackpot lottery winner. An honest-looking couple from Jefferson City, Missouri, a fifty-three-year-old company supervisor and his fifty-two-year-old wife, a substitute teacher, had won an enormous amount of money, $130,600,000, from a five-dollar investment and had been pulled into a press conference to explain how they planned to use their winnings.

After the husband explained that he planned to replace his 1950s-era tractor, and the wife said she wanted a new kitchen refrigerator to replace the one they had from the "Nixon days," the husband added, "I'd also like to buy a new gun."

At that moment, I understood perfectly well that an "amendment" of the Second Amendment, as suggested by both houses of Congress, just wouldn't happen.

The Conversion of Professor Tribe

The influence of the NRA is likely to grow, as is demonstrated by the work of a particularly noteworthy constitutional scholar. With regard to the Second Amendment, his position has evolved from a previous recognition of conventional state rights as indicted in the *Miller* decision to the human rights position favored by the NRA. The scholar is Laurence H. Tribe, the Ralph S. Tyler Professor of Constitutional Law at Harvard Law School. His primary work, *American Constitutional Law,* is an established textbook used not only at Harvard but also in law schools all over the United States. It is said to have been cited in more than fifty Supreme Court rulings. The popular professor also appears on television programs discussing the constitution and is known for his liberal opinions.

Professor Tribe presented a significantly different interpretation of the Second Amendment in his third and most recent edition of *American Constitutional Law* in 2000 than he did in the first and second editions published in 1978 and 1988, respectively.

I first learned of this from a headline in the August 27, 1999 edition of *USA Today* that proclaimed, "Scholar's Views on Arms Rights Anger Liberals." The article reported that Professor Tribe had recognized the right to bear arms by all American citizens as a human right, perplexing a great many of his colleagues. The NRA was pleased at this development. Richard Poe, a journalist sympathetic to the NRA, happily proclaimed in his controversial 2001 book, *The Seven Myths of Gun Control: Reclaiming the Truth About Guns, Crime, and the Second Amendment,* that Tribe's "modest assertions proved sufficient" to send his "liberal colleagues into a rage and confusion." Poe quipped, "The real shocker was that a man called 'the most influential living American constitutional scholar' had waited twenty years before deciding to do so."[8]

I ordered the 2000 edition in question and compared it to the first and second editions. I found it to be quite different from what was reported in *USA Today* and the boasting in the NRA publications. Not only is it modest, as Poe states, it is also quite delicate in its language. Nevertheless, it is unquestionably a change in interpretation.

In my view, Professor Tribe is making a painful effort to adapt to the times. It appears to be a scholar's acceptance of responsibility toward the use of force evident in the DNA of America's founding that I am trying to document in this book.

In the 1978 first edition of *American Constitutional Law*, Professor Tribe clearly takes the position that those who drafted the Second Amendment were concerned only with state rights. He remarks that the "sole concern" of the Second Amendment framers was to prevent a situation in which the federal government could intervene in a state's militia and destroy local autonomy with a standing national army. Therefore, he argues the Second Amendment does not apply to purely private acts. As for the *Miller* decision, Tribe explains that the decision takes the position that the Second Amendment is not the only constitutional guarantee of state sovereignty, but merely supplements other guarantees.

He addressed this issue only in footnote 6 to chapter 5, "Federal Legislative Power: Congressional Authority and the Implications of State Sovereignty." The following quote provides the essence of his interpretation:

> The sole concern of the Second Amendment's framers was to prevent such federal interferences with the state militia as would permit the establishment of a standing national army and consequent destruction of local autonomy. Thus, the inapplicability of the Second Amendment to purely private conduct. [9]

The treatment in the notes column of the second edition of 1988 is almost identical. However, there are substantive changes in the third edition published in 2000. Taking up the subject in the book's preface, the professor skillfully maneuvers with prudence and irony, touching upon even the Columbine shooting, and changing his position as quoted below.

> Although a few terrible episodes of school shootings, most dramatically that in Littleton, Colorado, in April 1999, seem to have galvanized public opinion in the direction of gun control for the time being—a direction I personally applaud strictly as a matter of policy—nothing that has happened since 1988 has altered the legal landscape on which the Second Amendment sits.
> Yet an avalanche of scholarly investigation, including my own research on the subject (not previously published), has required me to revisit the meaning of that amendment, with its peculiar preamble about 'a well regulated Militia, being necessary to the security of a free State'—peculiar, that is, for provisions of the

federal Constitution; state constitutions regularly contain such purposive preambles. My conclusions, without giving the whole game away, are:

1. That it's extremely misleading to frame the debate in terms of a clash between those who think the Second Amendment protects only the militia and the rights of states, and those who think the Second Amendment protects individual rights to keep and bear arms and therefore makes pretty much all forms of gun control presumptively unconstitutional;

2. That the Second Amendment does indeed protect individual rights as well as collective rights—but not in a way that creates significant obstacles for any program of gun control short of a federal disarmament campaign designed to eliminate all private gun ownership, which isn't remotely in the cards anyway; and

3. That the biggest payoff from studying the Second Amendment is the value of being forced to grapple with difficult interpretive issues in a politically and emotionally charged environment.[10]

Professor Tribe continues discussing the issue further in the main text of chapter 5 in a section titled "The Second Amendment and State Sovereignty." The main point of this discussion is as follows:

Whether the Second Amendment might restrain various forms of gun control is a topic that has attracted much academic and popular, if not judicial, attention. The topic gains in poignancy and interest from the enormous strength of most people's policy views on the need for, and desirability of, much more sweeping sorts of gun control than exist in this country at present, and from the inescapable tension, for many people on both sides of this policy divide, between the reading of the Second Amendment that would advance the policies they favor and the reading of the Second Amendment to which intellectual honesty, and their own theories of constitutional interpretation, would drive

them if they could bring themselves to set their policy convic-
tions aside. . . . For this reason, and for the further reason that
the Second Amendment provides fertile ground in which to till
the soil of federalism and unearth its relationship with individual
as well as collective notions of rights, few constitutional provi-
sions offer a richer opportunity to sort out the strands of one's
approach to constitutional interpretation.

   Today, the jurisprudence of the Second Amendment is
radically underdeveloped, largely because it has been mistak-
enly interpreted in binary terms: either the Amendment con-
fers a personal right, in which case all forms of gun control are
presumptively (or perhaps conclusively) unconstitutional, or it
does not, in which case there is assumed to be no constitutional
issue at all. If the Second Amendment does indeed play a role
in securing some kinds of individual rights as well as securing
a degree of state sovereignty, that role will have to be defined
by careful argument from constitutional text, structure, and
history.[11]

While this is a form of self-criticism on the part of Professor Tribe, it
is also a declaration that the Second Amendment needs to be reexamined
in order to provide a clear interpretation. The evolution of Professor Tribe's
work is extremely important because of the huge influence he commands,
and such a change of view may further influence a change in the Supreme
Court's approach to this amendment. The timing of new appointments to the
Supreme Court to replace the aging justices retiring to private life will have a
critical effect on U.S. politics. The appointments made to the Supreme Court
during the Bush administration have been of a profoundly different nature
than those during the Clinton presidency, and the change in the Court's
treatment of the Second Amendment in the future must be watched right
along with the conversion of Professor Tribe.

   In the meantime, the one thing I can do is to finish reading my American history, as Professor Tribe suggests.

   Moreover, it is incumbent upon Japan, with its increasing contact with
America, to comprehend the degree to which the permission of gun ownership exists in contemporary American society. For this very reason I, too,
must continue the work on which I have embarked.

On October 17, 1992, a sixteen-year-old Japanese exchange student, Yoshihiro Hattori, was shot and killed from inside the doorway of a home in Baton Rouge, Louisiana, his only "crime" having been to go to the wrong house for a Halloween party. The shooter, however, was found not guilty in court.[12] As I honor Yoshihiro's soul anew, I believe it is becoming more critical to grasp the true face of this country called America, where such a tragedy thrusts into relief.

THREE

Birth from "Disorder"

A Bundle of Compromises

In order to understand the logic contained in the Second Amendment, we must first go back to the birth of the United States and the original documents that created the nation. These date from the nation's establishment at the Constitutional Convention in Philadelphia in 1787, the Constitution's ratification the following year in 1788, and the ten amendments known as the Bill of Rights added three years later. The Constitution and the Bill of Rights have been in force continuously for more than 214 years.

As the history books tell it, the government structure set down by this Constitution took twelve years to enact after the Declaration of Independence of 1776 and represents the work of the Founding Fathers. This elite group of men—President George Washington, John Adams, Thomas Jefferson, James Madison, and Alexander Hamilton, among others—created, out of passion and determination, an original form of democracy, one found nowhere in Europe.

Their passion and conviction was in the challenge of developing an original democracy for the new-world United States that differed from the democratization of Britain or France. Their determination was in weaving a democratic system unique to the United States into a constitutional document.

The Constitution was a product of compromise between thirteen former British colonies that had united as states to form a de facto, newly independent nation, and involved fine tuning the various controversial issues of the day: state rights versus the federal government, large states versus small states, the East versus the South, industry versus agriculture, cities versus rural communities, and standing army versus militia.

In this manner the U.S. Constitution adopted the following main points:

- While stipulating the state rights of the former colonies, the new nation would assume a federal form.

- A small, centralized federal government would be established as a "necessary evil" to manage such national matters as foreign diplomatic relations and the economy.

- The president would be placed at the center of this federal government as head of state, with Congress and the Supreme Court as counterbalances on either side, thus establishing popular sovereignty with a system of checks and balances through the so-called separation of powers.

Although the constitution represented the birth of what later was sometimes called "100 percent American-style democracy," it was also described as a "bundle of compromises."

The addition of the Bill of Rights, of which the Second Amendment is a part, represents the last compromise and could be called the final act of a drama that vividly thrusts the true face of this country into relief even now after over 210 years.

The debates at the Philadelphia Constitutional Convention in May 1787 were a tug of war between two groups, the Federalists and Anti-Federalists. The former were optimists who immediately wished to launch a new, unified nation under a federal system with a small central government. While recognizing the value of preserving state rights, they saw the necessity of placing foreign relations and economic functions in the hands of a central government. The latter, on the other hand, were pragmatists who desired maximum preservation of the rights of each autonomous entity, that is, the thirteen states, but who recognized the inauguration of a federal central government as a necessary evil.

The Constitutional Convention convened in secret on May 25, 1787, with former Continental Army Commander George Washington as chairman and fifty-five representatives participating from twelve states. The colony of Rhode Island did not take part. The debates progressed based upon the Virginia Plan submitted by James Madison, later called the father of the U.S. Constitution. It is said to have been a hot and humid summer. Although those convened included eight veteran statesmen who had signed the Declaration of Independence, such as the eighty-one-year-old Benjamin Franklin, half of the convention's members, including the thirty-six-year-old Madison, were young, energetic founders in their thirties.

The greatest issue concerned to what degree the Articles of Confederation of 1781, which recognized the thirteen states as actual independent republics, should be amended to establish a central power within a federation. The Virginia Plan proposed a bicameral system that assigned seats in proportion to population. The New Jersey Plan proposed a unicameral system with one vote per state. Out of these two diametrically opposed views came a third plan, the Connecticut plan, that called for a House of Representatives with its seats determined by population and a Senate with two votes per state without regard to size. Adopted by a slim margin, this arrangement was dubbed The Great Compromise.

Next followed arguments between the southern states, which sought to increase their population by counting black slaves—thus boosting the number of their seats in the House even though no state recognized the suffrage rights of the black slaves—and the northern states, which opposed this effort. The resulting Three-Fifths Compromise recognized each black slave as three-fifths of a person for the purpose of the population count. Furthermore, the northern states, proposing the abolition of the slave trade itself, agreed to a compromise under which they would not raise the abolition issue in Congress for at least twenty years. With those compromises, the draft document was finally concluded that September.

The Second Amendment as *Fait Accompli*

Toward the end of the deliberations, Virginia delegate George Mason proposed a bill of rights that introduced freedom of speech and press, freedom of religion, and a system of trial by jury in the preamble. It also specified the right to bear arms. According to the constitutional scholar Leonard W. Levy,

Mason reasoned that this would provide ordinary citizens with a sense of security. In a matter of hours he produced a draft he thought would be adopted satisfactorily. Accordingly, there were no notable speeches on the topic.

The Massachusetts delegation agreed with Mason's proposal. Connecticut delegate Roger Sherman, however, argued that bills of rights were already embodied in the constitutions of the states, and since the new constitution in effect recognized the rights of the states, such a bill was unnecessary. Sherman's motion was not debated, and the Constitution was approved with no dissenting votes. A motion to insert at least one line guaranteeing freedom of speech was also dismissed, and the Constitutional Convention concluded three days later on September 17. Levy theorizes that the delegates had become fatigued and did not wish to engage in new debate.[1]

Though Mason was unsuccessful, he had some basis for his optimism since the political situation in 1787 made a separate Bill of Rights a fait accompli. This point is critical since it influenced the origin of the U.S. political system that remains to this day. Since the arrival of the advanced information society in the latter half of the twentieth century, this framework may have undergone some superficial changes, but it can still be seen as the core of American democracy and civilian life.

In those days, each state was a de facto sovereign republic with its own rights, in other words an independent country. Moreover, almost all the states, including Mason's native Virginia, had state constitutions that included bills of rights. The Declaration of Independence of 1776 declared a union of these de facto independent countries. Five years later, the Articles of Confederation, ratified by agreement of the former colonies, used the words "United States of America" for the first time as the name of the union. It ensured that "each state retains its sovereignty, freedom, and independence, and every power, jurisdiction, and right, which is not by this Confederation expressly delegated to the United States, in Congress assembled."

In the case of Virginia, five days prior to the adoption of the Declaration of Independence on July 4, 1776, the Constitution of Virginia outlined a bill of rights and government structure. Section One loudly heralds the basic principle of democracy as it proclaims:

> That all men are by nature equally free and independent and
> have certain inherent rights, of which, when they enter into a
> state of society, they cannot, by any compact, deprive or divest

their posterity; namely, the enjoyment of life and liberty, with the means of acquiring and possessing property, and pursuing and obtaining happiness and safety.

Article 2 continues with the statement:

That all power is vested in, and consequently derived from, the people, that magistrates are their trustees and servants, and at all times amenable to them.

A central feature of American democracy—that democracy begins with the guarantee of each citizen's democratic rights at the state level—is clearly understood. The Virginia Constitution was the world's first written constitution and serves as the prototype for the U.S. Constitution.

Constitutions and bills of rights followed in the other states: New Jersey in July 1776, Delaware and Pennsylvania in September 1776, Maryland in November 1776, North Carolina in December 1776, Georgia in February 1777, New York in April 1777, South Carolina in March 1778, Massachusetts in October 1780, and New Hampshire in June 1784.[2] Many states had their own independent constitutions already in place long before the federation progressed from the loose union provided under the Articles of Confederation to the establishment of a central federal government in June 1788 through the U.S. Constitution. This marked the change to the current national structure of a president, congress, and supreme court, with its features of checks and balances and separation of powers.

A prototype for the Second Amendment was also specified perfectly in the Articles of Confederation. Article 6 clearly states that:

Every State shall always keep up a well-regulated and disciplined militia, sufficiently armed and accoutered, and shall provide and constantly have ready for use, in public stores, a due number of filed pieces and tents, and a proper quantity of arms, ammunition and camp equipage.

The clearest specification in a state document is contained in Article 13 of the September 28, 1776 version of the Constitution of the Commonwealth of Pennsylvania, which reads:

The right of the citizens to bear arms in defense of themselves and the State shall not be questioned. No standing army shall, in time of peace, be kept without the consent of the Legislature, and the military shall in all cases and at all times be in strict subordination to the civil power.

Section Thirteen of Virginia's constitution similarly states:

That a well-regulated militia, composed of the body of the people, trained to arms, is the proper, natural, and safe defense of a free state, therefore, the right of the people to keep and bear arms shall not be infringed; that standing armies, in time of peace, should be avoided as dangerous to liberty; and that in all cases the military should be under strict subordination to, and governed by, the civil power.

Virginia's Bill of Rights is, incidentally, Mason's composition.

Other states, including Maryland, Delaware, and New Hampshire, used more direct expressions to define the necessity of a well-regulated militia for the proper, natural, and safe defense of a free government. In Pennsylvania, even the pacifist Quakers owned arms and reportedly took part in militia training.

The Dignity of State Rights

In any event, a strong wariness of standing armies existed owing to the hostility among colonists toward the British regular army dispatched from the mother country. Some states had militias that approached the status of standing armies. These selected their members from the regular militia, similar to the minutemen of Massachusetts that started the War of Independence. The Second Amendment's controversial beginning, "a well regulated Militia," is the root of the division within American society, the explanation for why gun control is unchecked, and the reason that even Professor Tribe has stated that the matter must be reexamined.

The enactment of the Constitution and the founding of the republic were not necessarily on the formal agenda of the Philadelphia Constitutional Convention itself. The decision to convene a meeting specifically for the clear single purpose of revising the Articles of Confederation had been made only in February. Preparations for establishing a more powerful federal system and federal central government were skillfully devised after the realists judged these features to be indispensable. They were particularly concerned with such pressing problems as the need to set up diplomatic and foreign commercial relations (including customs duties), the domestic economic market, and the establishment of domestic order, especially in light of Shays' Rebellion in Massachusetts the previous year.[3] These men came to be called federalists during the course of the constitutional debates. As such, the building blocks of America were founded upon the strength of the original system of state rights.

State rights are a unique and important part of American democracy. An appropriate example of their power can be seen in the 2000 presidential election.

In this election George W. Bush was defeated by Al Gore in the popular vote, but was nevertheless inaugurated as the forty-third president because of his one-vote victory in the Electoral College. As defined in the U.S. Constitution, art. 2, sec. 1, cl. 3, each state appoints electors equal to its total number of senators and representatives. While the number of representatives for each state changes according to the population, the number of senators for each state is fixed at two. This is a mechanism of equal state rights, and it can be said to have worked well for Mr. Bush in this close election.

The Founding Fathers were the top elite of the day from each colony. They had taken precautions against a government elected by an unknowledgeable mob and opposed elections by popular vote, a process distrusted by many of the nation's founders. The election of a president not from the elite class was not to take place until 1828 with the election of Andrew Jackson. The Seventeenth Amendment, ratified in 1913, eventually specified that the election of U.S. senators would be decided by popular vote rather than by the vote of state legislatures as had been originally provided in the Constitution.

In Japan there is the view that Electoral College decisions constitute a crisis in the American governmental system. However, the final settlement of President Bush's election in the form of a Supreme Court determination, despite the trouble in Florida, reflects a successful application of the U.S. constitutional system with checks and balances. Former Vice President Gore, who conceded after his narrow loss, bore no grudge against the system but affirmed his loyalty to the U.S. Constitution and went on with his life. Constitutional amendments to change the Electoral College system have been proposed over seven hundred times but have always fallen by the wayside.

In other words, Mason, an advocate of state rights, judged that the insertion of a Bill of Rights could provide citizens with a sense of security regarding the Constitution. Mason felt that on top of the militias' accomplishments in achieving a guerilla war victory over the British Army during the War of Independence, such a Bill of Rights offered a safety valve designed to quell voters' fears of a resurgence of tyranny and to secure their support to a new government that went by the name of the United States of America.

In order to understand this point, we must go back into history even further. Among the ten amendments that constitute the Bill of Rights, the phrase "a well-regulated Militia, being necessary to the security of a free State" appears only in the introduction to the Second Amendment. We will see how and why it got there.

Secession from England

It is important to realize that the entire Second Amendment is a holdover from the former British monarchy. The U.S. Bill of Rights was modeled after the English 1689 Bill of Rights, which was enacted as a result of the Glorious Revolution, a bloodless uprising that banished James II for attempting to reestablish Catholicism in England. The seventh declaration of this bill specifies "that the subjects which are Protestants may have arms for their defense suitable to their conditions and as allowed by law." Ninety-eight percent of the English people were, incidentally, Protestant.

By the time the British Parliament created the Bill of Rights enumerating the rights of subjects, about four centuries had passed since 1215 when the Magna Carta was written and feudal aristocrats succeeded in forcing rule of law on the king. The constitutional monarchy was established by two milestones: Charles I's acceptance of the Petition of Right in 1628, and the Puritan Revolution that led to Charles I's execution in 1649. It was a bloody history. The right to bear arms has certainly traveled a bumpy road.

During the twelfth and thirteenth centuries, the duty to bear arms was imposed by the king upon his subjects, and the "extent of appropriate armament" was periodically checked by the royal family. Preservation of peace, community defense, and de facto police powers were granted to regional authorities. The duty to bear arms also applied to serfs without land, an arrangement which was the beginning of the militia system. The system made sense for a Britain that was aiming to establish itself as a maritime powerhouse. While the nation's powerful navy could deal a heavy blow, the army's combat forces were put on the back burner.

In the sixteenth and seventeenth centuries, however, the kings moved to establish a more powerful standing army in response to colonial territorial expansion. They also began to restrict ownership of arms to a handful of aristocrats, large landowners, and the wealthy. These actions were in response to the civil disorder occurring as the result of the spread of weapons. At the same time a new, widespread movement was deepening solidarity among small landowners, free farmers, merchants, tradesmen, attorneys, and scholars as free people. They confronted and fought the king's despotism and oppression while demanding a civic right to bear arms. This was the beginning of the debate over a standing army versus militias that was later brought to the American continent. For those involved, the bearing of arms was not only the right of self-defense for a free people but also a political right, or in contemporary language, a democratic right.

The Birth of the "Well-Regulated Militia"

In this fashion, free men came to believe that the most effective means of preserving freedom was through arms. Andrew Fletcher, one of the Scottish Enlightenment philosophers who greatly influenced American revolutionary thinking, put it this way in 1698: "Arms are the only true badges of liberty. The possession of arms is the distinction of a free man from a slave."

Fletcher further appealed,

> Let us now consider whether we may not be able to defend
> ourselves by well-regulated militias against any foreign force,
> though never so formidable: that these nations may be free from
> the fears of invasion from abroad, as well as from the danger of
> slavery at home.

Here the phrase "well-regulated militia" appears for the first time. A "well-regulated militia" was a militia of free men in contrast to a standing army organized as the "king's militia." This distinction is important.

Thus, the right to possession of arms by a well-regulated militia was included in the Bill of Rights of the constitutional monarchy that the English and Scottish Enlightenments achieved through the Glorious Revolution. To Algernon Sydney, a leading philosopher of republicanism known for his criticisms of the English king and his encouragement of American independence at the time of the Glorious Revolution, the arming of citizens is a legitimate and godly thing that only a tyrant hates. He also stressed the right of citizens to bear arms as indispensable to republicanism. Sydney reportedly had an influence on Thomas Jefferson, the drafter of the Declaration of Independence, and his opinions were quoted—along with those of John Locke and Charles-Louis Montesquieu—in press editorials in the years between the Declaration of Independence and the establishment of the Constitution.

Jefferson also was influenced by the opinions of Italian Enlightenment thinker Cesare Beccaria, who wrote:

> The laws that forbid the carrying of arms are laws of such a nature. They disarm those only who are neither inclined nor determined to commit crimes. Can it be supposed that those who have the courage to violate the most sacred laws of humanity, the most important of the code, will respect the less important and arbitrary ones, which can be violated with ease and impunity, and which, if strictly obeyed, would put an end to personal liberty—so dear to men . . . and subject innocent persons to all the vexations that the guilty alone ought to suffer? Such laws make things worse for the assaulted and better for the assailants.

Beccaria's work *Of Crime and Punishment* is called the origin of criminal jurisprudence and is known for its influence on the French Revolution.[4]

The most extreme aspect of the enlightenment of the eighteenth century, the defense of militias in opposition to standing armies, or rather the arming of citizens to oppose the despotism of standing armies, had as part of its genealogy the classic republicanism of Greece and Rome and the further medieval republicanism of Nicolo Machiavelli, who claimed that civil war is better than oppression. This way of thinking had crossed the Atlantic and was destined to become still more extreme after being planted on the new

American continent, which, unlike Britain, had not one fragment of a feudal infrastructure.

Since, on American soil, all migrants and settlers were free people, the well-regulated militia was established from the outset. On April 18, 1775, special units of this well-regulated militia, known as the minutemen, fired on the standing British Army after it had seized militia armories at Lexington and Concord, Massachusetts, and arrested the caretakers. The fuse of revolution and the American War of Independence was lit.

The Bill of Rights Revived

Ratification of the Constitution required passage by nine states, and in the state debates the concept of inserting Mason's proposed Bill of Rights into the Constitution was revived. With the bitter exclamation that "I would sooner chop off my hand than put it to the Constitution as it now stands," Mason and the anti-Federalists argued against ratification of the Constitution because it lacked a Bill of Rights.

After insisting that the Constitution itself was a Bill of Rights, federalist leaders James Madison and Alexander Hamilton changed their position after the states of Pennsylvania, Massachusetts, and Maryland officially and unofficially announced that they would ratify the Constitution only if a Bill of Rights was inserted. In order to keep the Constitution intact, they promised to submit a Bill of Rights as amendments during the first congressional session, and the immediate addition of the Bill of Rights became the top order of the day for the Founding Fathers.

The clincher came when Madison changed his attitude during the ratification meeting in Virginia in June 1788. In order to put the building of the new nation on track immediately, Madison decided that the anti-Federalist demand must be accepted. Not long before, Madison had received a letter from Thomas Jefferson, then in Paris as minister to France, in which Jefferson stated that, as a result of the thirteen states uniting into a single nation, "a Bill of Rights is what the people are entitled to against every government on earth, general or particular, and what no just government should refuse, or rest on inference." Such advice from an old and close friend is said to have deeply influenced Madison.

Madison concluded that the most important point was that no government had the power to interfere with basic human rights. Since not every state constitution contained a bill of rights, it made logical sense to add amendments to the new Constitution as a form of "double security," in the words of Leonard W. Levy, to insert a guard against abuse of power by the federal government of the United States.

Consequently, Madison proposed adding the Bill of Rights to the just-completed document during the first congressional session. When it opened in accordance with the new Constitution in June 1789, both houses acted to summarize a bill of rights into twelve articles of amendment. In December 1791, about two years after the states had appealed to President Washington for ratification, the Bill of Rights—reduced to the present ten amendments—finally became a part of the Constitution of the United States. After a process of repeated persuasion, conflict, and compromise, the ingredients of the earliest written constitution in the world had been set.

Jefferson proudly reported to France's Marquis de Lafayette, by whose side he had fought during the War of Independence, that with the establishment of these ten amendments, the anti-Federalists had lost their supporters and opposition to the Constitution had nearly completely disappeared.

Still, the three states of Massachusetts, Connecticut, and Virginia did not ratify the constitution until its 150th anniversary in 1939. From this it is clear to see that the Bill of Rights was a document born of much toil. In addition, the Constitution was also established as both a product of the great pains taken by the Founding Fathers in their quest to build a nation and their devotion to and passion for the uniqueness of American democracy.

The late prominent American historian Samuel Elliot Morison, known for his book about Admiral Perry and the coming of the "black ships," commented on the Founding Fathers in his book, *The Oxford History of the American People*, as follows:

> One of the most remarkable things about the American Revolution is the fact that the radicals of 1774–76 who started it, also saw through to a point—that point being 1787, when younger men took over to put a capstone on the edifice. All modern history proves that it is easy enough for a determined minority to pull down a government, but exceeding difficult to reconstruct, to re-establish law and order on new foundations. And in no other great revolution have the initial agitators long survived

liquidation by their successors. Dozens of nations since World War II have won independence—but how many have secured liberty?[5]

I think this is an appropriate point. The materialization of the ten amendments that constitute the Bill of Rights in 1791 indeed marked the Founding Fathers seeing their effort "through to a point," and was "exceedingly difficult."

The Foresight of Adam Smith

The process by which the DNA of military might assumed the form of a "well-regulated Militia," crossed the Atlantic, secured victory in the War of Independence, and established itself as the Second Amendment to the U.S. Constitution, is highlighted in the interesting work of Adam Smith.

In his famous work, *An Inquiry into the Nature and Causes of the Wealth of Nations*, published four months before the Declaration of Independence in March 1776, Smith stated that the colonization of the United States had its roots in disorder and injustice. Furthermore, he demonstrated that the nation was built freely in the absence of formal policy decisions by the British Empire.

Smith criticized mercantilism that depended upon the plundering of another nation's wealth and advocated laissez-faire economics supported by the "invisible hand of God." These ideas secured his place in history as the father of modern economics. While Smith's theory was put into practice over the past three centuries, materializing into today's American market economy, its antithesis has also been explored elsewhere in various forms of controlled economies like the New Deal.

According to Irving Kristol, one of the founders of the neoconservative movement and a strong influence on President Bush's decision to go to war with Iraq, Madison and the Founding Fathers referred to *The Wealth of Nations* as "the new political science." Upon reading the book's summary, they were confident they could build a capitalist democratic society as the American way of life.[6]

Certainly when I read Smith's precise analysis of the country, written in March 1776, I can see how the Founding Fathers were encouraged by it.

Not only an economist, Smith also occupied a high position—together

with Locke and David Hume—as one of the English and Scottish Enlightenment philosophers who influenced the American independence movement.

In chapter 7 of Book 4 of *The Wealth of Nations*, a section titled "Of
Colonies" describes the situation in America as follows:

> The policy of Europe, therefore, has very little to boast of, either
> in the original establishment or, so far as concerns their inter-
> nal government, in the subsequent prosperity of the colonies of
> America.
>
> Folly and injustice seem to have been the principles which
> presided over and directed the first project of establishing those
> colonies; the folly of hunting after gold and silver mines, and the
> injustice of coveting the possession of a country whose harmless
> natives, far from having ever injured the people of Europe, had
> received the first adventurers with every mark of kindness and
> hospitality.
>
> Upon all these different occasions it was not the wisdom
> and policy, but the disorder and injustice of the European gov-
> ernments which peopled and cultivated America.
>
> The leading men of America, like those of all other coun-
> tries, desire to preserve their own importance. They feel, or
> imagine, that if their assemblies, which they are fond of calling
> parliaments, and of considering as equal in authority to the Par-
> liament of Great Britain, should be so far degraded as to become
> the humble ministers and executive officers of that Parliament,
> the greater part of their own importance would be at end. They
> have rejected, therefore, the proposal of being taxed by Parlia-
> mentary requisition, and like other ambitious and high-spirited
> men, have rather chosen to draw the sword in defence of their
> own importance.
>
> From shopkeepers, tradesmen, and attornies, they are
> become statesmen and legislators, and are employed in contriv-
> ing a new form of government for an extensive empire, which,
> they flatter themselves, will become, and which, indeed, seems
> very likely to become, one of the greatest and most formidable
> that ever was in the world.
>
> They are very weak who flatter themselves that, in the state

to which things have come, our colonies will be easily conquered by force alone.

The distance of America from the seat of government, besides, the natives of that country might flatter themselves, with some appearance of reason too, would not be of very long continuance. Such has hitherto been the rapid progress of that country in wealth, population, and improvement, that in the course of little more than a century, perhaps, the produce of American might exceed that of British taxation. The seat of the empire would then naturally remove itself to that part of the empire which contributed most to the general defence and support of the whole.

The discovery of America, and that of a passage to the East Indies by the Cape of Good Hope, are the two greatest and most important events recorded in the history of mankind. Their consequences have already been very great; but, in the short period of between two and three centuries which has elapsed since these discoveries were made, it is impossible that the whole extent of their consequences can have been seen.[7]

This analysis has many poignant propositions that do not lose their freshness even now, 228 years later. In conclusion, *The Wealth of Nations* wraps up its exposition by condoning the independence of the American states:

The rulers of Great Britain have, for more than a century past, amused the people with the imagination that they possessed a great empire on the west side of the Atlantic. This empire, however, has hitherto existed in imagination only. It has hitherto been, not an empire, but the project of an empire; not a gold mine, but the project of a gold mine; a project which has cost, which continues to cost, and which, if pursued in the same way as it has been hitherto, is likely to cost, immense expense, without being likely to bring any profit; for the effects of the monopoly of the colony trade, it has been shown, are, to the great body of the people, mere loss instead of profit. It is surely now time that our rulers should either realize this golden dream, in which they have been indulging themselves, perhaps, as well as the people, or that they should awake from it themselves, and endeavour to awaken the people. If the project cannot be completed, it ought to be given up.

Thus, George III, Prime Minister Frederick North, and other British whom Smith called the "very weak" were defeated by the guerrilla tactics of the "well-regulated Militia," and a country called the United States was born.

FOUR

Of the Mayflower's *Origin*

A Democracy with No Model

There was, of course, an established British royal colonial order on the North American continent. As the colonies entered the eighteenth century, a governor appointed by the Crown managed each colony. Even at the time of the Battles of Lexington and Concord in 1775, of the three million residents in thirteen colonies, the number that supported independence did not exceed one-third. Another third consisted of loyalist Tories opposed to independence, and the remainder were politically neutral.

Among these, some entrusted their dreams in economic ventures in the vast South with Virginia as its hub. There were those who sought a religious new world in the areas around Plymouth and Boston in New England. There were those in New York who had lived through the city's transformation from Dutch to British territory. Within each of these widely diverse groups there were American colonists who believed that the greatest advantages for the colonies could only come through subordination and loyalty to the British Crown.

They believed that it was possible to preserve economic, religious, and social freedom even while accepting loyalty to the Crown as long as the "wisdom and policy" of that institution (which Adam Smith held to be nonexistent) and British governmental control were relatively loose.[1]

Regarding the situation in the pre-revolutionary thirteen colonies, Yale

University historian and professor Robert R. Palmer, known for his comparative studies of European and American democracies, offers a clear-cut analysis of the social structure of the thirteen pre-revolutionary colonies, stating that, unlike France, there was no feudalism, no systems of lords and estates, and no sharecroppers. Feudal lords and aristocrats did not exist, and there were no magnificent, privileged churches such as the Church of England. [2]

According to Palmer, Americans had had no experience with taxation, public offices, the army, and diplomacy until the start of their confrontation with England. There were no medieval economic holdovers like the guilds of Europe, alongside the banks, businesses, and trading companies of Europe's advanced capitalism. The colonies had none of the great wealth or extreme poverty of large cities like London or Paris, and nothing comparable to the road networks of some parts of England and Europe. Apart from a few institutions like Harvard, the College of William and Mary, and Yale, there were no institutions of higher learning.

There was no publishing industry to speak of; most books circulated were imported from Britain. In fact, there were no real intellectuals. A handful of the Founding Fathers, such as Benjamin Franklin, Thomas Jefferson, and John Adams, frequently read works from Europe and possessed great knowledge and intellect, but they were from the second generation of successful colonists. The southerners among them, such as Jefferson and George Mason, were from the slaveholding class. Such men were exceptions among exceptions.

In short, America in 1776 was a newly emerging country with no common inheritance of human rights, religion, linguistics, or politics. As Palmer states, the thirteen colonies, on achieving independence, constituted a nation that simply had no role model.

Ironically, the fuse of the American Revolution was lit when the British Empire changed its formerly loose governing style. Seeking to pay for the seven-year war between England and France that lasted from 1756 to 1763, Parliament levied a succession of unpopular taxes through the Sugar Act, Stamp Act, and Tea Act. These brought strong opposition from the colonists.

The American theater in the war between England and France, known to this day in the United States as the French and Indian War, actually began in 1754. The French army went so far as to involve the Indians on its side, fighting south from Canada onto the plains of the Ohio and Tennessee river valleys west of the Appalachian Mountains.

This war was just one part of a further and simultaneous worldwide colonial scramble between the two empires of France and Britain in Europe and India. It was arguably the final decisive battle between the two powers following King William's War of 1689–97 (part of the War of the League of Augsburg), Queen Anne's War of 1702–13 (the American version of the Spanish Succession), and King George's War of 1744–48 (similarly a part of the Austrian Succession).

The result was the final victory of the co-mobilized British regular army and colonial militias. At the Battle of Plassey in India, the army of the British East India Company defeated the Governor of Bengal and the French army in 1757. Thereafter Britain exerted substantial influence over the Indian subcontinent.

Nevertheless, as a result of the 90 million pounds spent for these wars, England fell into serious financial difficulty. The heavy taxation inflicted on the American colonies eventually drove Britain into a corner. Long years of colonial objections to "taxation without representation" were ignored by the Crown. With the imposition of one law after another by the British Parliament, colonists began to despair. Gradually the flashpoint of revolution approached and the idea of rebellion against British tyranny by the "well-regulated" colonial militias was born.

In this way, the DNA of the use of force ultimately became embedded in the Constitution itself, and it has remained a part of American democracy ever since. This is the reason that the Second Amendment continues to function as a part of the Bill of Rights.

The NRA and other gun lobbies vehemently argue that the Second Amendment is a "right that our founders so divinely captured and crafted," as Charlton Heston stated in the 1999 speech mentioned at the beginning of chapter 2. Gun-control groups still find themselves on the defensive despite such events as the assassinations of the Kennedy brothers and Reverend King while the Supreme Court evades a clear ruling on the issue. The reason for all of this lies in the country's lineage, which has incorporated the use of force in its DNA.

The War of Independence was no mere coup d'etat or armed uprising, and it was through military might that the nation achieved independence and produced an original democracy. Therefore, it became a citizen's duty not to condone tyranny, and the DNA of the use of force was embedded as a part of the idea of democracy in the name of a well-regulated militia.

Virginia's Survival by Tobacco

So, how did this order known as American democracy come about?

For an explanation, we must reach back to 1620. We must tell the story of the group of 102 settlers who arrived off the shore of Cape Cod (about 30 miles south of present-day Boston) in November after having endured a severe sixty-five-day voyage across the Atlantic from England packed aboard the 180-ton *Mayflower*.

But first it is important to examine the group that built the first English colony in North America. These were the 105 settlers sent to Jamestown in present-day Virginia in May 1607 by the Virginia Company, a colonial-development company chartered by the British Crown. In modern-day language, these were the employees of a venture business, or rather, of its branch location.

Prior to this settlement, Captain John Smith had explored the Atlantic coast of the new continent repeatedly since the beginning of the seventeenth century and had published maps with place names at the behest of the Virginia Company. He had incidentally left a journal of his travels.

According to this journal, the only concern of this get-rich-quick group was to "dig gold, wash gold, refine gold, load gold." When no gold materialized, dissension erupted. After a year had passed, about half the settlers had perished, and the other half were on the verge of death. As one of this remaining group of settlers, Captain Smith brandished a gun and demanded supplies of corn from the chief of the nearby Powhatan tribe. The surviving colonists narrowly escaped doom thanks to the affection of the chief's daughter, Pocahontas, who later married another Jamestown colonist.

For a number of years the settlers struggled on the brink of starvation, reduced to eating anything they could get their hands on, including, it is said, dogs, cats, snakes, and, for the less fortunate colonists, poisonous mushrooms. Smith reported that the governor dispatched from the Virginia Company ran the colony like a forward-deployed military base—an exile stronghold in which everyone woke each morning to a drum signal and was put to labor, and people were sentenced to death for stealing just one ear of corn.[3]

However, taught by the Native Americans to cultivate tobacco, starting in 1612, the colony began to succeed. Later, cotton was planted, adding to the prosperity of the colony. The boon, described by Adam Smith as the "surplus of produce of the land," was immeasurable. In 1619 the first twenty black slaves arrived aboard a Dutch merchant ship, and with their labor, the colony got underway as a venture business. A new governor arrived that same year who was under orders to discuss important matters of management with the local colonists. A colonial legislature was soon installed by the governor and his appointees. Before long, these legislators came to be chosen by election, and thus the first colonial assembly in the history of the colonies was born.

Virginia's political base and abundant financial power eventually produced elites on a level with those of Boston. This class of men eagerly absorbed the philosophies of the Enlightenment movements of the European Continent as well as those of England and Scotland. Virginia produced a large number of such people, including Washington, Jefferson, Madison, and Mason, who were recognized for rendering distinguished service in the founding of the nation.

An example of the affluence of this group can be seen in Jefferson's book collection. He had two thousand volumes by 1773, and he added twelve hundred more during his tenure as Minister to France following independence. This was during a period when nearly all books in America were imported and expensive. In 1815, during the financial difficulties of his later years, Jefferson sold a total of 4,500 titles, constituting 6,700 volumes, to the federal government. Congress appropriated $23,000 for this purchase, and these books became the foundation of today's Library of Congress.[4]

According to Professor Levy, Jefferson was also known as a collector of rifles and handguns, and developed exchangeable parts. Where firearms were concerned, his motto was: Let your gun be the constant companion of your walks, as "it gives boldness, enterprise and independence to the mind. It would seem that a true portrait of Jefferson, the embodiment of the American Revolution, would depict a man holding a book of the Enlightenment's philosophy in one hand and a gun in the other.[5]

But my interest in Virginia is not yet exhausted. I will speak later of my further study of this irony-filled state, but at this point I would like to provide the following observation by Professor Levy, Pulitzer Prize winning scholar of the Bill of Rights, because I believe it is an excellent summary of the mindset of the Founding Fathers on the use of force:

> The right to keep and bear arms still enables citizens to pro-
> tect themselves against law breakers, but it is a feckless means
> of opposing a legitimate government. The so-called militias of

today that consist of small private armies of self-styled super-patriots are entitled to their firearms but deceive themselves in thinking they can withstand the United States Army. The Second Amendment as they interpret it feeds their dangerous illusions. [6]

The Signing of the *Mayflower Compact*

Now, let's turn back to the *Mayflower*.

The 102 people who landed ashore on December 21, at a place Captain Smith had previously explored and named Plymouth, were not mere settlers. Their purpose was altogether different from that of the Virginia group.

With the Puritans at their core, these were the Pilgrim Fathers, to be canonized by future generations. This group originated in the region surrounding the way station of Scrooby, 150 miles north of London, along the Great Northern Road leading straight to Edinburgh, Scotland.

This congregation of reformist Puritans opposed the authoritarianism and decadence of the Church of England. They had been persecuted for their purist faith, so unlike that of the Church, and for insisting on a church independently managed by free men. These were the people who, after spending thirteen years in hard exile in Amsterdam and Leiden in the Netherlands, eventually arrived on the new continent in search of self-reclamation.

Plymouth itself, however, was not their intended destination. Originally, the *Mayflower* had headed for New York's Hudson River region, but was unable to navigate past the Cape Cod area. The settlers had no choice but to land at Plymouth, located a mere one degree north of the area approved by the Virginia Company.

In addition to the Puritans, the 102 included hired hands, craftsmen servants who built barrels to collect water, and "strangers." The latter were ambitious men and women seeking to make their fortune with the permission of the monopolistic Virginia Company and funded by the London venture fund known as "The Adventurers."

On November 11, 1620, they signed the historical document known as the *Mayflower Compact*, which became a starting point in the history of American democracy. With tensions between the separatist Puritans and the strangers reaching their limit aboard ship, the Compact was hurriedly concluded as an emergency measure, prior to landing in the severe winter conditions. Still, its content was epoch-making in its clear enunciation of democratic principles. The text, in full, is as follows:

> IN The Name of God, Amen. We, whose names are underwritten, the Loyal Subjects of our dread Sovereign Lord King James, by the Grace of God, of Great Britain, France, and Ireland, King, Defender of the Faith, &c. Having undertaken for the Glory of God, and Advancement of the Christian Faith, and the Honor of our King and Country, a Voyage to plant the first colony in the northern Parts of Virginia; Do by these Presents, solemnly and mutually in the Presence of God and one another, covenant and combine ourselves together into a civil Body Politick, for our better Ordering and Preservation, and Furtherance of the Ends aforesaid; And by Virtue hereof do enact, constitute, and frame, such just and equal Laws, Ordinances, Acts, Constitutions, and Offices, from time to time, as shall be thought most meet and convenient for the general Good of the Colony; unto which we promise all due Submission and Obedience. In WITNESS whereof we have hereunto subscribed our names at Cape Cod the eleventh of November, in the Reign of our Sovereign Lord King James of England, France, and Ireland, the eighteenth and of Scotland, the fifty-fourth. Anno Domini, 1620.[7]

It was a written oath to confirm by mutual contract the creation of the power of a civil body politic for the communal life to follow, and was signed by forty-one adult men from all four groups, seventeen Puritans who referred to themselves as saints (as indicated in the table below), seventeen strangers who were the settlement enterprisers participating in the equity regardless of faith, four servants, and three hired hands.[8]

MAYFLOWER PASSENGERS

	Saints	Strangers	Servants	Hired Hands	Total
Men	17 (17)	17 (17)	11 (4)	3 (3)	48 (41)
Women	14	9	1	–	24
Children	10	14	6	–	30
Total	41	40	18	3	102

(Numbers in parentheses indicate signers of the *Mayflower Compact*.)

It is interesting to note that the strangers, servants, and hired hands outnumbered the separatist Puritans. Within the Compact, the location of Plymouth was intentionally identified as "the northern Parts of Virginia" as an adjustment to preserve the king's charter. This indicates that what the Pilgrim Fathers had started was already one of the colonial disorders mentioned by Adam Smith. The history of America during the more than 170 years from the arrival of the Pilgrims until the enactment of the Constitution is a history of coexistence of prejudices, accommodations to various heterogeneous values, and ultimately a true and brilliant compromise of ideas to form a republic that could sustain itself.

In any event, the surprising thing about the *Mayflower Compact* was the way in which it foreshadowed what was to come. It was, in fact, the enlightened prototype for the country's political structure established about 150 years later by the Declaration of Independence (1776), the U.S. Constitution (1789), and the ten amendments known as the Bill of Rights (1791).

It can be safe to say that after the Pilgrim Fathers had signed the *Mayflower Compact*, there was no semblance of democracy anywhere on earth when the ship landed at Plymouth on December 21, 1620. Four centuries earlier, in 1215, the king and city merchants of England, after much conflict, had finally reached the agreement known as the *Magna Carta*, which established the rule of law and inaugurated a parliamentary system that engaged the aristocracy. However, it was not until 1628, eight years after the Plymouth landing, that the British Parliament forced Charles I to approve the Petition of Right. The next significant event did not occur until twenty-one years later, in 1649, when the Puritan Revolution created a temporary republican system, which was eventually followed by the establishment of the constitutional monarchy.

A Solid Bond among Three Leaders

At this point we must examine the leaders among the Pilgrim Fathers.

The career of Cambridge University graduate William Brewster was especially significant. Brewster was born the son of the caretaker of the Scrooby Manor House, the site of occasional meetings of the Privy Council during the time of Henry VIII and a place where the king, archbishop, and postmaster of Scrooby occasionally lodged. As the senior elder in Plymouth, he provided support and nurturing to groups until his death in 1644 at the age of eighty-four.

After graduating from Cambridge in 1584, he became a diplomat and served in the Netherlands for three years as assistant to William Davison, the ambassador dispatched by Elizabeth I. At that time, the Netherlands was a Protestant country that had found its way into an alliance with England after coming under pressure from the Catholic Spanish Empire. Brewster lived with the Puritan ambassador Davison and gained a strong sense of religious freedom whenever he visited Leiden and the other various Dutch regions where the Pilgrim Fathers would eventually live. [9]

One incident, however, set Brewster on the path to becoming the founder of the Pilgrim Fathers and playing a central role in the opening of America.

This incident began when Ambassador Davison returned to England to assume the post of acting secretary of state under Elizabeth I. Mary Stuart, the former queen of Scotland, had been executed for treason in 1587. Immediately afterward, Elizabeth I, worrying over domestic backlash and hoping to shirk her own responsibility in the matter, claimed to have been deceived by Davison into signing the execution order. He was then sentenced to London Tower as a scapegoat. With the loss of his post, Brewster returned to his hometown of Scrooby where he eventually inherited his father's official post.

Brewster's religious activities commenced at this point. Re-igniting the passion of his experiences with religious freedom in the Netherlands, he enrolled in Peterhouse College, a constituent of Cambridge, where he was influenced by the separatist activities of the Puritans who were becoming active on campus. He began to follow the path of the separatist Puritans as a result of his relationship with John Greenwood with whom he lived on campus. Greenwood ultimately sacrificed himself for the separatist cause, choosing death in 1593. In 1606 Brewster began holding secret meetings at the Manor House. It can be argued that the Pilgrim Fathers would never have existed were it not for the conversion of Brewster with his high social status and career in the English court.

The sixteen-year-old William Bradford, the orphan of a rural farm owner, showed his face often at the Scrooby Manor House meetings where he studied Greek and Latin under Brewster and became a Brewster disciple. He later served for thirty years as the second governor of the Plymouth Colony.

During these years he built friendly relations with the Native Americans, negotiated with greedy venture financiers in London, and haggled in the beaver trade. Not only was he a man who demonstrated his talents by performing great deeds, he also left meticulous records of overall colony management in order to pass down knowledge of colonial life to future generations.

There is one other important person in this story, the pastor John Robinson, who also hailed from the Scrooby region and studied theology at Cambridge. Robinson received his master's degree at Cambridge University's Corpus Christi College and remained with the university as a fellow. Influenced by the anti-Anglican movement then at its peak, he was ousted from the university and became a pastor at Norfolk. He was later expelled from Norfolk as well for violating James I's rules against secret meetings and for the content of his sermons. He became the quintessential separatist, appearing on the scene as the pastor of the Scrooby Manor House Church.

The secret bond of faith forged in Scrooby between Brewster, Robinson, and Bradford remained firm throughout the rest of their lives.

When a spy for the authorities exposed the Manor House meetings and Brewster was cited and fined by the high court for religious disobedience, the three men assembled about sixty of their colleagues, designated themselves Pilgrims, and fled to the Netherlands. At the time, Brewster was forty years old, Robinson was thirty-two, and Bradford seventeen. Of course, nobody could have imagined that thirteen years later they would be knocking on the front door of the North American continent.

The path, however, had not been simple. On one occasion they attempted a desperate escape from eastern England's Boston Harbor where the entire group was betrayed by the ship's captain and arrested. They also had confrontations in Amsterdam with an earlier Puritan settlement there, which resulted in a migration to Leiden a year later. After spending twelve years in the Netherlands, they found that they still could not get acclimated, because they sought an even stricter standard of order modesty, simplicity, thrift, resistance to temptation, purity, reflection, and diligence[10] than was practiced by the other Puritans. For the Pilgrims, many of whom hailed from the farm villages around Scrooby, life in the college town of Leiden was painful.

Concerned about their future children's education and the prospect of the reappearance of the great shadow of the Spanish Empire—suggested by the imminent expiration of the thirteen-year non-aggression compact between the Netherlands and Spain—Brewster, Robinson, Bradford, and their followers decided to make the trip to the New World with about one hundred new associates, a final voyage to attain religious freedom.

I will not recount here the details the thirteen-year drama that followed, Pastor Robinson's venture fund investment negotiations with London, the setting out of the *Mayflower* and the *Speedwell* across the Atlantic, the immediate loss of the *Speedwell* soon after its launch, and the tribulations following the Scrooby escape. Nevertheless, it is worth noting that the voyage of the *Mayflower* was made possible by the Pilgrims' firm bond of faith under good leadership and their noble, undaunted determination to hold on to their heretical views.

The Significance of the Robinson Letter

Pastor Robinson wrote two letters of historical significance, one to the husband of his younger sister, John Carver, who was to become the first governor of Plymouth, and one addressed to all parties. The importance of this second letter must be discussed.

Dated July 27, 1620, the letter included advice on relationships with the strangers and an appeal for brotherly patience in communal life. It is preserved in Bradford's priceless account titled *Of Plymouth Plantation: 1620–1647*.[11] In his letter, Robinson told the Pilgrims:

> Whereas you are become a body politic, using amongst yourselves civil government, and are not furnished with any persons of special eminency above the rest, to be chosen by you into office or government; let your wisdom and godliness appear, not only in choosing such persons as do entirely love and will promote the common good, but also in yielding unto them all due honour and obedience in their lawful administrations.

If we dare to translate the phrase "civil government" as used in 1620 into contemporary terms, the innovation implicit in Robinson's thinking is evident. The advanced nature of the method by which the separatist Puritans chose their pastor, by decision of the general church congregation, is uncanny. Behind the choice of death at the hands of "the wild savages of America" over the prisons of Catholic Spain, one can well perceive a concealed but strong anti-tyrannical way of thinking.

Pastor Robinson departed this earth at the age of fifty, without ever having set foot in Plymouth, while rounding up the remaining groups in Leiden.

The *Mayflower Compact* uses Robinson's concept of a civil government as its foundation. In the intense cold of that fall of 1620, without having reached the mouth of the Hudson as planned, and having lost their legitimacy to found a colony even as they brandished the king's charter, the Pilgrims' only recourse was to entrust their survival to the creation of authority by a contract among all members, including the strangers who had been expressing their dissatisfaction. Such was the reality that the Pilgrim Fathers had to face.

In this way, the Robinson letter, which hastily hammered out the democratic concept of a civic government, became a model for the *Mayflower Compact*, drafted for an emergency situation.

According to Bradford's account, after the Plymouth landing, everyone participated in general assembly meetings and annually elected the governor and his assistant. Sermons were delivered by general congregation members in pastorless churches, and a militia system under Captain Miles Standish was adopted for times of crisis. These put the "body politic" of the Robinson letter into practice.

An Armed Group of a Sort

The Pilgrim Fathers, who set foot upon American soil with the seed of American democracy in hand in the form of the *Mayflower Compact*, were an "armed group of a sort."[12] The DNA of the use of force, which I have been following, unquestionably landed with them at Plymouth Rock, and American democracy and military might are bound together in a unified and indivisible relationship to this day.

According to Bradford's account, when they arrived near Cape Cod, the actions of the thirty-six-year-old professional soldier Standish were particularly notable. He led a search party aboard a two-mast sloop and determined the landing spot. A stranger with a history of military service in the Dutch War of Independence, he became a companion of the Pilgrim Fathers after encountering them in Leiden. Bradford records,

> It was conceived there might be some danger in the attempt, yet seeing them resolute, they were permitted to go, being sixteen of

them well armed under the conduct of Captain Standish, having such instructions given them as was thought meet. They set forth the 15 of November; and when they had marched about the space of a mile by the seaside, they espied five or six persons with a dog coming towards them, who were savages; but they fled from them and ran up into the woods. . . . But about midnight they heard a hideous and great cry, and their sentinel called "Arm! arm!" So they bestirred them and stood to their arms and shot off a couple of muskets, and then the noise ceased.

From this first step, the history of American use of force begins.

While battling the diverse climate and topography of the huge continent, the Pilgrims and their successors in the new land contacted and then eliminated the Native Americans. They then ran up against the advanced colonial powers of Spain and France that had already set foot upon the new continent. Combining a life of religious and political confrontation with the need to hunt for food and fur supplies, naturally gave rise to the use of armed force in all aspects of life. In short, the use of armed might was present at the start.

Standish was formally appointed captain during a colonial general assembly the following year. Under his authority and leadership, the assembly soon resolved that colony members would abide by military law and participate in armed training and drills specified by the governor and the governing council. It was the first instance of the American-style militia.

Later militias were established as low-level administrative organizations with police functions in each colonial town. At the same time they represented a military organization for the entire colony in the event of emergency. An armed services committee established under the "body politic" that derived its power from the colony can be seen as the prototype of the civilian control of the military that exists to this day.

In late September 2002, I visited the *Mayflower II* and the Plymouth Plantation Village, which has been restored to reproduce the life of the period. I also visited the first landing point of Plymouth Rock. I had been blessed with fine weather on my arrival and the place was filled with American flags and tourists. Plymouth Rock was housed in a building like a relic from the Roman era. The entire *Mayflower Compact* was proudly displayed aboard the restored *Mayflower II* as "the foundation of the U.S. Constitution."

At the 1627 Pilgrim Village, the settlements of the native Wampanoag people were also reproduced. As soon as I entered the site, I was guided to the orientation center, where a video presentation introduced the Pilgrim Fathers as "a new kind of people" who were unlike the white men who had earlier pillaged the Native Americans. The film also alluded to the recent fixation with multiracial power. This was reportedly a change that had been instituted during the Clinton administration.

At the center of the village was a town house with six cannons on the second floor, their muzzles facing in all four directions. I understood very well that these "new kind of people" were an armed group, indeed.

I asked one of the staff members, "What kind of weapons did the *Mayflower* carry?" He looked befuddled at this question, said he didn't know off the top of his head, and would have to research it. Later, when I pressed for the answer again by e-mail, they answered that, although it was not 100 percent certain, the Pilgrims were thought to have brought muskets, swords, and three types of cannons—minion, saker, and base—that differed primarily in size.

They also told me that they thought the research by the scholar Harold L. Peterson might be helpful. After inquiring of the Pilgrim Society in Plymouth, I was finally able to get my hands on one book, the precisely titled *Arms and Armor of the Pilgrims: 1620–1692.*[13]

In this book, Peterson describes the military might of the Pilgrim Fathers in detail:

> A completely armed man, especially in the first years, was usually equipped with one or more articles from each of the three groups, usually a helmet and corselet, a sword, and a musket. . . . The most common type of firearm that came to America on the Mayflower was the musket. This was a smooth-bored weapon, usually slightly more than five feet long with a caliber ranging between .69 and .80. The majority of those that the original settlers brought with them were matchlocks . . . (but) the matchlock was in many ways inferior to the Indian's bow. The ball from a matchlock musket was superior to an arrow in the size of the hole it tore, the bones its smashed, and the amount of blood it spilled. The bow was superior in accuracy and rapidity of fire. Moreover, it was light and easy to carry while the gun was heavy and clumsy.

The matchlocks were eventually replaced with "snaphance" muskets, thrusting Plymouth technologically years ahead of Europe.

Presumably, the Pilgrims also had cannons. Bradford recorded that the crew pulled minions up from the beach on February 21, 1621, before the *Mayflower* returned to England, so it is possible that the cannons from the *Mayflower* were left behind. Peterson writes that a traveler in 1627 "visited Plymouth and noted that the Pilgrims had six cannon of unspecified types in their fort and four 'patreros' (small guns) mounted in front of the governor's house." The largest were the 2.7-inch caliber minions weighing 1,200 pounds and having a range of nine-tenths of a mile. The 2.7-inch sakers were somewhat smaller, also having a range of about nine-tenths of a mile. The smallest cannons, the bases, could be installed on wooden platforms that allowed artillerymen to change the direction of fire. Peterson indicates that, following the *Mayflower*'s return, the colony imported paper-cylinder ammunition cartridges "not widely used by European infantry until after 1700" aboard a continuous flow of British ships.

Peace and Friendship Treaty with Native Americans

At first, the Pilgrim Fathers did not use their armed power against the original native inhabitants. During the first spring in 1621 they had signed a peace and friendship treaty with Massasoit, the chief of the Wampanoags who lived near the landing site. This treaty remained in effect until Governor Bradford died in 1657. According to the historian Dwight Heath, who has commented on another record of the Plymouth plantation, *Mourt's Relation: A Journal of the Pilgrims at Plymouth*,[14] this was the first mutual-security treaty, military alliance, and trade agreement in the history of the United States.

Thanks to this treaty, the trade in beaver and other furs eagerly awaited in London got off the ground. It may be concluded that coexistence with the native people was indispensable to the Pilgrims' survival. According to Heath, Governor Bradford concluded similar trade and military agreements with other tribes as well. Even today, a statue of Massasoit stands in the center of Plymouth.

Such practicality is evident in the Pilgrim Fathers and the characteristics of the *Mayflower Compact*, and it is also one of the traits of the United States that continues to the present day. These origins should not be forgotten.

An official Plymouth Plantation Village pamphlet states that this treaty

came about due to the efforts of the Indian Squanto, who had been introduced to the Pilgrims by his friend Samoset and acted as an intermediary
to the chief. Squanto had earlier been taken as a showpiece to England by
Captain Hunt—who explored the same region in 1614—but fled home by
another ship two years later.

Bradford regarded the arrival of Squanto, who spoke English, as "a special instrument sent of God." Squanto took the lead in teaching the settlers
what was and wasn't edible, and showed them how to sow corn and catch
herring, eel, and game birds. Squanto's teaching of survival know-how in a
harsh environment was the greatest blessing that first winter when over half
the crew died from malnutrition.

This unemotional account by Bradford—who had been hit by terrible
misfortune when his wife Dorothy fell into the sea and drowned just before
the landing—is quite moving and firmly conveys his gratitude for not having
to use armed force.

In autumn of that year, on the occasion of the first harvest after the landing, the Pilgrims invited ninety Indians, including Massasoit, to a celebra-
tory dinner. The following year, the third year after the landing, on Thursday,
November 29, 1622, the day was officially designated Thanksgiving Day, and
was held as an observance of goodwill toward the Indians. This was the first
Thanksgiving, which Americans now revere as a holiday for family gathering.

In 1637, when the extermination of the Indians by the English settlers
in central Connecticut began in what was known as the Pequot War, the
Pilgrim Fathers prepared to mobilize a sloop with fifty militiamen, but they
never joined the fighting.

The Rise of Boston

Around this time, however, the power of the Boston-centered Massachusetts
Bay Colony rose to the forefront. The Massachusetts Bay Colony began ten
years after the *Mayflower* when one thousand non-separatist Puritans emigrated to America under the leadership of London lawyer and Cambridge
graduate John Winthrop, a member of the British gentry class, which was
second only to the aristocracy.

History records that aboard the ships bound for the New World in 1830,
Commander Winthrop quoted from the Sermon on the Mount (Mathew
5:14): "You are the light of the world. A city on a hill cannot be hidden." This

is regarded as a typical example of how the country was founded by settlers possessing a religious sense of mission as a chosen people and their country as blessed by God.

In fact, although they also were Puritan, these colonists—unlike the Plymouth separatists—did not cut their ties with the Church of England but proudly displayed a loyalty that surpassed that of Plymouth in the Crown's eyes. The Virginia settlement was completely under the control of the Church of England, and the region from Manhattan to the Hudson River Valley, which later became New York, was occupied by the Dutch. So for the Puritans who had escaped persecution under Charles I, Boston was a suitable shelter. The population of the Massachusetts region quickly grew to twenty thousand by 1640.

The Pilgrim Fathers proved that Englishmen could live on the desolate rocky shore of nearby Plymouth,[15] and settlers continued to arrive in the Massachusetts Bay Colony. In 1636, Harvard University was founded as a center of training for future leaders of the clergy.

The potential military power within the colonies was enormous. Personnel required to engage in special combat operations were assembled from militia troops of all regions and ranks and organized into "trainbands" led by specially appointed commanders. Militia units also conducted military exercises. One record exists documenting the proper execution of one such exercise in which about 1,200 militiamen participated under the orders of militia commander-in-chief Colonel Winthrop. According to Morrison Sharp in an article titled "Leadership and Democracy in the Early New England System of Defense":

> Early New England society approached a total unity for certain major purposes ... all of New England was by virtue of its purposes and organization a total system of defense of which the trainbands and fighting companies were the most important parts.... It may seem somewhat surprising that the clergy, although excused from training, kept closely in touch with trainbands, fighting companies, and other defense activities ... they opened training with prayer and closed it with prayer; they voted in trainband elections; they gave advice in trainband quarrels; and in time of war, marched with their soldiers to exhort, strengthen, and advise.[16]

The makings of the American War of Independence pitting the well-regulated militia from this region against the regular army deployed from England can already be seen.

According to Sharp's analysis, the military might of New England centered on the rise of the Massachusetts militia in which even the clergy were enlisted, reflecting arrangements for defense markedly more powerful than was to be found in Virginia and New York. Furthermore, religious control was as strict as the founders' religious piety: four Quakers who had come to Boston after escaping persecution in England were hanged in 1655 for their refusal to condone the use of armed force.

The Pequot War represented a kind of dress rehearsal for later developments. Resulting from expansion into Pequot tribe-controlled areas, the war turned into a slaughter in which all four hundred Pequots holed up in a sandbank fort were exterminated by a Massachusetts militia unit possessing overwhelming military might. A wartime pastor named Stone devised the strategy that led to the victory.

It seems clear that the religious sense of mission in building "a city on a hill" is nearly inseparable from the DNA of the use of force.

The Last Days of Plymouth

For additional security against the Native Americans, in 1643 the Plymouth Plantation merged with the colonies of Massachusetts Bay, Connecticut, and New Haven to form the New England Confederation.

In 1675, when the number of English settlers in New England numbered more than forty-five thousand, an all-out war began with many Native American tribes in which Plymouth played a leading role. Fifteen years after the death of Chief Massasoit, who had built a trusting relationship with Governor Bradford, he was succeeded by his second son Metacom (who also went by the English name of King Philip). Frustrated by the increasing number of land acquisitions by white immigrants and Christian missionary activity, local tribes, led by the Wampanoag, revolted in what was known as King Philip's War.

The war was set off by the assassination of a converted Indian who had studied at Harvard, and many battles were fought in a wide area from Maine to Rhode Island over a period of about a year. One hundred militiamen from Plymouth and three hundred from Massachusetts were mobilized.

Once again, the clergy took an active role by assuming command and collecting war funds. One account says that a thousand Indians died, and another account reports that a thousand more were sold off into slavery in the West Indies.

Of the casualties among the white settlers, it is said that twelve towns were burned and six hundred died. In the end, some Native Americans defected to the Caucasian side. King Philip was shot, and his head was displayed in the center of Plymouth for a long time. This was the last major occasion in which colonial military force was employed to eliminate the Native Americans in New England.

With the help of the Native Americans the Plymouth colony had survived and steadily developed its agriculture and fishing industries following the *Mayflower* landing. It had also prospered and profited from the supply of foodstuffs to Boston only 30 miles away. Finally, in 1691 it was completely absorbed into the Massachusetts Bay Colony.

The events of these years brought about the first manifestation of England's growing concern about the wealth produced by the colonies on the new American continent. England had endured the trial and error of Cromwell republicanism, restoration of the monarchy, the Glorious Revolution, and the founding of the constitutional monarchy. As England tightened its grip over the colonies year by year, Governor Bradford met the expectations of the London strangers' commercial venture and made the beaver trade a success. Ironically, Plymouth was absorbed into the larger Massachusetts colony not long after it had finally received a charter for self-government.

The Role of the Great Awakening

In the Massachusetts Bay Colony, the colonization company that had received the charter from the king came to play the role of the autonomous colonial government. Steeped in their Cambridge educations, the Puritan elite under Governor Winthrop exploited an ambiguous loophole in the royal charter regarding the location of the general shareholders meeting and formed the organization and charter of the Massachusetts Bay Company in Boston. Having done this, the Puritans engaged for a while in an oligarchic religious rule of a kind no different than the government-sanctioned terror imposed in England. The execution of Quakers and the burning of witches were two prominent aspects.

At the same time more "liberal" elements rebelled with the establish-ment of the Rhode Island Colony by Roger Williams and the Connecticut Colony by Thomas Hooker. The end result was the establishment of bicameral legislative systems and the incorporation of the English Bill of Rights into the governments of the colonies that ultimately became the United States.

In this way, the *Mayflower Compact* itself, as well as its heart and soul, was absorbed into the DNA of the use of force by the democracies of the Massachusetts Bay Colony and all of New England. The armed group to which Captain Standish gave great care also became a part of the military might of New England's "well-regulated militia."

Against the background of such power, the Massachusetts Bay Assem-bly soon issued a resolution to Charles II declaring that English common law was not applicable in America. It stated further that the British Parlia-ment should not restrict trade of the Crown's subjects in America if they had no representation in Parliament. Angered, the king revoked their charter and appointed himself governor in direct control of the territory. Thus, the stage was set for the American War of Independence that was to come a half century later.

Taking advantage of its excellent harbor, which was deeper than that at Plymouth, Boston developed into a commercial city with a huge mari-time business and prosperity on a par with that of Virginia. In particular, investments in education, such as the foundation of Harvard, produced an intelligentsia of excellent quality who fed the spirit of autonomy. Thus, the republican movement grew increasingly, not only in Boston but throughout New England.

During this period a religious development arose that would prove of great significance. Referred to as the Great Awakening, this was a revivalist movement that spread from New England south to Georgia starting in the 1720s. Pastors and believers went out to preach the gospel directly to settlers in all regions, disregarding established religious authorities, denominations, parishes, and churches. This led to a great shift in popular conscience and touched one of the Founding Fathers, Benjamin Franklin, who heard and was moved by these sermons. Japanese scholar Makoto Saito has observed that "the Great Awakening created individual self-consciousness on the one hand and a self-consciousness of being American on the other," and thus laid a popular foundation from which the American Revolution would soon be born.[17]

In fact, it is fair to conclude that, going into the 1760s, the change in consciousness sparked by the Great Awakening helps account for the suddenness with which protests were organized against the Stamp Act where even women took part. As the independent United States entered the mid-nineteenth century and began to expand westward, it had gone through Second and Third Great Awakenings that helped raise American self-consciousness to its present-day level.

In this way, the Great Awakening planted the seeds of republican philosophy not only among the elite but among the common settlers as well. The curtain of the drama of secession from the British Empire known as the American Revolution was raised.

Many Kinds of People

Thus, the judgment of Adam Smith in referring to the United States as having been born in "disorder" is illuminated in the histories of the colonies of Plymouth, Massachusetts Bay, and Virginia. Groups of immigrants from various backgrounds set out from Europe on a two-month, three-thousand-mile voyage across the Atlantic to the new continent. The roots of the nation can be seen in how each group survived through the attainment of statehood.

Even so, such "disorderly" pluralism did not exist only within the English colonies. Spain, for whom Columbus had discovered the New World in 1492, expelled the first French to arrive in the Florida region in 1565. France had already advanced into the Quebec region in 1533, and later into Louisiana. In 1626 the Netherlands founded three colonies centered on New Amsterdam (present day New York) along the Hudson River Valley in order to counter the ground gained by Plymouth after the *Mayflower*.[18] The power of Smith's thesis is very persuasive.

In *The Wealth of Nations* he reports:

> The declension of the naval power of this latter nation (Spain),
> in consequence of the defeat or miscarriage of what they called
> their Invincible Armada, which happened towards the end of the
> sixteenth century, put it out of their power to obstruct any longer
> the settlements of the other European nations. In the course of
> the seventeenth century, therefore, the English, French, Dutch,

Danes, and Swedes, all the great nations who had any ports upon the ocean, attempted to make some settlements in the new world.

And, before long, the Germans arrived as seasonal indentured servants. In short, if I follow the style of presentation at the Plymouth Plantation Village orientation video, the foundation of America began with the assembly of "many kinds of people."

The religious, economic, and political motives of the various settlers from England and other countries may have differed, but they all had in common the energy of free men who, while governed by the king, had escaped from a far more restrictive order in Britain. So these settlers had a sense of liberty that was at odds with the "order" upon which the British authorities relied, although, formally, they were under the control of the royally sanctioned charters issued by the colonial companies. The governor in each of these colonies represented the interests of the Crown and was appointed directly by the English government.

Nevertheless, as the example of Plymouth demonstrates so eloquently, the settlers were able to decide freely where to land and to freely agree to opt for the creation of their own "body politic." Accordingly, the *Mayflower Compact* in this sense represents the origin of the pluralistic foundation of a nation with its beginnings in "disorder." One should think of it as the base upon which the United States was founded.

The difficulty of understanding the contemporary United States, its ascendant neoconservative ideology, its pride, and its excitement grows out of this "order" borne of "disorder." These things will be analyzed next.

FIVE

Faith in Manifest Destiny

The Glorification of Plymouth

The tale of Plymouth will always live on in the hearts of Americans. The epic account of the New England settlement during the severe winter, in which half died by springtime, and the struggle for survival, strikes the heart with romantic wonder. But that isn't the whole story. The *Mayflower Compact*, born aboard the *Mayflower* just before the landing, still lives today. One can feel the originality of this democratic innovation and understand, even four centuries later, how it was ahead of its time.

The various tales of the Plymouth settlement and the Pilgrim Fathers were revered throughout the period that followed the founding of the United States. In addition, modern-day Plymouth is treated as the holy land of American democratic origins and is a tourist destination for many.

Regarding this glorification of the Plymouth settlers, there is a voluminous Japanese work entitled *Pirugurimu Faazaazu to iu Shinwa* [The Myth of the Pilgrim Fathers] by International Christian University Professor Naoki Onishi.[1] This history of the Pilgrim Fathers illustrates precisely how the United States needed the Plymouth myth as a symbol of national unity after the nation's founding.

According to Professor Onishi, the mythologizing of Plymouth Rock, the famous tourist spot and symbol of the Pilgrim Fathers' first step onto the new continent, began more than a century later in 1741. A ninety-four-year-old man who had heard about the landing from his father started talking about it publicly. The father had landed on the ship *Ann* in 1623, three years after the *Mayflower*. The story quickly became revered during the subsequent escalation of the independence movement. Pieces of the rock that had been split in two were rejoined into one, and a roofed shrine-like structure that still houses the rock was constructed in 1880.

As the country moved into the nineteenth century, the lore surrounding the settlement's first winter and the celebration of the first harvest with the Indians was glorified as a blend of self-sacrificing piety, passionate patriotism, and love for family and mankind. A movement arose advocating that Thanksgiving be designated a national holiday as a symbol of American social unity. Influenced by the movement's female leaders, President Lincoln, with the Civil War turning in his favor in 1863, declared Thanksgiving Day a public holiday falling on the last Thursday of November, the same date noted in the official records of the Plymouth settlement.

Most of the presidents after Lincoln observed this declaration, and in 1941, just before the outbreak of war between the United States and Japan, Congress finally declared Thanksgiving a legal holiday falling on the fourth Thursday of November.

Reportedly, the first person to associate the *Mayflower Compact* with the origin of the U.S. Constitution was John Quincy Adams. According to Professor Onishi, in an oration marking the anniversary of "Forefathers' Day" in Plymouth in 1802, the senator from Massachusetts, who would become the sixth president, touched upon the *Mayflower Compact*, remarking, "Here was a unanimous and personal assent, by all the individuals of the community, to the association by which they became a nation." Adams praised this as an example of the French philosopher Rousseau's concept of a social contract put into practice, a comparison not made idly, since Rousseau had been read and admired by several of the Founding Fathers.

At the time, Federalist Party leader Adams and his father, John Adams, a former president, had taken up the mission of carrying the U.S. Constitution into the expanding western territories. The tale of Plymouth and the *Mayflower Compact* were effective tools of persuasion in this mission.

"Actors on a Most Conspicuous Theatre"

American pride in the originality of American-style democracy, which began with the *Mayflower Compact* and the glorification of the Plymouth myth, became obvious in other ways. I think it is important to understand this point, and I want to call attention to a relevant comment by George Washington.

After winning the War of Independence with Britain, General Washington disbanded the Continental Army, went into seclusion at his home in Mount Vernon, Virginia, and delivered the following circular to each state governor in June 1783:

> The Citizens of America, placed in the most enviable condition,
> as the sole Lords and Proprietors of a vast Tract of Continent,
> comprehending all the various soils and climates of the World,
> and abounding with all the necessaries and conveniencies of life,
> are now by the late satisfactory pacification, acknowledged to be
> possessed of absolute freedom and Independency; They are, from
> this period, to be considered as the Actors on a most conspicuous
> Theatre, which seems to be peculiarly designated by Providence
> for the display of human greatness and felicity.

I believe the phrase "actors on a most conspicuous theatre" is most important, because the impulse to demonstrate this greatness soon bore fruit.

Washington didn't know he would become president six years later. For a man of such modesty, the statement displayed a sense of ambition. He further went on to say:

> There is an option still left to the United States of America, that
> it is in their choice, and depends upon their conduct, whether
> they will be respectable and prosperous, or contemptible and
> miserable as a Nation; This is the time of their political proba-
> tion, this is the moment when the eyes of the whole World are
> turned upon them.

For the states gathered under the Articles of Confederation prior to the appearance of the federal government, this statement must have had strong national appeal. The point of the "eyes of the whole World" already watching was profound.

Another work beautifully illustrates this concept of "the impulse to demonstrate" forty-six years after the Washington circular.

The Americans, in their intercourse with strangers, appear impatient of the smallest censure and insatiable of praise. The most slender eulogy is acceptable to them, the most exalted seldom contents them; they unceasingly harass you to extort praise, and if you resist their entreaties, they fall to praising themselves. It would seem as if, doubting their own merit, they wished to have it constantly exhibited before their eyes.

. . . Their vanity is not only greedy, but restless and jealous; it will grant nothing, while it demands everything, but is ready to beg and to quarrel at the same time.

If I say to an American that the country he lives in is a fine one, "Ay" he replies, "there is not its equal in the world." If I applaud the freedom that its inhabitants enjoy, he answers: "Freedom is a fine thing, but few nations are worthy to enjoy it."

It is impossible to conceive a more troublesome or more garrulous patriotism; it wearies even those who are disposed to respect it.

These passages were extracted from the so-called bible of American studies, *Democracy in America* by Alexis de Tocqueville.[2]

This twenty-six-year-old French aristocrat traveled about the United States for only nine months in 1831. This was during the administration of Andrew Jackson, the seventh president and the first to realize the dream of going from a log cabin to the White House. It was a time when American democracy was still growing, and the sharp observations that he left behind are nothing short of astonishing.

Unlike any other country, America came into the world with a message for mankind—that all are created equal, and all are meant to be free.

These words were part of a speech delivered by the current president, George W. Bush, during an Independence Day celebration in 2002. The United States is a nation that continues to believe and proclaim there is "no better country" and to view itself as "unlike any other."

The Empire of Liberty

In this way, the glorification of Plymouth raised spirits in the United States. The "garrulous patriotism" of Washington's "actors on a most conspicuous theatre" evolved into a consciousness of the nation's responsibility as the *empire of liberty*. Amid the growing excitement, people latched onto the call of Manifest Destiny, put their faith in the same, and commenced the expansion westward.

At this point an explanation of the term *empire of liberty* is warranted.

The term is often used by the influential neoconservative groups in Washington today. Max Boot, a prominent young neoconservative, polemicist, and Olin Senior Fellow of the Council on Foreign Relations, is the author of *The Savage Wars of Peace: Small Wars and the Rise of American Power*. In this 2002 work Boot argues that, if required, the United States should not fear fighting the savage wars of peace to extend its empire of liberty, and concludes by saying that the United States has always thus far done so.

Boot, however, was not the first person to use the term *empire of liberty*. Thomas Jefferson, author of the Declaration of Independence and third U.S. President, also used it. According to Mr. Norio Akashi, a Japanese Jeffersonian scholar, during the War of Independence, Jefferson, then governor of Virginia, wrote on December 25, 1780, to George Clarke, a militia commander who was fighting an alliance of the British and Native Americans in what is now the state of Kentucky. Part of that letter reads:

> In the event of peace on terms which have been contemplated
> by some powers we shall form to the American union a barrier
> against the dangerous extension of the British Province of Canada
> and add to the Empire of liberty an extensive and fertile country,
> thereby converting dangerous enemies into valuable Friends.

On another occasion, Jefferson wrote:

> By enlarging the empire of liberty, we multiply its auxiliaries, and
> provide new sources of renovation, should its principles, at any
> time, degenerate, in those portions of our country which gave
> them birth.[3]

At the end of the War of Independence in 1783, Congressional Representative-elect Jefferson, already conscious of the westward expansion of this empire of liberty, recognized the establishment of new states with rights equivalent to those of the existing states. He had in mind the so-called Northwestern Territory north of the Ohio River and the still vaster lands west of the Mississippi River.[4]

There is no shortage of episodes illustrating the "empire consciousness" of the Founding Fathers, who considered U.S. expansion westward the duty of man. Another such incident was the discussion surrounding the design of the Great Seal of the United States of America, adopted by Congress on June 2, 1782.

According to Samuel Morison's *Oxford History of the American People*:

> Although some members wished to adopt a distinctly American bird like the wild turkey, or a dove of peace, Congress chose the eagle, symbol of imperial Rome. Over its head is a "glory" of thirteen stars, a new constellation in the galaxy of nations. In one talon the eagle clasps an olive branch and in the other a sheaf of arrows, to represent peace and war. In his beak is a ribbon inscribed E Pluribus Unum, and on his breast a shield with thirteen vertical stripes for the states, surmounted by a horizontal "chief" for Congress. On the reverse of the seal is a pyramid of thirteen courses of stone, to indicate permanence, with room for a few more at the top; and over it, in another "glory," the all-seeing eye of Divine Providence. On this reverse are two Latin mottoes: Annuit Coeptis, meaning, "He has favored our undertakings"; and Novus Ordo Seculorum, "A New Cycle of Centuries." Both were suggested by the poetry of Virgil: Aeneid, ix.625 and Eclogues, iv.5-7, best known by Shelley's paraphrase:
>
> > The World's great age begins anew,
> >
> > The golden years return.
>
> The classically trained leaders of the American Revolution were very fond of this prophecy. They believed that the Declaration of Independence had inaugurated a new order; and they hoped that they themselves were the nova progenies, the new Heaven-born generation predicted by the Latin poet.

I think this illustrates the origin of the United States splendidly. It matches precisely the same sense of mission that existed in the days of Governor Winthrop of the Massachusetts Bay Colony, who believed the Puritans had received a special commission from God and had come to the New World to fulfill their mission.

Facing the Pacific

It was thus that President Jefferson concluded the Louisiana Purchase with Napoleonic France in 1803 and doubled the territory of the United States in one stroke. With this purchase, the vast area west of the Mississippi River—now known as Louisiana, Missouri, Iowa, Nebraska, South Dakota, North Dakota, Minnesota, Montana, Wyoming, and Colorado—was acquired for $16 million.

Napoleon had been troubled by the need to subdue a slave rebellion in Haiti, which stranded sixty thousand expeditionary troops scheduled for stationing at New Orleans. In consequence, he decided to give up his dream of building a New France on the North American continent in place of Canada, a territory his Bourbon predecessors had lost before he was born. In fact, he had only recently acquired the Louisiana Territory by secret treaty with Spain in 1801.

The prospect of both the Spanish and French colonial powers—sitting at the flank of the newly emerging United States along the Mississippi Valley—soon clearing out of the area was a turn of good fortune.

President Jefferson immediately stepped in and dispatched the first official western expedition with a budget obtained from Congress. In May 1804 he sent his secretary, Meriwether Lewis, and Lewis's partner, William Clark, with a "Corps of Discovery" to explore their new lands beginning in St. Louis. It is interesting to note that Jefferson instructed Lewis and Clark to observe and record everything they encountered—the conditions of each Native American tribe, the types of plants and animals, and the changes in topography and climate—much as he had done himself in Virginia. There was one other strict order they were not to forget, to reach the Pacific Ocean and map out their route along the way.

Blessed with the good fortune of having a Native American guide, on November 15, 1805, a year and a half after setting out, Lewis and Clark found themselves facing the Pacific Ocean at the mouth of the Columbia River.

At this moment, Jefferson's strategy and calculations in aiming for the West were accomplished. Lewis and Clark returned home in September 1806. Today, the portrait of Sacagawea, the female Native American guide who provided distinguished service, is engraved on the reverse side of the golden dollar coin.

The foundation of America's westward expansion was built upon the success of the Lewis and Clark Expedition, which charted the Louisiana Purchase and the Pacific coast, making possible the era of Manifest Destiny that followed.

The Truth behind the Monroe Doctrine

At this point we need to examine the career of James Monroe, who, in a shrewd diplomatic contest with Napoleon, negotiated the Louisiana Purchase as President Jefferson's special envoy to Paris. This action ultimately led to the formulation of the doctrine which bears Monroe's name.

Like Jefferson, Monroe was born into a wealthy Virginia family and had been fascinated with Jefferson from an early age. During his career he served as an attorney, state legislator, congressional representative, and U.S. minister to France. After succeeding with the Louisiana Purchase, he followed in Jefferson's footsteps to become governor of Virginia.

He then served as secretary of state under President Madison, and after that, as secretary of the army during the difficult War of 1812, also known as the Second War of Independence. This war started out as a difficult test for the United States, with the British Army having burned the White House, but in the end victory was achieved through direct combat, unlike the guerrilla tactics employed during the War of Independence.

As a result of his distinguished service, Monroe won the presidential election of 1816. He gave the country its first taste of real nationalism and increased the nation's confidence in its own economic independence. Politically, he successfully reconciled party factions and built the period known as the Era of Good Feelings. He served two terms as president.

In 1819 he acquired Florida from Spain, and together with Britain, demarcated the border with Canada along the forty-ninth parallel from the present-day Lake of the Woods to the Rocky Mountains. Amid all of this, the concept of Manifest Destiny emerged as the opening act of the Monroe Doctrine.

The Monroe Doctrine was introduced as a key element of his foreign policy during a presidential address to Congress on December 2, 1823. This doctrine clearly asserted the special right of the United States to resist encroachments by European powers in the Western Hemisphere. At issue were pressures by Czarist Russia in present-day Alaska and movements by Spain to regain its lost territories in South America. At the same time, the United States had worked out a principle of mutual noninterference with Europe by which the United States pledged not to interfere in European affairs.

Specifically, the doctrine was a statement of intent by the United States to remain neutral in European wars, if the European powers would respect the independence of the fledgling nations of the Western Hemisphere.

While the Monroe Doctrine is misunderstood even today as the beginning of U.S. isolationism, the part of the doctrine mandating noninterference with Europe can certainly be called isolationism. This principle was maintained until the United States entered World War I in 1917.

On the other hand, since the United States regarded South America as its back yard and itself as representing all of North and South America, the Monroe Doctrine became the basis for justifying various interventions. Furthermore, there is no mention at all of isolationism or unrelated interference toward Asia and the Pacific region, including Japan and China. Rather, the preservation of its free hand is made clear.

> She goes not abroad in search of monsters to destroy. She is the well-wisher to the freedom and independence of all. She is the champion and vindicator only of her own.

These were the words of John Quincy Adams—later to become the sixth president—as secretary of state under President Monroe in 1821 regarding the realization of Monroe's declaration. Today Patrick Buchanan and other isolationists—once affiliated with neoconservative groups but in opposition to those groups over the war in Iraq—quote this passage often as the teachings of the Founding Fathers.

Adams returned to the House of Representatives in 1829 after serving one term as president. In the 1840s he fully supported Massachusetts Congressman-elect Caleb Cushing, who advocated that measures be taken to preserve U.S. mercantile rights against British interests in the Pacific. This was at the time of China's defeat in the Opium Wars and the ceding of Hong Kong by the Treaty of Nanking. In 1843, while serving as Chairman of the House of Representatives Committee on International Relations, Adams demonstrated his zeal by submitting a resolution to the House supporting Cushing's mission in his new post as President Tyler's special envoy to China.

In July 1844 Cushing successfully concluded the Treaty of Wanghsia, which opened five Chinese ports to merchant trade, extended special trading status to China, and included an extraterritoriality provision. Cushing carried a message from President Tyler to the Chinese emperor that read:

> The twenty-six United States are as large as China.... Our territories extend from one great ocean to the other; and on the west we are divided from your dominions only by the sea ... going constantly toward the setting sun, we sail to Japan and the Yellow Sea.

Cushing himself reportedly wanted to play a role in the opening of Japan after China.[5] It seems the Monroe Doctrine's true intention in "following the sun" westward had been revealed.

Incidentally, the first step toward China was a visit to Kwangtung (formerly Canton) made by the New York merchant ship *Empress of China* on August 28, 1784. In the following years trade progressed, and fourteen American merchant vessels were at Kwangtung Port when President Washington was inaugurated in 1789.[6] This preceded the visit of Commodore Perry's fleet to Japan by sixty-nine years.

Sometime I must undertake the new challenge of writing about the deep relationship of the United States with China, which started out not with military ships but merchant vessels, and which predates its relationship with Japan.

A Sun That Doesn't Set

Max Boot has provided his own interpretation of the Monroe Doctrine in the work mentioned above. After recognizing that, unlike Europe, the United States has continued to extend its influence into the Caribbean and Pacific, Boot states:

> Much of the growing American role overseas ... was the result of the restless Yankees' inexorable progress across the North

American continent and beyond, a process dubbed "manifest destiny" by journalist John O'Sullivan in 1839. Many of the obstacles in the path of American expansion were summarily knocked aside by military might. The army had the primary job of fighting the Indians, in wars that would drag on until 1890. The army, navy, and marines all pitched in to defeat Mexico in 1846–48 and Spain in 1898. America's small wars abroad were mostly the province of the navy and Marine Corps.

Put another way, the arrival of the Perry fleet to demand the opening of Japan in 1853 is interesting as one of the "small wars" along the path of westward expansion contained between the lines of the Monroe Doctrine. We must slowly digest the fact that, although the two did not actually engage in combat, the relationship between Japan and the United States began essentially as an extension of the U.S.'s employment of military power in its expansion westward. Later, in the American "rear area" possession of the Philippines, these "small wars" were fought violently under the command of General Arthur MacArthur, whose son Douglas would one day be Supreme Commander of Allied Powers during the American occupation of Japan.

We must also understand precisely what is meant by the slogan Manifest Destiny, which entered into America's consciousness around the time of Perry's arrival.

There is something I always notice whenever I return home to Japan from Washington or New York aboard All Nippon Airways or Japan Air Lines, and that is the fact that, over the course of the fourteen-hour flight, the sun continues to shine above the clouds outside my window. The sun doesn't set until I arrive at Narita.

Once I asked the captain (through the flight attendants) if the sun also continued to shine when flying to Narita from Los Angeles, San Francisco, Honolulu, or other west coast cities. He answered, "Yes, as long as it's a daytime take-off." This is, of course, the same situation when flying west from Narita, such as traveling across Russia to Europe, so it's not a deeply scientific problem or anything of the sort.

Still, why does it impress me? Because the westward journey from the United States appears to be under the protection of the sun, always bringing to mind the words Manifest Destiny.

"Armed with the Plough and the Rifle"

The term Manifest Destiny was made popular by the versatile writer John O'Sullivan. Born in Europe and educated in France and England, O'Sullivan went on to study at Columbia University and become a New York attorney. He became acquainted with authors and poets such as Nathaniel Hawthorne and Edgar Allen Poe and in 1837 published a literary magazine, the *United States Magazine and Democratic Review*. In 1839, in an editorial titled "The Great Nation of Futurity," he discussed the concept of the development of the western United States. He called on the idea of providence, that is, divine will, as follows:

> America is destined for better deeds. . . . We have no interest in the scenes of antiquity, only as lessons of avoidance of nearly all their examples. The expansive future is our arena, and for our history. We are entering on its untrodden space with the truths of God in our minds, beneficent objects in our hearts, and with a clear conscience unsullied by the past. We are the nation of human progress, and who will, what can, set limits to our onward march? Providence is with us, and no earthly power can . . . the nation of many nations is destined to manifest to mankind the excellence of divine principles. . . . Yes, we are the nation of progress, of individual freedom, of universal enfranchisement. . . . This is our high destiny, and in nature's eternal, inevitable decree of cause and effect we must accomplish it. All this will be our future history. . . . For this blessed mission to the nations of the world . . . has America been chosen.

With the astonishing territorial expansion resulting from the Louisiana Purchase of 1803 and the acquisition of Florida in 1819, the United States set its sights on the Pacific Ocean and its heart on the dream of further expansion westward. This editorial conveys the pride of the eastern intellectuals of the day perfectly.

In 1845, just after Texas was annexed into the Union, John O'Sullivan once again published an editorial in the *United States Magazine and Democratic Review*, in which he mentioned "checking the fulfillment of our manifest destiny to overspread the continent allotted by Providence for the free development of our yearly multiplying millions." This was the first time the words Manifest Destiny were used.

After conjecturing that "It is wholly untrue, and unjust to ourselves, the pretence that the Annexation has been a measure of spoliation, unrightful and unrighteous—of military conquest under forms of peace and law—of territorial aggrandizement at the expense of justice due by a double sanctity to the weak," the piece goes on to talk frankly about the ambition of acquiring California:

> Imbecile and distracted, Mexico never can exert any real govern-
> ment authority over such a country. . . . The Anglo-Saxon foot is
> already on its borders. Already the advance guard of the irresist-
> ible army of Anglo-Saxon emigration has begun to pour down
> upon it, armed with the plough and the rifle, and marking its trail
> with schools and colleges, courts and representative halls, mills
> and meeting-houses. A population will soon be in actual occupa-
> tion of California, over which it will be idle for Mexico to dream
> of dominion. They will necessarily become independent. All this
> without the agency of our government, without responsibility of
> our people—in the natural flow of events. . . . And they will have
> a right to independence—to self-government—to the possession
> of the homes conquered from the wilderness by their own labors
> and dangers, sufferings and sacrifices. . . . Whether they will then
> attach themselves to our Union or not, is not to be predicted with
> certainty. Unless the projected railroad across the continent to
> the Pacific be carried into effect, perhaps they may not; though
> even in that case, the day is not distant when the Empires of the
> Atlantic and the Pacific would again flow together.

The importance of John O'Sullivan's coinage of Manifest Destiny is that it clearly demonstrates the self-confidence, pride, and democratic originality in the DNA of the use of force that is central to American principles.

Like the westward territorial expansion aiming at the Pacific Ocean by Anglo-Saxon emigrants with "ploughs and rifles" and later "schools and colleges, courts and representative halls," the construction of various systems of democracy including schools, colleges, and representative politics, which were "exported" to the west, were regarded by many Americans as something in accord with the providence of God, expressing the idea that the United States is a chosen country and an instrument of divine will. "Ploughs and rifles" is an honest expression.

Thus, the United States evolved from its founding in "disorder" on the "barren North American continent," through the Declaration of Independence, the enactment of the U.S. Constitution, the establishment of the "necessary evil" of the federal government, and the manifestation of the diplomatic declaration of independence from Europe known as the Monroe Doctrine. Americans' growing consciousness of their success in creating "order" became both a source of national excitement and a form of self-made trap, pushing the country willy-nilly into further adventures.

In 1845, under James Polk, the eleventh president, the path of Manifest Destiny became national policy. Within just four years the United States achieved the annexation of Texas (1845), the cession of Oregon (1846), and won a two-year war with Mexico, thereby acquiring California and New Mexico (1848).

This marked the birth of a United States ranging from the Atlantic Ocean to the Pacific for the first time in the country's history, and it was just beginning to participate as a major nation in international politics. Polk's achievements consistently contribute to his rating as one of the top ten presidents by U.S. historians.

De Facto Discrimination

The North Carolina–born President Polk employed military force along the path of Manifest Destiny to connect two great oceans and complete the empire of liberty. He constantly maintained an intense sense of being one of the "chosen" Anglo-Saxons, superior to Native Americans, blacks, Mexicans, and Asians.

Robert Walker, secretary of the treasury under Polk and a strong advocate of territorial expansion, suggested that the United States should send Negro slaves to Texas, Mexico, and Central America, where the "brown people" live. Cushing, the advocate of active commerce with China, remarked that "colored" people were inferior to the whites of world and must be governed. There are many such statements on record by the leading adherents of Manifest Destiny, including O'Sullivan.[7]

James MacPherson, professor of American history at Princeton University, who has authored numerous books on black issues in the nineteenth century and Civil War, wrote as follows:

"The Mexican War fulfilled for the United States its self-proclaimed manifest destiny to bestride the continent from sea to shining sea   the manifest destiny that represented hope for white Americans thus spelled doom for Red Americans."[8]

We must face the reality of the de facto discrimination on this path of Manifest Destiny. Moreover, the attitude led to the immigration restrictions on Japan and China in the nineteenth and twentieth centuries as well as the incarceration of Japanese American citizens in concentration camps during World War II while Germans and Italians continued to be permitted to immigrate.

In 1846, President Polk sent the warships USS *Columbus* and USS *Vincennes* to Uraga under the command of Admiral James Biddle, who had experience making port calls in China. However, the ships encountered strong resistance from the Edo Shogunate—a little-known episode of failure in the history of the opening of Japan. The sea was calm, and it was a humiliating scene for the United States when its two ships had to be pulled out by a sailing boat when they left.

Through the Civil War and into the twentieth century, the spirit of Manifest Destiny was translated into the development of American sea power and the gunboat diplomacy of Theodore Roosevelt.

Secretary of State John Hay declared an "open door policy" toward China in 1899. This followed the Alaska Purchase (1867), the Hawaii Annexation (1898), and the Philippine Possession (1898). Though the final point of arrival for Manifest Destiny had already been reached, the concept underlying the policy served as a remote cause of the war between the United States and Japan. Secretary Hay referred to the Spanish-American War, in which the United States gained the Philippines, Guam, and Puerto Rico from Spain, as a "splendid little war."

It cannot be overemphasized that the four ships of the East India Fleet under the command of Commodore Matthew Perry that arrived at Uraga on July 8, 1853, were just one step on the westward movement to follow the sun. Incidentally the flagship *Susquehanna,* on which Commodore Perry sailed, was also the top warship among seven steam battleships that the navy built after the war with Mexico. The necessity of demonstrating overwhelming military might in the opening of Japan was a lesson learned from the Biddle fleet's previous failure.

Thus, the opening of Japan fulfilled a sense of mission as one part of the path of Manifest Destiny. Implicit in this mission was the DNA of the use of force. Nine more ships arrived in Japan only seven months later in February 1854, and the Treaty of Amity was signed on March 31. Townsend Harris, the first U.S. consul general to Japan, wrote the following entry in his journal on August 19, 1856, two days prior to landing at Shimoda. Eighty years after the United States was born out of "disorder," the diplomat's use of the phrase "new order" is interesting:

> I shall be the first recognized agent from a civilized power to reside in Japan. This forms an epoch in my life and may be the beginning of a new order of things in Japan. I hope I may so conduct myself that I may have honorable mention in the histories which will be written on Japan and its future destiny."[9]

The U.S. posture toward Japan, or rather the Manifest Destiny mindset always present in the roots of that posture, must never be forgotten.

The Civil War as the Starting Block

The Civil War, which took place from 1861 to 1865, could be called the greatest resolution of compromises since the nation's founding. This war was fought when the states of the South resisted the efforts of the North to directly abolish slavery. On a more fundamental level, a second cause of the war erupted from disputes over the "necessary evil" functions executed by the federal government. These, too, played a central role in the confrontation between the North and South.

The war broke out as a result of Lincoln's insistence on preserving the federal system after rejecting the kind of compromise that the Founding Fathers, now gone, had forged between North and South. In addition, an impending crisis loomed on the horizon with the possibility of European countries diplomatically recognizing the South as a separate nation.

The major battles of this long, miserable war were fought in the South, with 2,900,000 soldiers participating in both the Union and Confederate armies. Over a period of five years 620,000 soldiers died, counting both the

North and South. The total number of deaths surpasses that of all "American wars," World Wars I and II, and the Vietnam, Persian Gulf, Afghan, and Iraq Wars.

It must not be forgotten that not only did the victory of the Union Army result in the permanent establishment of the federal system and the end of slavery, it also solidified the modern United States of America diplomatically, providing the foundation of an empire. According to Professor MacPherson, a mature United States had appeared on the scene.

This war showed that America had reached a stage where the Industrial Revolution underway in the North was fully reflected in the nation's military and economic might. The defeat of the slavery-dependent South, which lagged behind in the Industrial Revolution, was a natural development.

The rivalry and competition generated by the Civil War not only spawned a modern infrastructure of railroads and telegraph communications throughout the country, it also promoted the development of the techniques of mass production and new technologies in weaponry. These included new Colt revolvers and repeating rifles; the use of landmines and torpedoes; the appearance of new-type cannons, machineguns, armored warships, and submarines; and reconnaissance and battlefield photography from manned balloons. Furthermore, the first draft lottery system was established in 1863, from which the standing military known as the United States Armed Forces was born, and various new technologies and know-how were employed that served as forerunners of modern war. The Civil War was also the war that built the foundation of the United States as the number one military nation of our time.

The proliferation of guns in the United States exploded after the end of the Civil War. When the soldiers were demobilized, three million new-type small arms manufactured for the Union Army, along with 2.5 million old-style muskets, were sold at low prices and scattered across the country. Experts say that the Civil War made the United States into the definitive gun society.[10] In 1871, the NRA was established with the support of New York State for the purpose of helping ex-Union Army officers maintain their marksmanship skill during peacetime. In this way, the path of Manifest Destiny rode upon the back of America's infrastructure from the twentieth into the twenty-first century, extending to the West, to Asia, to Europe after World War I, and to the entire world. Today, as the sole victor of the Cold War, the United States is spreading its wings to Iraq.

I believe that the nineteenth-century American triad of the Monroe Doctrine, Manifest Destiny, and the Civil War is indispensable in understanding this country called America. Commodore Perry's arrival at Uraga, World War II, the Vietnam War, the demands upon Japan for structural reform, and the current path taken by the neoconservatives have all derived from these factors.

The United States today is unquestionably "an actor on a most conspicuous theatre." The intense self-consciousness displayed immediately following George Washington's victory in the War of Independence is still alive today more than 220 years later. The whole world takes silent notice of every move the actor now makes because these moves affect all corners of the world, and for some countries they are a matter of life or death. As Alexis de Tocqueville so harshly concluded, many nations and people are "wearied" by the "garrulous patriotism." The Iraq War is a fresh example.

SIX

Discrimination and Exclusion

A Nation Founded on Discrimination

With its trust placed in Manifest Destiny, the United States continued to expand ever westward to the Pacific Ocean, dragging a large black shadow along with it. The import of black slaves began in 1619, the same year as the first colonial assembly in Jamestown, marking the beginning of black discrimination. However, the colonists' treatment of Native Americans, a policy of exclusion, was even harsher.

This discrimination and exclusion were first clearly enunciated when the U.S. Constitution in 1788 was drafted. As discussed in chapter 3, the slave states of the South and the free states of the North, compromised in how the population of each state was calculated to be calculated for elected representation. In art. 1, sec. 2, clause 3, the Constitution states that:

> Representatives and direct Taxes shall be apportioned among the several States which may be included within this Union, according to their respective Numbers, which shall be determined by adding to the whole Number of free Persons, including those bound to Service for a Term of Years, and excluding Indians not taxed, three fifths of all other Persons.

As the text of the document clearly shows, the men who drafted the

Constitution did not treat the Native Americans as citizens who could be taxed. Where black Americans were concerned, the indirect expression "whole Number of free Persons, and excluding . . . three fifths of all other Persons" omits the remaining two-fifths of the population.

There is only one other passage that mentions Native Americans. Article 1, section 8, clause 3, defines the authority of Congress and stipulates that, as well as enacting laws regarding foreign and interstate commerce, Congress is also "To regulate Commerce . . . with the Indian Tribes."

A discriminatory attitude toward blacks can also be seen in art. 4, sec. 2, clause 3 of the Constitution:

> No Person held to Service or Labour in one State, under the
> Laws thereof, escaping into another, shall, in Consequence of
> any Law or Regulation therein, be discharged from such Service
> or Labour, but shall be delivered up on Claim of the Party to
> whom such Service or Labour may be due.

This clause indirectly recognizes that slave flight from the southern slave states to the free North had already become a social problem at the time of the Constitutional Congress. In fact, in 1793, immediately following the establishment of the U.S. constitutional system and the Bill of Rights, Congress passed a law recognizing the right of owners of fugitive slaves to recapture or kidnap them from other states and take them home.

This law clearly set forth a plan for excluding the application of the writ of habeas corpus and Bill of Rights—that is, basic human rights—to black slaves. Forty-nine years later, in 1842, a Supreme Court composed largely of judges from the South upheld this 1793 law.

The Underground Railroad

Before talking about the exclusion of Native Americans, I would like to continue discussing the origins of slavery in the early years of democracy. This comes out in the drama of the fugitive slaves, and is a shameful episode on the part of the "actors on a most conspicuous theatre" in whom George Washington was so proud. The DNA of the use of force also shows its face here.

Let's examine the detailed circumstances surrounding the Supreme Court's constitutional ruling of 1842. It began with the Fugitive Slave Act passed in 1826 by the state legislature of Pennsylvania, which had come to typify the free states. Slavery abolitionists had stood up and established a nationwide watch committee for the protection of runaway slaves. In 1837, the state authorities of Pennsylvania used this law to find guilty on charges of kidnapping a man named Edward Prigg, who had kidnapped a fugitive slave woman and her child and returned them to their owner in Maryland.

Prigg's attorney appealed the decision to the Supreme Court, and the 1842 ruling *Prigg v. Pennsylvania* found the Pennsylvania Fugitive Slave Act of 1826 unconstitutional. It also declared that the 1793 federal law recognizing the constitutional right to recapture runaway slaves invalidated any contradictory legislation by free states. The court also declared that neither slave nor free-state authorities need recognize this right to return fugitive slaves, noting that the federal government was solely responsible for returning slaves.

As already seen in the examples involving the Second Amendment in the *Miller* and *Emerson* decisions in chapter 2, the rulings of the U.S. Supreme Court were very political affairs that keenly reflected the social situation of the time. The *Prigg v. Pennsylvania* ruling represented a skillful but ultimately futile effort by the Court to come to terms with a situation that was already leading slowly but surely to the Civil War. In addition, the court skillfully balanced competing interests, recognizing the right to return slaves as a concession to the South while at the same time defying Southern insistence on state rights by assigning authority to the federal government.

In fact, after this ruling, the free states enacted a large number of acts designed to preserve freedoms. These outlawed the use of state facilities in the kidnapping and return of fugitive slaves and at the same time guaranteed human rights through the use of the courts and trial by jury.

Protection and surveillance committees were organized in the free states to fight kidnappers from the South as well as those in the North who were in league with the kidnappers.

As a result, hundreds of fugitive slaves each year were sent into the Boston-centered free North and further into Canada by way of a secret support network known as the Underground Railroad that escaped the notice of the federal marshals.

George Mason, one of the Founding Fathers who contributed to aspects of the Constitution and the Bill of Rights, especially the Second Amendment, commented that the loss of honor from the flight of slaves was greater than the loss of property.[1]

Like Jefferson and others, Mason was a wealthy landowner who possessed slaves. During the Second Continental Congress of May 1776, which rejected the authority of England over the colonies, Mason received appeals to establish an independent government. He was the star performer in drafting both the Bill of Rights and the Virginia Constitution.

Article 1 of this constitution proclaims:

> That all men are by nature equally free and independent and have certain inherent rights, of which, when they enter into a state of society, they cannot, by any compact, deprive or divest their posterity.

This drafter did not expound upon the human rights of slaves, which he himself owned, and I believe the true face of the country at the time of its founding is contained in the concept of "Southern honor."

In 1850, a new Fugitive Slave Act was passed, establishing a new federal commissioner's office specializing in the control of slave flight and the return of fugitive slaves.

This legislation was also much stricter than the law of 1793 in specifying that:

1. Slave owners recognized the right of the federal commissioner's office to arbitrate the status of slaves that they found.

2. Federal marshals or their deputies who refused to cooperate with slave owners were assessed a fine of one thousand dollars.

3. Those who sheltered fugitive slaves or blocked their return were punished heavily.

4. The federal Department of the Treasury funded the expenses of finding and returning fugitive slaves entirely.

Statistics show that, during the 1850s after this Act was passed, 332 slaves were returned to the South by arbitration of the federal commission while only eleven made it to freedom. In 1859 the U.S. Supreme Court ruled that the law was constitutional.

The Underdog South

Still, the defensiveness of the slave states was clear. The crafting of the Fugitive Slave Act of 1850 was just one part of the Compromise of 1850, which dealt with the confrontation over whether to make the California and New Mexico territories, which had just been won from Mexico, slave states or free states.

The slave states were forced to:

1. Accept the petition of California as a free state.

2. Leave the decision of New Mexico up to the residents.

3. Outlaw the slave trade in Washington, D.C., the nation's capital.

When Missouri became a slave state in 1819, Maine separated from Massachusetts to maintain an even balance of eleven free states and eleven slave states. Compared to the Missouri Compromise, which had ended a crisis of national division,[2] the Compromise of 1850 indicated that the influence of the South had clearly weakened.

Over a period of ten to twenty years, various Underground Railroad organizations arose in each of the free states. Meanwhile, the slave states were pouncing on runaway slaves who had succeeded as craftsmen in cities such as New York and Boston. About three thousand fugitive slaves had been sent into Canada in the last three months of 1850 alone. As a result, the black population of Ontario increased to eleven thousand during the 1850s.

On September 11, 1851, a bloody incident occurred in the Quaker village of Christiana, Pennsylvania, near the border with Maryland. A Maryland slave owner and a group of federal marshals who had come to kidnap fugitive slaves were unable to collect their bounty after being met by fierce resistance from a group of Caucasians and blacks with a Quaker in charge who pressed them to abandon their kidnapping intentions. A fight ensued. The slave owner died, and his son was seriously injured. In addition two whites and two blacks on the other side were hurt. The three black men who were the targets of the kidnapping escaped to Canada.

Local Pennsylvania papers and the *New York Tribune* printed reports with sensational headlines such as "Civil War—The First Blow Struck," causing the abolitionists in the free states to rise up. President Fillmore went so far as to call in the Marines. Thirty-six blacks and five whites were arrested and prosecuted, not only for violation of the Fugitive Slave Act but for treason as well.

These strong measures backfired as they spawned fierce public opposition and deep-rooted dissatisfaction in the free states not only against slavery but against the South as well. In the end the grand jury released as innocent the white Quakers who appeared as the first defendants. The federal government eventually dropped all charges.

Opposition to slavery continued to grow in the free states after California itself elected to become a free state. On the other side a pro-slavery group known as the Fire-Eaters began speaking of secession from the Union. The three states of South Carolina, Georgia, and Mississippi convened a meeting to discuss the merits of secession, and the governor of South Carolina announced that there was no longer any room for doubt about Southern independence. Though no action was taken by these states to secede at the time, ten years later, on April 11, 1861, the Confederate Army fired on Fort Sumter outside of Charleston, South Carolina, beginning the Civil War that raged for the next four years.

Ironically, with defeat of the Confederacy imminent after its loss at Gettysburg, General Robert E. Lee began requesting the militarization of the black slaves. At the same time France and Britain were offering recognition on the condition that the slaves would be freed.[3]

Discrimination against Blacks Is Tantamount to the Gas Chambers

I have dared to describe at length the involvement of fugitive slaves in the process of the North-South catastrophe because it took a tragic Civil War in which a total of 620,000 people died to knock down the wall of black slavery built into the nation's founding.

The introduction of extraordinary use of force must be reexamined when, without it, the United States could not have even begun to erase the original sin of black discrimination. The DNA of American use of force really did show its face in different ways as this country established its "order."

I refer once again to Samuel Morison's *The Oxford History of the American People* because it provides a fair generalization about racial attitudes in the Southern slave states. In chapter 32, "The Southern States, 1820–1850," Morison writes:

> Whilst the average Englishman or free-state American disliked the Negro as such, Southern slave-owners understood and loved him as a slave. . . . There was no physical repulsion from color in the South. White children were suckled by black 'mammies' and played with their children.

This was the world portrayed in the film *Gone with the Wind*. At the same time, however, Morison also notes:[4]

> Instances of sadistic cruelty to slaves are so numerous in the records that they cannot be dismissed as mere abolitionist propaganda. These were extreme cases; no doubt the majority of masters were kind and humane; but should not a system be judged by the extremes that it tolerates? May we not judge Hitler's regime by the gas chambers, or Stalin's by purges, forced-labor camps, and firing squads?

I deeply respect the values that Americans harbor when they equate slavery to the atrocities of Hitler and Stalin. I believe such values reflect America's open-mindedness and generosity.

In 1865 the Thirteenth Amendment abolished slavery in response to President Lincoln's Emancipation Proclamation of 1863. Discrimination as a principle on the constitutional level disappeared further through the Fourteenth Amendment, sec. 1, which was enacted in 1868 and stipulated that "All persons born or naturalized in the United States and subject to the jurisdiction thereof, are citizens of the United States and of the State wherein they reside." The Fifteenth Amendment of 1870 prohibited the denial of the right to vote based on race or color.

Furthermore, the Thirteenth Amendment completely annulled the portion of the U.S. Constitution, art. 4, sec. 2, clause 3, that had caused so much pain for fugitive slaves and become the flashpoint of the Civil War. A century and a half later, the status of the black population, now referred to as African American, has improved to the point where blacks epitomize the multiracial power that helps explain why the United States has become the sole superpower. Even though conditions of discrimination still exist, they have become a catalyst for American pluralistic energy.

In contrast, Native Americans were thoroughly disregarded and excluded. Pushed onto reservations, they are still far from being in a position to contribute to this pluralistic energy.

While blacks had been held in slavery, they were released. In contrast, Native Americans continued to be alienated from many of the rights that blacks gained. The Fourteenth Amendment recognizes the black population as a part of the population of the states, but the clause referring to "excluding Indians not taxed" has never gone away.

A Population Unchanged after Four Centuries

The exclusion of Native Americans was total. Let's begin with a few numbers.

What was the population of the native Indians, then called "savages," at the time the future Americans landed at Jamestown and Plymouth?

The "Important Events" page on the *Blue Cloud Abbey* website run by a Benedictine Monastery in South Dakota reports that the North American Native American population was approximately sixty million in the year 1500, about a century before the Jamestown settlement or the arrival of the *Mayflower*. This population had declined to about one million in 1900. The basis for these numbers, however, is not clear.

In contrast, the high school American history textbook, *The American Nation*, quoted in chapter 2, tells us, in addition to changing the name *Indians* to Native Americans, many experts have concluded that, as of the year 1500, there were probably about 2.5 million people divided into hundreds of tribes. So, let's keep this number in mind for the time being.

Returning to the present, in September 2002 the staff of the U.S. Census Bureau released a document titled "Historical Census Statistics on Population Totals By Race, 1790 to 1990, and By Hispanic Origin, 1970 to 1990, For The United States, Regions, Divisions, and States" in a series of working papers based on the results of the 1990 census.

The year 1790 was two years after the U.S. Constitution was enacted and one year after the first president, George Washington, assumed office. This was the year the national population census began as one of the systems peculiar to American democracy. It is based on a provision of the Constitution, art. 1, sec. 2, clause 3, which states:

Representatives and direct Taxes shall be apportioned among
the several States which may be included within this Union,
according to their respective Numbers. . . . 'The actual Enumera-
tion shall be made within three Years after the first Meeting of
the Congress of the United States, and within every subsequent
Term of ten Years, in such Manner as they shall by Law direct.

Under this system the number of seats in the House of Representatives
allocated to each state changes every ten years with the population census.
According to the results of the most recent census of 2000, Texas, Florida,
and California, states that increased in population, gained a total of eleven
representatives, while Pennsylvania and Michigan lost a total of eleven seats.

In presidential elections as well, the number of state representatives is
related to the number of electors for each state. In the election of 2000, the
change in state population was a critical factor in President Bush's victory.
The Supreme Court determination that Bush won Florida reflected that
state's increased electoral importance.

The first year that Native Americans were included in these critical
statistics was 1860. Through the seven censuses until that time, the data for
Native Americans was marked "NA," not applicable. Even so, the census of
1860 lumped together "Indians, Eskimos, and Aleutians," after "Caucasians"
and "Negroes."

The numbers themselves, however, are small: 40,021 in 1860. Ten years
later in 1870, the numbers are still fewer: 25,731. In 1880 there were 66,407.
Even if all of these figures represented Indians, I think these numbers are
extremely small.

A U.S. Census Bureau note attached to these figures states that only
those Indians who were taxed were counted. As previously discussed, the U.S.
Constitution, art. 1, sec. 2, clause 3, stipulates that the population is to be calculated "excluding Indians not taxed" for the purposes of determining the number of elected representatives. This stipulation appears to have been faithfully
executed. How many, then, of these "Indians not taxed" were there?

The answer to this question lies in the census of 1890. Two types of
numbers are indicated for that year, the number 58,604 in the same column
as before, and for the first time, the six-figure number of 248,253 is reported as
"including the population of Indian territories and reservations." Beginning
with the census of 1900, these numbers have been combined into one.

In other words, the number of "Indians not taxed," people driven into the Indian territories and reservations in the remote, barren regions, was included for the first time and appeared in the final official statistics. Later, in 1930 the number was reported as more than three hundred thousand, in 1960 more than five hundred thousand, in 1970 more than eight hundred thousand, in 1980 more than 1.4 million, in 1990 more than 1.9 million, and in 2000, the census counted the Native American population as 2,475,956.

So, why is it that almost the same Native American population of 2.5 million is presumed for the year 1500, as recorded in the American high school textbook over four centuries later? I think the answer lies in the various forms of slaughter that had exhausted the Native American populations. I think the DNA of the use of force shows its face throughout the history of Native American exclusion. The reason for following these numbers in detail was to illustrate this fact.

A Record of Slaughter

The accounts of this slaughter are unpleasant. There are, of course, a few dramas of friendship: the story of the Pilgrim Fathers and Wampanoag Chief Massasoit and their treaty; the sparing of Captain John Smith's life; the saving of the Jamestown colony; Chief Powhatan's visit to London and the tale of his daughter Pocahontas.

Still, these are exceptional episodes that took place at a time when the Native Americans stood in a position of relative advantage over the colonists. When the Plymouth Plantation merged into the neighboring Massachusetts Bay Colony with its military strength, the combined colonists fought the Pequot and King Philip wars described in chapter 4.

Similarly, Jamestown to the south fought the first colonial war against Native Americans in 1622. As the population of the colony grew year by year, Native Americans' concerns over increasing demands for land had become a trigger.

The Blue Cloud Abbey website records that the first Native American reservation was set aside near the Connecticut Colony in 1636, the same year as the Pequot War. It is said that King Philip was driven to war by a sense of impending crisis over the Christian evangelical activities of the colonial pastors together with his opposition to the reservation plan. The Native Americans were pushed onto reservations and forced to "civilize" to white and Christian cultures, and this constitutes the basis of the reconciliation policies in effect from the early days of settlement to this day.

The full-scale use of force against the Native Americans, however, started with the French and Indian War, also known as the Seven Years' War, between England and France over control of North America. We have already seen how this war, which began in 1755, laid the groundwork for American independence.

France had built numerous forts stretching from Quebec down the St. Lawrence River to the Great Lakes rand throughout the vast area along the Mississippi River to the Gulf of Mexico. The entire area was known as New France.

Meanwhile, England, which had solidified its thirteen Atlantic seaboard colonies from New England to the South, wanted more land for its rapidly increasing number of settlers, particularly in the three colonies of New York, Pennsylvania, and Virginia. England decided to push forward across the Appalachian Mountains into the Ohio and Tennessee River valleys and the Northwest.

In consequence, both France and England began forming alliances with leading native tribes such as the Algonquin and Huron in the Northwest where the two countries had clashed for many years. One Native American saying went, "England and France are like the two edges of a great scissors. We are like a cloth that has been cut by them."

The Native Americans in these regions, who made the "sacred woods" their livelihood, offered little resistance to the French, who were fur hunters and traders. In contrast, the British agricultural settlers cleared the woods, stole the land, and took the Native American women in marriage. For these reasons, the Algonquin and Huron tribes decided to ally themselves with France. A union of six Iroquois tribes from upper New York State, however, had been hostile to the French for many years and aligned themselves with England.

In this way, the Native Americans were divided against one another and fought or were forced to fight in tragic combinations in the confrontation between the French army, British army, and American colonial militia. Furthermore, the colonial powers used the situation to justify their slaughter of the Native Americans.

The American high school textbook mentioned earlier reports the record of this slaughter coolly and conscientiously. Its stance is fair and painfully moves readers to sympathy for the plight of the Indians through descriptions of the frightful armed force used against them.

A pair of incidents offer a vivid picture. In 1760, a year after the French defeat, the British army and Carolina Militia attacked a settlement of Cherokees living along a route to the Mississippi River Valley. The Cherokees counterattacked, causing damage to the British army, but the final toll represented about five thousand Cherokee deaths, including noncombatants. It was after this tragedy that a peace treaty was finally concluded.[5]

The second incident of note was the slaughter known as Pontiac's War. Following the French retreat, the British army in the Ohio River Valley arrogantly set the prices of trade goods higher than they were during the French period. They also calmly provided land to settlers from New England and the South. As a result, the Huron and other tribes in the region who had fought on the side of the French revolted.

The leader of this rebellion was Pontiac, the chief of the Ottawa Tribe. In April 1763, as the treaty concluding the French and Indian War was about to be signed in Paris, Native Americans attacked British army forts and settlements over a period of two months, reportedly killing two thousand English settlers. However, the attacks on Fort Pitt (present-day Pittsburgh), the most important British army base, and the attempted capture of Fort Detroit both failed. When news arrived of the defeat of the French army, the rebellion tapered off.

The Use of Biological Weapons

What must be recorded is the fact that during the battle of Fort Pitt, the British army employed biological weapons, to use terminology from the present-day Iraq War.

Under the direction of Lord Jeffrey Amherst, the commander-in-chief of the British army who won the French and Indian War, the British garrison handed over two blankets and one handkerchief from the fort's smallpox ward as a gift to the Delaware Tribe that had surrounded the fort. Smallpox spread instantly among the Delaware, and the dead dropped one after another "like grape vines." Observers called it a "spectacle defying description."[6]

This incident is not recorded in the American high school history book.

There is the opinion among some scholars that the spread of smallpox was "unintentional." However, a paper by Peter Derrico of the University of Massachusetts Legal Studies Department that was published on a Native American website argues otherwise. A study of a letter that General Amherst had written to Captain Simeon Ecuyer, a Swiss mercenary and the garrison's senior officer, revealed that Amherst had approved Captain Ecuyer's proposal to infect the Native Americans. According to Derrico, the letter reportedly said, "You will Do well to try to innoculate the Indians by means of Blankets as well as to try every other method that can serve to Extirpate this Execrable Race." This letter has been microfilmed and preserved in the U.S. Library of Congress.

General Amherst also likened the Indians to pests and wood-dwellers that need not be considered human, and called for their total extermination. He was later appointed governor general of British North America and promoted to commander-in-chief of the British Army. A college town named for this general still remains in Massachusetts. Incidentally, Native Americans began to be vaccinated in 1832.

As a result of Pontiac's War, the British government issued the Proclamation of 1763, signed by King George III, that simultaneously prohibited the migration of British settlers west of the Appalachians "until further notice" and ordered those settlers already living there to leave immediately. It also protected Indian territories in the Ohio River Valley, known then as the Western Frontier from white settlement. To execute this proclamation, a standing army of ten thousand soldiers was deployed from England.

This action did not mean the British had given up trying to acquire land by force. Instead, it was an attempt to guarantee the security of British settlers based on the lessons learned from Pontiac's War. The new policy recognized that peaceful coexistence through conciliation was indispensable. At that time, the majority of British government authorities controlling the settlements west of the Appalachians had judged it wiser to promote settlement in Atlantic Seaboard regions such as Nova Scotia in Canada and Florida in the South.

The new policy, however, was set forth unilaterally without consulting those concerned, and strong protests arose from the three colonies of New York, Pennsylvania, and Virginia. For these areas, westward expansion was already a necessity for development. Records show that the proclamation was largely ignored, and nine hundred thousand settlers crossed the mountains. Furthermore, the British Army did not deploy troops to frontier areas such as Pittsburgh, Detroit, and the Carolinas, but kept them stationed around large cities like New York, a move that was meant to curb retirements in its officer corps.

When the British government forced the costs of stationing its troops back onto the colonies, protests increased even further. The huge budget deficit incurred from the victory in the French and Indian War and the establishment of worldwide hegemony was the beginning of a financial burden that was part of the British Empire.

Later, the British government tried to overcome its financial difficulties and tighten its control of the colonies by churning out such revenue-boosting measures as the Sugar Act, Stamp Act, and Tea Act. We have already seen the process that caused the thirteen colonies from New Hampshire to Georgia to unite in chapter 4.

The protest movement that developed under the slogan "no taxation without representation" developed into armed clashes following the Boston Massacre of 1770. The War of Independence began five years later. Thus, the battle at Fort Pitt, or Pontiac's War, in which the Native Americans were on the receiving end of a bacteriological attack, had in a roundabout way pulled the trigger of revolution. This is the irony that I want to point out.

In 1765 in Detroit, the British and Pontiac laid down their weapons and secured peace. Pontiac was assassinated by a Native American in 1769.

A Scrapped Treaty

The drama of slaughter continues about a century later in the 1890 massacre at Wounded Knee, though there was no intention of slaughter at the beginning.

The desire for peaceful coexistence displayed in the Proclamation of 1763 during the British colonial period continued, and the Continental Congress concluded a peace and friendship treaty with the Delaware Tribe in 1778. The Northwest Ordinance of 1787, one of two land bills enacted by Congress immediately after achieving independence, established the principle of governing the territories outside the thirteen states by declaring:

> The utmost good faith shall always be observed towards the
> Indians; their lands and property shall never be taken from them
> without their consent; and, in their property, rights, and liberty,

they shall never be invaded or disturbed, unless in just and lawful wars authorized by Congress.

Efforts at Christianization based on the Puritan traditions from the Plymouth Plantation period, called civilizing, were also being continued. Even Thomas Jefferson, a central founding leader of the nation, dreamed of converting the traditional hunting lifestyle of the Native Americans in the new territories west of the Appalachians and infinitely further west of the Mississippi to one of agriculture. His design was to peacefully acquire vast tracts of land that could absorb the white population.

During the War of Independence, however, many native tribes fought on the side of the British, persuaded by the British claim that vast numbers of white settlers would cross the Appalachians and steal Native American land if the colonists won the war. One hundred and thirty thousand Native Americans reportedly fought on the British side and thus became direct enemies of the United States.

The standing army, which now went by the name of the United States Army, soon cemented the nation's foundation by fighting and winning the War of 1812. Then, during the Seminole Wars as part of the territorial expansion along the path of Manifest Destiny, which included the Louisiana Purchase and the Florida Acquisition, Native Americans were banished from the new territories. The abominable slaughter was repeated again.

In 1830 the Indian Removal Act was passed under President Jackson mandating the relocation of the Cherokees to the frontier lands west of the Mississippi. This action embodied the country's true intentions after Jefferson. Driven from their ancestral lands in the east by the U.S. Army, about sixteen thousand Cherokees crossed the Mississippi westward into present-day Oklahoma. No less than four thousand died of malnutrition and other causes on this journey that came to be known as the Trail of Tears.

The employment of military force became unstoppable. The years following saw the Texas Annexation, the Mexican-American War, the acquisition of California and New Mexico, and the Union Army victory in the Civil War. When gold was discovered on the reservations, the treaties with the Indians were scrapped in the blink of an eye.

In 1890 members of the Lakota Tribe were feverously participating in a Ghost Dance ceremony to invoke their messiah and restore their land at

Wounded Knee, South Dakota. Three hundred were shot dead without resistance by the U.S. Army's 7th Cavalry Division. This was the Wounded Knee Massacre, a tragedy said to have been carried out as revenge for an incident that happened fourteen years earlier. In 1876 General George Custer and 250 men of the 7th Cavalry Division had been ambushed and killed by an alliance of the Lakota Sioux and Cheyenne.

The Wounded Knee Massacre was the final act in the "exclusion" of Native Americans. That same year the Census Bureau declared the disappearance of the frontier. The Western frontier has been lauded for its special role in the development and enhancement of American democracy, including the implementation of the first popular election.[7] Still, Frederick Turner, the flag-bearer of the Frontier Thesis—which posited that the exceptional vigor of the nation was derived from its interaction with the frontier—had himself supported "exclusion," stating that "The Indian was a common danger, demanding united action."[8]

More recently, however, the name of the Custer Battlefield National Monument, established by the descendants of Custer's annihilated cavalry, was changed to Little Bighorn Battlefield National Monument and a Sioux woman assumed the office of park superintendent. This national park attracts a half million tourists each year. The sale of neckties and other souvenirs made by the Custer Association have been forced out of the market in Chicago, and every year on June 27 a memorial parade is held in mourning of the massacre during which nobody utters the name of General Custer. Finally, Native Americans are no longer Indians.

Among the six famous marines depicted in the photograph of the raising of the Stars and Stripes atop Mount Suribachi on Iwo Jima is a Native American of the Pima Tribe, Private First Class Ira Hayes. This was reported widely by the U.S. media during World War II, and PFC Hayes was paraded all over the nation as a hero. However, his glory was short-lived. He became an alcoholic and froze to death along a road on a reservation. Compared to African Americans, the condition of Native Americans has been treading a step or two behind.

Days of Managing Casinos

What are the Native Americans doing now? This is what I wish to report in the end. It is a story filled to the brim with painful irony. They are now discovering the benefits of cash income through the management of casinos on their reservations.

According to the Bureau of Indian Affairs, as of September 2003 there were 554 Native American tribes, of which 330 owned casinos. There were casinos in twenty-eight states, with California having the most at thirty-three. Oklahoma was second with eighteen, and there were seventeen each in Arizona, Michigan, Minnesota, and Washington. Nationwide there was a total of 212 casinos with slot machines as the primary attraction.

Among the largest were the Foxwoods Resort Casino in Connecticut with eight hundred rooms, and the Mystic Lake Casino in Minnesota, with three thousand slot machines and eighty-eight blackjack tables. The casino industry had its beginnings in Las Vegas in the 1930s and has expanded to 430 locations nationwide since opening in Atlantic City in 1978. "Indian casinos" constitute a majority.

Furthermore, their earnings are considerable. In 1998, when there were only seventy casinos nationwide, their total revenue amounted to $211 million. In 1997 casino income was $700 million, and in 2002 this figure jumped to $14.5 billion.

As described in the previous chapter, native reservations were a product of exclusionary policies established on top of a belief in Manifest Destiny. Some tribes narrowly protected their ancestral grounds. Others were pushed westward to the very edge of the barren land known as the frontier. A common factor among all the tribes, however, is that they secured their own sovereignty as independent nations on the reservations in exchange for treaties with the United States. Even today, 373 of these treaties remain in force as does the portion of the Constitution that gave Congress the authority to "trade" with them.

Accordingly, residents of reservations have no obligation to pay taxes as U.S. citizens, including federal or state income taxes or corporate taxes. Nor are they under obligation to disclose casino accounting, including profits and operating costs. Payments to obtain the cooperation of state administrative authorities to guarantee access to the reservations have become routine, enabling these businesses to secure net profits of 10 to 30 percent. In the case of the Foxwoods Resort Casino and the Mohegan Sun Casino (also in Connecticut), 25 percent of slot machine profits are being paid to the state. There are also many instances where casinos make no payments, such as those in Verona, New York.

As a result many Native Americans have reportedly become millionaires. According to the 2000 census, the success of the Sioux casinos in Minnesota have resulted in average incomes of $84,500 per person, exceeding the average income of affluent areas like Scarsdale, New York, and Beverly Hills, California.

Still, according to a report by the National Indian Gaming Association, 55.5 percent of the profits from all Indian casinos in 2000 was generated by the top twenty establishments, so it's difficult to say that tribal casino operations have resulted in universal benefit. According to the same census, the average annual income for Native Americans was $12,893, which is $21,587 less than the national average. In general, the current conditions on reservations are marked by the slow development of infrastructure and their dependency on Bureau of Indian Affairs subsidies of only $13 million a year.

Schwarzenegger Seizes the Opportunity

Regarding these circumstances, Jacob Levy, assistant professor of political science at the University of Chicago and author of *The Multiculturalism of Fear*, commented in the *New Republic*:

> None of which is to say that a heavily casino-dependent economy is good for Indians. Casinos in the current legal structure are a bit like oil and diamonds in the resource-curse theory of development—they don't require any broad-based development of the tribal economy, they tend to loosen the ties of accountability between leaders and the led, and they tend to concentrate power at the center. But the interests of reservation Indians in broad-based and decentralized development is the last thing on the minds of those who see Indian gambling revenues as a juicy target for taxation.

He then proposes:

> The key point is that Indians are, once again, looking down the barrel of some especially adverse and arbitrary treatment by a political system in which they make up a tiny minority. If I were

in their shoes and had some money on hand, I'd probably spend it on political campaigns, too.

This point, perhaps, gets to the core of the matter.[9]

The activities of Native American group lobbies are already conspicuous, Mr. Levy's advice notwithstanding. Although political donations to federal lawmakers in Washington have been established for the direct purpose of preserving the rights and interests of the Indian casinos, they have also proven useful in the growth of unprecedented political influence. According to the figures of "responsible political centers" in Washington, political donations from Indian casino groups, which totaled only $1,750 in 1990, jumped up to $6.6 million in 2002.

The path for the Indian casino business was paved by a 1987 Supreme Court decision that stated a state government may not prohibit the construction of casinos on Indian reservations. With this ruling in hand, the National Indian Gaming Association was inaugurated in accordance with the Indian Gaming Regulatory Act of 1988. With a firm grasp of the act's political implications, Robert Loescher, the commission's sole Native American member, wrote:

> In my view, the benefits from Indian gaming are just a tiny down payment on the deficit of stupendous social and economic needs facing the vast majority of Native American citizens . . . it's natural that Native Americans would begin investing in Capitol Hill.

In 2002, for example, one tribe donated the significant sum of $512,000 to the Democratic Party, twice the amount contributed to the Republican Party.

The California governor recall election of October 2003 threw into the spotlight the relationship of Native American power to politics. Indian casinos were a factor in the victorious election of popular actor Arnold Schwarzenegger to the governorship of the nation's most populated state when the Democratic front-runner, incumbent Lieutenant Governor Cruz Bustamante, came under harsh criticism for accepting political contributions in the neighborhood of $10 million from Indian casinos.

These funds were donated to protect a gaming business with sales ranging from $3 billion to $6 billion. Of California's 108 tribes, fifty two enjoyed benefits from this business and supported the election of the until-then cooperative Bustamante as governor. Native Americans also had a track record of contributing nearly $1 billion a year to the state's Democratic legislators. This was the first time in California's political history that Indians had participated openly in the political process.

What is interesting is that after Schwarzenegger was elected governor, he reversed his position and agreed to discuss both the licensing of casinos in cities outside the reservations and ending the two-thousand-slot-machine-per-casino limit.

It has been said that the new governor's real intention was to reorganize the state's huge budget deficit of $8 billion by reallocating the $2 billion of the money paid by the tribes to the state.

Since the founding of the United States, there is perhaps no greater irony than the power of exclusion, which has ranked second only to that of the DNA of the use of force.

As a side note, California's Native American population dropped from one hundred thousand in 1850 to seventeen thousand in 1870 as a result of massacres, starvation, and disease due to the encroachment of settlers.

SEVEN

The Standing Army and Multiracial Power

The Philosophy behind Rejection of a Standing Army

Among the ironies surrounding the exclusion of Native Americans is the fact that the U.S. military played a major role in their plight—another telling example of America's DNA of the use of force.

Through the arming (or "militarizing") of all citizens, the Second Amendment, which is woven into the very soul of America's origin, prevents the federal government from becoming the seed of new tyranny. Nevertheless, that concept has waned. The small standing army envisioned in the drafting of the Constitution has, in two centuries, grown into the greatest armed force in the world.

In order to grasp the significance of this development correctly, I want to touch once again upon the philosophy behind the strong rejection of a standing army at the time of the nation's founding. Here is a quote from James Madison—the Virginia-born father of the U.S. Constitution and a leading federalist—from the *Federalist* No. 46, titled "The Influence of the State and Federal Governments Compared," which was published as a public-relations piece supporting the Constitution's ratification:

> Besides the advantage of being armed, which the Americans possess over the people of almost every other nation, the existence of subordinate governments, to which the people are

attached, and by which the militia officers are appointed, forms a barrier against the enterprises of ambition, more insurmountable than any which a simple government of any form can admit of. Notwithstanding the military establishments in the several kingdoms of Europe, which are carried as far as the public resources will bear, the governments are afraid to trust the people with arms. And it is not certain, that with this aid alone they would not be able to shake off their yokes. But were the people to possess the additional advantages of local governments chosen by themselves, who could collect the national will and direct the national force, and of officers appointed out of the militia, by these governments, and attached both to them and to the militia, it may be affirmed with the greatest assurance, that the throne of every tyranny in Europe would be speedily overturned in spite of the legions which surround it. Let us not insult the free and gallant citizens of America with the suspicion, that they would be less able to defend the rights of which they would be in actual possession, than the debased subjects of arbitrary power would be to rescue theirs from the hands of their oppressors. Let us rather no longer insult them with the supposition that they can ever reduce themselves to the necessity of making the experiment, by a blind and tame submission to the long train of insidious measures which must precede and produce it.[1]

By Madison's logic the federal government, under the watchful eye of an armed citizenry, is a necessary evil. This logic was most persuasive at the time, and thus boosted the Constitution's chances of being ratified. The militia's track record of fighting the regular British army, securing victory, and achieving independence remained a vivid memory. Furthermore, Madison's text is dated October 29, 1788. A year later the French Revolution occurred as he predicted, and the system of monarchical rule collapsed in France.

Moreover, Madison and his contemporaries promised to weave this thesis into the Constitution's Bill of Rights early in order to placate the concerns raised by the anti-Federalist groups who had for some time been making an issue of the lack of a rights provision and, therefore, opposed ratification. In this way, the Second Amendment was born with the opening statement, "A well regulated Militia, being necessary to the security of a free State . . ."

The United States is now divided into two camps over the Second Amendment, a gun control faction that claims the issue to one of state rights and an anti-gun-control faction claiming the issue to be one of individual rights. It can be said that America's runaway gun possession is the price paid for the fear of tyranny some 210 years ago. The greatest sponsor of the individual rights theory, the NRA, makes a point of glorifying George Washington and other Founding Fathers in every respect, but especially in their roles as soldiers, hunters, and frontiersmen, which is to say, gun owners. I think it is important to understand this connection.

In large part this arming of the citizenry—this defense of democracy by militia—was the manifestation of distrust of a standing army as a tool of tyranny. The militia system itself, which was inherited from England, hails historically from opposition to the Crown's standing army during the Glorious Revolution. On top of this, there is the fact that the first shots of the War of Independence came from colonists resisting the burden of quartering the king's army. In this way, objections to a standing army became well entrenched at the time of the country's founding.

The DNA of Washington's Democracy

At the outset of the War of Independence, each colony's militia responded with guerrilla tactics against its British opponents. However, in June 1775 the Continental Congress, which was formed to resist British oppression, decided to organize a Continental Army, starting with the New England and New York militias, as the means by which all thirteen colonies could fight as a whole. George Washington was selected as commander in chief. He had entered military service during the French and Indian War as a twenty-two-year-old major and was taken prisoner in that war. Nevertheless, he was highly regarded by British army officials. This was his first appearance on the stage of history.

Washington concluded that a simple band of armed farmers and citizens would not succeed. He proposed to the Continental Congress, and received approval for, the formation of a full-scale army whose members, in contrast to the militia organizations of each colony, all wore the same uniform and served for a fixed period. Such an army could move freely about the continent to fight the British Army. One condition for approval was that the force be under the direct control of the Continental Congress and exist only for a limited time.

The army consisted of volunteers and draftees from each colony. It also included presently serving militiamen as well as foreign officers from France and Germany, what Washington himself referred to as "rabble."

The foreign officers were drawn from two groups, those who supported U.S. independence as a matter of principle and those driven by ambition and profit. Among the former was the Marquis de Lafayette, a twenty-year-old French aristocrat whose statue to this day stands in a park in front of the White House. Lafayette participated in numerous military exploits and was a lifelong friend of and advisor to Washington, Jefferson, and the other Founding Fathers.

In fact, the Continental Army was established two years before the Declaration of Independence of 1776, and it can be said that, in addition to being the first de facto federally centralized organization, the fact that its composition included international volunteers gave it a character that helped the new nation win support across the globe.[2]

Opposing this force, the British Army of George III recruited close to thirty thousand German mercenaries from related royal family domains in Hanover. These soldiers were known for their bravery and cruelty in battle, but the colonies repelled them strongly, further paving the way to independence. The Declaration of Independence even lists the use of foreign mercenaries as one of its grievances. Thus, both Germany and France were deeply involved in the American War for Independence.

At the time the colonies were not necessarily unified in their support for independence. The number of colonists who supported the Crown was quite substantial. These supporters reportedly made up close to one-third of the entire colonial population of 3.22 million.

In any event, the six and a half years from the clashes in the towns of Lexington and Concord near Boston in April 1775 to the British army's surrender at Yorktown, Virginia, in October 1781, were dramatic. Toward the end, the French fleet, which had joined forces with the Continental Army in 1778, played a key role in the final victory. In addition, new, improved rifles with significantly higher accuracy began to be used in the Continental Army, outnumbering the increasingly obsolete British muskets by more than three to one. In this way, armed revolution and the establishment of a new, independent nation progressed simultaneously.

What I want to emphasize here, however, is the fact that the Continental Army imposed strict controls upon itself as a necessary evil required to fight the regular British army, evidence going clear evidence of the principle of rejection of standing armies.

In June 1776, one year after Washington was appointed commander in chief, the same type of committee that had previously existed at the Plymouth Plantation was established to oversee the army. John Adams, who would succeed Washington as president and a leading figure in the revolution, was one member of the Board of War and Ordnance that controlled the general administration of the Continental Army's personnel, organization, supply, and other matters. The tradition of civilian control, which the Pilgrim Fathers had established at Plymouth Plantation 150 years earlier, was securely entrenched.

General Washington faithfully endorsed civilian control at all times. Washington's staunch republican philosophy contributed to the birth of American democracy, compensating for various strategic errors as commander and a lack of charisma as a leader. I believe that he was the person who, more than any other, embodied the DNA of American style democracy.

An episode in 1782 illustrates his republican philosophy. A Continental Army officer wrote a letter suggesting that Washington should be king. Surprised, Washington replied, "I must view (such ideas) with abhorrence and reprehend with severity."[3]

Specifically, he always treated the Board of War and Ordnance and its parent Continental Congress as the authority that his own Continental Army served. Accordingly, toward the end of the War of Independence, he perpetuated the continuing existence of the militias that had been substantially absorbed into the Continental Army. In June 1783 he sent the previously mentioned circular dissolving the Continental Army. In other words, he faithfully accepted the principle of civilian control and reaffirmed the tenet, inherent in the first documents adopted by the new nation, that the central government would be monitored by a militia of armed citizens.

The Withering Militia

This tradition of civilian control has been maintained to this day, and must be understood as a central factor in the establishment of the armed forces of the United States today as the strongest military force in history. Although there had been a movement among the Continental Army officers resembling a non-confidence motion against Washington during the Revolutionary War, that sentiment died out. There has been no really serious attempt at a coup d'etat in the history of the U.S. military.

It is because of this tradition of civilian control that the preemptive nuclear strike against the Soviet Union recommended by General LeMay was averted. During the Vietnam War and even in the present-day Iraq War, it was the administrators of civilian control who pushed the skeptical uniformed officers to the use of force. This, I believe, is worth noting once more.

Still, civilian control, which was born from a militia perspective, has as a result cleared the path toward the militia's disappearance. It began with Washington, who cared deeply for the militia structure and valued the practice of civilian control.

In the circular regarding the dissolution of the Continental Army, which compared the United States to "actors on a most conspicuous theatre," Washington explained the necessity for the militia system and described it as follows:

> The Militia of this Country must be considered as the Palladium
> of our security, and the first effectual resort in case of hostility;
> It is essential therefore, that the same system should pervade the
> whole; that the formation and discipline of the Militia of the
> Continent should be absolutely uniform, and that the same spe-
> cies of Arms, Accoutrements and Military Apparatus, should be
> introduced in every part of the United States.

The phrase "and for governing such Part of them [the Militia] as may be employed in the Service of the United States," which accepts the authority of Congress to regulate the militia, was inserted into the U.S. Constitution (art. 1, sec. 8, clause 16) in response to a compromise between those led by George Mason who opposed the formation of a standing army and those led by Alexander Hamilton who saw a need for one. This phrase, "as may be employed in the Service of the United States," essentially created the nation's armed forces.

Just as the minutemen, which were organized for self-defense in the Massachusetts Bay Colony as early as 1636, ultimately became leading players in the War of Independence, militias throughout the colonies were absorbed and evolved into the present-day armed forces of the United States.

After Washington was inaugurated as the first president, one of his first acts, in conjunction with Secretary of War Henry Knox, was to propose a bill imposing obligatory military service. He had in mind the first volunteer corps of "rabble" he commanded during the War of Independence. Nevertheless, Congress rejected the proposed legislation, demonstrating the unease surrounding the militia's transformation into a standing army.

In 1792 Congress finally passed the Militia Act that allowed the president to call up and command the militias of the states. The law further required all white males between the ages of eighteen and forty-five in all states to register for military service and to supply themselves with muskets, bayonets, belts, and ammunition.

President Washington and Secretary Knox asked for a budget of $400,000 to standardize the militia's equipment. However, Congress twice rejected the request, which resulted in the birth of a weak militia with used equipment. It is interesting to compare these developments to how Napoleon during the same period built a powerful army by means of a draft. The saving of $400,000 was the newly established federal government's first order of business.

However, almost at the same time, a five-thousand-man Legion of the United States was organized for the purpose of fighting the Native Americans. Separate from the weak army with self-supplied equipment, this army directly served the federal government. This was the first appearance in U.S. history of a regular army of professional soldiers.

The Legion was commanded by General Anthony Wayne, a veteran of the War of Independence. After the war, Wayne attempted to negotiate with the native tribes. When these peace talks failed, the government faced fierce resistance from Native Americans who had allied themselves with the British in Canada and the Spanish in Florida. It was therefore judged that the creation of a standing army was indispensable after all for the expulsion of the Native Americans—an irony surrounding the birth of the armed forces in the United States. In 1802 the United States Military Academy at West Point was opened for the education of professional officers.

In the beginning there were few members in this standing army. The total military strength maintained throughout the nineteenth century topped out at a maximum of thirty- to forty thousand.

Even during the War of 1812, the U.S. military consisted of 10,000 soldiers while the militia made up about 490,000. During the Mexican-American War, the U.S. military numbered 40,000 and the militia about 73,000, indicating that the leading role was still being played by the militia.

Although President Madison proposed legislation for the conscription of soldiers during the War of 1812, Congress once again rejected it. The first such legislation was enacted for the Union Army during the Civil War.

As of 2003 the total number of army, navy, air force, and marine personnel in the U.S. armed forces numbered 1,410,000 people (including 196,100 women) in the regular active-duty forces, 1,259,300 in the Army Reserves, and 464,300 in the National Guard. This huge military force is now maintained on a 100-percent volunteer basis.

What Would George Washington Think?

The draft was implemented in earnest during World War I (September 1917 to November 1918) and World War II (November 1940 to October 1946). The Selective Service Act was passed 1947 with the advent of the Cold War, and it continued through the Korean and Vietnam Wars. Immediately after the U.S. withdrawal from Vietnam in July 1973, the draft was eliminated.

The obligation for eighteen-year olds to register for the draft, a basic foundation of this law, was also abolished in 1975. Later, however, in response to the former Soviet Union's invasion of Afghanistan, the requirement to register was revived and remains in effect to this day. Even so, there are only minor penalties for failing to register.[4]

The concentration of the militia under civilian control begun by Washington was completed with the Union Army victory in the Civil War. With the coming of the twentieth century, this "Army of Democracy" advanced into the Asia-Pacific. Notable landmarks on this trail were the possession of the Philippines and acquisition of Hawaii in the wake of the Spanish-American War, as well as troop deployments during the Boxer Rebellion and Siberian Intervention.

Europe and, indeed, the world became a stage for the U.S. military in World War I. By the end of World War II, the United States possessed the greatest military force in the world, putting into actual use its nuclear capacity to conclude the war decisively at Hiroshima and Nagasaki. Over the decades, the American military achieved victory after victory.

While the United States was defeated in Vietnam just over twenty years after the Korean War ended in a truce, in more recent years the latest high-tech weapons—developed during a period of monopolistic nuclear predominance following American victory in the Cold War—have led to the overthrow of Saddam Hussein in what was termed a regime change. Now, however, through nation-building, counterterrorism, and anti-guerilla warfare in Iraq, the country is having its legs pulled out from under it. I would very much like to ask George Washington his opinion of the military path that the United States has followed.

The Militia Act of 1792 was superseded by the Militia Act of 1903, which separated organized militia forces from reserve forces. Incidentally, when the Marquis de Lafayette once again visited the United States in 1824, he coined the name "national guard" for the militia after the name of the revolutionary army under his command during the French Revolution. The New York militia adopted this name, which later spread nationwide.

In 1908 U.S. reserve forces were inaugurated focusing on military doctors. In 1916, just prior to entering World War I, the federal government enacted the National Defense Act, authorizing payment for training and standardization of equipment for the National Guard. Two revisions of this act, in 1922 and 1933, formally established the name "National Guard" and coupled the service with the regular armed forces.

Forty percent of the U.S. forces deployed during World War I were militia, and since that time, the proportion of National Guardsmen in World War II, the Korean War, and other large-scale conflicts has been very high. The National Guard has been mobilized for the current Iraq War, as well.

Today, the army and Air Force National Guards (the navy has no national guard) are part of a combined total force that has employed active duty, reserve, and National Guard forces since 1970. During the Vietnam War, because of the domestic political situation he faced, President Johnson avoided mobilization of the National Guard. Instead the military had to rely on the active-duty draft, which spurred the rise of the domestic antiwar movement. The National Guard must answer to the chiefs of staff of both the army and the air force and, at the same time, can be mobilized by state governors for use in disaster mobilization and drug control. This is one example of the continuation of the tradition of state rights.

The National Guard constitutes the main force supporting the Ready Reserve and Selective Reserve. A National Guard Bureau exists within the Department of Defense. The Army National Guard comprises 54 percent of the army's total military strength, and the Air National Guard provides 33 percent of the total air combat power. Six percent of the total National Guard is stationed at bases and barracks for their exclusive use, and they account for 10 percent of the national defense budget.

Forty Percent Minorities and Women

At this point, I must relate another irony involving the U.S. military.

It is a fact that the world's most powerful military, the military of the sole superpower, requires racial integration to maintain its forces, and as a result has contributed to the integration of U.S. society. It is ironic that this is a way the country has begun to overcome its negative inheritance of exclusion of Indians and discrimination against blacks.

America's sole victory has many aspects: overwhelming military strength; economic power and a consumer culture that sweeps over the world by means of a market economy faithful to Adam Smith; and its undeniable track record of democracy; indeed, many other examples could be cited.

Nevertheless, it seems to me that the multiple races and multiracial power reflected in the U.S. military are of great importance to the United States. If nothing else, the devotion of effort to that achievement, of a kind not possible in Japan, is the greatest asset for the nation's future.

Of course, the negative legacy has not disappeared. Neither the black ghettoes nor the Indian reservations have gone away. The reality is that the black unemployment rate is still twice that of whites, a fact that has not changed in the forty years that have passed since the late Reverend King's "I Have a Dream" speech of August 28, 1963.

Still, one mustn't mock the multiracial power that has absorbed minorities to such an extent. As a journalist who has followed events in the United States for more than forty years, I feel this most from my own experiences.

At the very least, the Armed Forces of the United States underscore this multiracial power. Let us begin by examining this fact.

I believe that the televised Iraq War, which transmitted the images of combat in real time, was also a showroom for this multiracial power by featuring such African American figures as Secretary of State Colin Powell, who had filled the post of chairman of the joint chiefs of staff during the Persian Gulf War; National Security Advisor Condoleezza Rice; and Brigadier General Vincent Brooks, who took charge of the daily press briefings at the U.S. Central Command Headquarters in Qatar. General Brooks, who calmly fielded the interviews, was reportedly at the top of his West Point class of 1980. A second-generation black general, he also studied at Harvard University's Kennedy School of Government.

On April 9, 2003, the soldier who draped the statue of Saddam Hussein with the Stars and Stripes the instant it was toppled in Baghdad was Marine Corps Corporal Edward Chin, an American citizen of Burmese descent. He became a hero.

Corporal Chin, the son of Stanley Chin, who emigrated from Burma (or, to use its present official name, Myanmar) in 1980, was born one week after his parents' arrival in the United States. He thus automatically became a U.S. citizen. Chin grew up in New York's Chinatown. His mother, Mrs. Chin, told CNN, "We like our children have a good life, good schools. We want American freedom. Now Edward bring American freedom."

Chin returned to the United States in late May, was promoted to Sergeant in June, and on July 10, threw the opening pitch at a Mets game at their home field of Shea Stadium in New York. Sergeant Chin, wearing a Mets jersey embroidered with the number 67 (representing June 7, his wedding anniversary), received a loud ovation from the spectators. Indifferent to being treated as a hero, he remarked, "I was just doing what I was told from down below. Throughout the whole war, that's how we all stayed alive, by taking orders and giving orders. . . . What I was thinking was this is a pretty big statue."

Sergeant Chin, who was soldier in the mechanized infantry, left the Marines that August to attend New York City College of Technology. The next day, every newspaper in New York printed the story along with Chin's photograph.

Immediately after the outbreak of the war, there was a female American soldier who became a prisoner of war of the Iraqi, twenty-year-old Army Private First Class Jessica Lynch. An attractive blonde, PFC Lynch's rescue by Special Forces from an occupied hospital was made into a hero's tale. I believe that, putting aside the Pentagon's manipulation of the media, the fact that a woman was taken captive in the Iraq war says something about American military power, which uses the strengths of both sexes. Captured along with PFC Lynch was a black soldier, a single mother. Among those killed in the action were a Native American mother and another single mother who had lost both her legs.

According to a report released by the Department of Defense in February 2002, women made up 18.8 percent of the entire U.S. military in fiscal year 2000. By service, they made up 20.9 percent of the army, 18.4 percent of the navy, 7.1 percent of the marines, and 25.9 percent of the air force. This same report announced that altogether, women, blacks, Hispanics, and other minorities made up 40 percent of the military.[5]

Frank Self-Criticism

One document particularly dramatizes the reality of the U.S. military's need for minorities. An amicus curiae (friend of the court) brief dated February 19, 2003, filed with the U.S. Supreme Court in support of a ruling by the Sixth Circuit Court of Appeals, argues:

> The services have programs that consider race both in selecting participants who broaden the pool of qualified individuals for the service academies and the ROTC and in admission to the service academies and ROTC scholarship programs. Currently, no alternative means to field a fully qualified, diverse officer corps exists. This limited use of race in furtherance of the compelling governmental interest it serves is, accordingly, constitutional.

The fourteen "friends" who submitted this joint brief included former NATO Commander and 2004 Democratic Party presidential candidate Wesley Clark, former Chairman of the Joint Chiefs of Staff William Crowe, and former Clinton administration Secretary of Defense William Cohen. This makes clear that the conclusion was the consensus of not only the court justices but of the entire military as well.

The brief concludes that complete racial integration is a military necessity—that is, "as a prerequisite to a cohesive, and therefore effective, fighting force." It frankly explains that the executive order prohibiting racial discrimination within the U.S. Armed Forces, issued by President Truman on July 26, 1948, was not adequately executed.

According to the brief, the army resisted racial integration until the Korean War, when, in the face of severe casualties, it had no choice but to assign black soldiers to undermanned white units. Even so, racial integration continued to lag at officer levels in the 1960s and '70s. Black soldiers lacked confidence in their white commanders, and several race riots broke out on marine bases and on aircraft carriers, including the USS *Constellation* and the USS *Kitty Hawk*. During the Vietnam War, some units found their combat capability weakened as a result of racial tensions.

The following figures were reported as of February 2003 and indicate the progress made during the intervening years:

- The active duty U.S. military was composed of 61.7 percent whites, 21.7 percent blacks, 9.6 percent Hispanics, 4 percent Asian-Pacific Islanders, 1.2 percent Native Americans, and 1.8 percent other.

- Among active duty officers, 81 percent were white and 8.8 percent black. Hispanics made up 4 percent, Asian-Pacific Islanders 3.2 percent, and Native Americans 0.6 percent.

- Black officers made up 1.6 percent of the officer corps in 1962, 2.8 percent in 1973, and 8.8 percent in March 2002. The percentage increase in the numbers of Hispanic, Asian-Pacific Islander, and Native American officers exceeded that of blacks, and minority officers represented 19 percent of the total.

- Thirty-eight blacks entered the U.S. Military Academy at West Point in 1968. This number rose to one hundred in 1971, and in 1993 minorities made up 16.5 percent of cadets. This number was expected to increase to 25 percent by the class of 2005. Of that number, 100, or 8 percent, were expected to be black, and 70, or 6 percent, were expected to be Hispanic. As of February 2003, 300 blacks and 150 Hispanics were enrolled.

- At the U.S. Naval Academy, 6 percent of the cadets were black and 3 percent Hispanic, with a policy in place of annually increasing the number of blacks by 7 percent and Hispanics by 4 percent. At the U.S. Air Force Academy, 18 percent of the cadets in the year 2000 were minorities.

- In any event, while the number of black personnel equaled 12.7 percent of rank and file, the number of black officers was only 8.8 percent. The fact that this has been frankly recognized as requiring improvement, and has been the subject of law suits strongly appealing for racial integration within the military, is impressive.

In a letter to Hamilton dated September 1, 1796, then former President Washington wrote:

The youth, or young men from different parts of the United States would be assembled together, and would by degrees discover that there was not that cause for those jealousies and prejudices which one part of the Union had imbibed against another part: of course, sentiments of more liberality in the general policy of the Country would result from it. What, but the mixing of people from different parts of the United States during the War rubbed off these impressions? A century in the ordinary intercourse, would not have accomplished what the Seven years association in Arms did.

At the risk of going out on a limb, it can be said that this comment, quoted in the amicus brief, develops the serious logic that diversity is critical to national security. In other words, the brief follows Washington's example when it supports the idea that racial integration must be built with officers "eating out of the same pot," a metaphor Washington used.

The fact that Washington had not included blacks and Indians as "people from different parts" has already been examined in chapter 6. I think the greatest irony is that Washington's letter was later used to justify the adoption of affirmative action for blacks and other minorities. And that is another question I would have for George Washington.

The amicus brief goes so far as to state that:

The crisis that mandated aggressive integration of the officer corps in the service academies and in ROTC programs is a microcosm of what exists in our society at large, albeit with potentially more severe consequences to our nation's welfare.

Affirmative Action: The Supreme Imperative

In January 2003 the Bush administration argued that the affirmative action program at the University of Michigan and its graduate school was "an unjust system based solely on race" and, therefore, unconstitutional. Those reportedly most shocked were the military authorities.

Democratic Senator Edward Kennedy issued a statement defending the military authorities and criticizing the Bush administration, saying:

> It is remarkable that this administration hasn't questioned the affirmative action programs for our military academies. Clearly, diversity in our military is a national priority.

This caused a White House spokesman to go on the defensive, explaining that the University of Michigan, which had set aside specific numbers of places for minorities, was not West Point. But the administration said it had no intent of making an issue out of the admissions policies at the military academies, its position being that methods of ensuring diversity solely on the basis of race were generally wrong.

The spokesman recognized the fact that West Point policy specified a target of 10 to 12 percent black cadets in its student body.

According to *Safire's New Political Dictionary*, written by sharp-tongued commentator William Safire,[6] the term affirmative action was first used in American politics in 1955 during the Eisenhower administration. The term turned up again in an official document in March 1961 in an executive order signed by President Kennedy six weeks after his inauguration that mandated firms contracting with the government to employ minorities.

Affirmative action policies were extended to university admissions after the Civil Rights Act of 1964 during the Johnson years. Although criticized by conservatives as "reverse discrimination," it supported improvements in the status of blacks and other minorities.

Some believe the Bush administration's position was aimed at winning conservatives' votes in the 2004 election. Nevertheless, since the terrorist attacks of 9/11, President Bush has been treading a dangerous path by undermining respect for the military's diversification efforts.

In the two University of Michigan cases the Supreme Court's decision was split. The court ruled that the admissions policy giving preferential treatment to minorities at the University of Michigan Law School was constitutional, but further stated that the policy of granting twenty admission points to minority undergraduate applicants was unconstitutional.

President Bush issued a statement supporting this ruling, saying, "My administration will continue to promote policies that expand educational opportunities for Americans from all racial, ethnic, and economic backgrounds. . . . I look forward to the day when America will truly be a color-blind society." The Republican Party commented that the brakes had been put on extremism, while Democrats claimed a victory for the American people, avoiding a division of public opinion and the breakdown of affirmative action.

I admire the political savvy, sense of balance, and spirit of compromise within the Supreme Court of the United States. I firmly believe that the coexistence of idealism and realism is a critical aspect of American DNA concentrated in the Supreme Court as part of the separation of powers.

This shows anew the importance of racial integration within the military, by way of further overcoming discrimination of a kind that has burdened the United States since the nation's founding. The frank opinions noted in the February amicus brief in the Supreme Court case support this:

> . . . (the) integration of the military, resulted not only from a principled recognition that segregation is unjust and incompatible with American values, but also from a practical recognition that the military's need for manpower and its efficient, effective deployment required integration.

Affirmative action and an increase in the number of minorities are, along with improvements in salaries and working conditions, indispensable to the functional maintenance of the U.S. Armed Forces.

With an all-volunteer force conducting the current Iraq War and force rotation posing a major problem, a multiracial armed forces is clearly essential.

With a draft in effect the number of U.S. troops at the peak of the Vietnam War in 1967 was 3,546,100, more than twice the current number. Thanks to the draft, Johnson could place a force exceeding five hundred thousand in Vietnam. However, the draft intensified the antiwar movement and, as previously mentioned, led to Johnson's downfall.

How long can the Bush administration fight "Rumsfeld's War" with a volunteer force? This is the test hidden in the U.S. efforts at nation-building in Iraq. This is a constant contradiction inherent in maintaining a standing army.

An Encounter with Mr. Edmond

This multiracial power impresses me because I can see how the United States has changed since I was first assigned to New York as a foreign correspondent in 1964. African American issues in particular stir me deeply, having seen racial integration progress so far from my own initial experiences in covering them.

The February 1965 assassination of Malcolm X, which happened three months after my arrival, the August 1965 riots in the Watts district of Los Angeles, the Martin Luther King, Jr. assassination of April 1968, and the subsequent riots in Washington—these and other black-white confrontations of the late 1960s were so intense they seem unbelievable now.

In 1967, at the peak of the black extremist confrontations with whites, I interviewed Black Power movement leader Stokely Carmichael. When I entered his room, he approached me, grabbed my necktie, and said, "The Japanese are people of color. Why do you wear the white man's clothes?"

I responded, "If that's how I look to you, then maybe that's what I am," after which I immediately took off my tie. Then we were able to talk cordially. To me, who had been subject to subtle discrimination in my negotiations with apartment landlords in New York, much like the "honorary white" Japanese in South Africa under apartheid, these words felt like a kick in the groin, and I remember this as though it happened only yesterday.

At this point, I must write about Mr. Lez Edmond, a black friend who cooperated in setting up the interview with Carmichael. In spring 1965, after the Malcolm X assassination, Mr. Edmond was introduced to me at the United Nations Press Club by the New York correspondent for Indonesia's ANTARA news agency. At the time, President Sukarno had declared Indonesia's withdrawal from the United Nations, and the nonaligned movement represented by Ghana, Guinea, and other African and Asian nations was at its peak.

Mr. Edmond was an intellectual and a friend of Malcolm X, and a picture of him with that leader appears in the latter's autobiography. He had contributed a report on the Harlem riots to *Ramparts* magazine, a journal founded as a left-wing Catholic magazine in the 1960s. He carried a U.N. press identification card from Howard News Service, managed by Peter Howard, a black man who actively distributed Africa-related news at the U.N. Press Club. We were the same age and got along well, and he taught me various things about black society in those days. He also took me to places where I would not have been able to go alone.

At that time, we frequented Micheaux's bookstore near the corner of 125th Street and Lenox Avenue in the middle of Harlem and The Truth coffee shop, a gathering place for the black intelligentsia on a corner in the so-called Black Village area. Micheaux's store was swamped with books about Che Guevara and the Third World.

I once asked Mr. Edmond to guide me to The Truth coffee shop with a famed author who was visiting from Japan, the late Ms. Sawako Ariyoshi, along with Mr. Yasushi Akashi, then a rising young staff member in the U.N. Secretariat and who later became Deputy Secretary General of the U.N. One of Ms. Ariyoshi's masterpieces is the novel *Hishoku* (Colorless) that tells the story of a Japanese woman who marries a black soldier in Tokyo during the U.S. occupation and who moves to the U.S. to live in East Harlem. While we were walking along 125th Street after having some nice coffee at The Truth, she confessed that "I only passed through Harlem once by bus." Nevertheless, I recall having admired her vivid description of Harlem in *Hishoku*.

I still have an old booklet titled "African History," which Mr. Edmond gave to me. This illustrated booklet asserts that Africa gave birth to much of the world's culture. It also explains how Egypt, Ghana, and the other empires of ancient Africa gave rise to chemistry, medicine, shoemaking, alcoholic beverages, the university system, libraries, construction, textiles, stenography, numbers, dentistry, and iron and paper manufacturing.

In short, this work is a public relations piece of the kind that spawned the Black Power movement in the late 1960s. Its message was that blacks should not hold inferiority complexes as the descendents of slaves, but rather that they should be proud.

The black nationalist movement espoused by Malcolm X and the Black Power movement were launched with this theme of "taking pride as Africans." Socially, these movements also influenced the fashion world of that period with the Afro look. Politically, however, as extreme elements like the Black Panthers were racing toward armed struggle, the nonviolence movement of the late Dr. King prevailed. The Black Power movement lost steam.

In 1969 Mr. Carmichael immigrated to Guinea with the assistance of his friend, President Sékou Touré. After changing his name to Kwame Touré, he published works on pan-Africanism and continued to lecture in the United States until his death from cancer in 1998. As I look at the booklet "African History," I replay in my mind the passion of those times.

After my family and I moved to Washington, Mr. Edmond visited us at our home and enjoyed my wife's Japanese cooking. However, I remember that my apartment superintendent in Arlington subtly complained the next day about his visit. After I responded, "He's an African diplomat," they reluctantly withdrew their complaint. In March 1969 when my first assignment to the United States was finished, he made a special trip from New York to help me sell my car to a young black man, and came to see me off at Dulles Airport.

Mr. Edmond later earned his doctoral degree, and he is presently the Director of Multicultural and Ethnic Studies at Saint John's University, a Catholic university located in Jamaica, New York. Founded in 1870, the school is renowned for its basketball team. When I saw him again in November 2003, he was quite well and planning to publish in book form a handwritten 1835 document by an Underground Railroad organization that protected runaway slaves. In response to my view about multiracial power, he answered, "That is true for upper-class blacks, but for lower-class blacks, nothing has changed since the 1960s."

The Afterglow of the Black Power Movement

Following the assassination of Reverend King on April 6, 1968, rage burst out in Washington. Black riots raged for several blocks near the White House and the National Guard fired tear gas into the crowd. While observing the start of the pillaging right before my eyes, I lost my eyesight for a considerable period of time. I have already described the comparative lightness of the tear gas I encountered one month later, during the May Revolution in Paris in 1968, when I journeyed there to cover the peace talks that had at last begun between the United States and North Vietnam.

At the Mexico City Olympics of 1968, Tommy Smith and John Carlos, two black athletes who won the gold and bronze medals in the 200-meter dash, raised their black-gloved fists in a sign of revolt during the playing of the national anthem and the raising of the U.S. flag. Black American athletes also frequently displayed gestures and signs of black protest on the winners' stand. Long-jump gold medalist Bob Beamon and bronze medalist Ralph Boston wore black socks, and the U.S. championship 1,600-meter relay team wore black berets. Smith and Carlos were banned from the Olympic Village.[7]

Thirty-six years later, the victory lap of black athletes waving the Stars and Stripes has become a regular feature of the Olympic Games, perhaps more noticeably after Carl Lewis's stunning performance in the 1984 Los Angeles Olympics, which has become a symbol of acceptance of the American flag by black Americans.

Ever since Jackie Robinson first tore down the wall of discrimination in Major League Baseball in 1947, African American participation in such sports as basketball, football, and track and field has grown steadily, and Arthur Ashe's pioneering achievements in the 1960s must be acknowledged. Finally, considering Tiger Woods in golf and the Williams sisters in tennis, the past walls of discrimination in sports are now nowhere to be found.

In 2000, Venus Williams won Wimbledon, the U.S. Open, and the Sydney Olympics. Together with her younger sister, Serena, they reigned for several years as the princesses of U.S. women's tennis. Their father, who is also their coach and manager, dreamed of raising a female pro champion from among his five daughters, and from the time Venus was four years old, he put her through a Spartan training regimen, forcefully hitting used tennis balls against a wall in the Los Angeles black district. Never once hiring a white coach, he raised her to where she is today by the strength of her family alone. Of the three other half-sisters, one is aspiring to become a lawyer and one a physician. Sadly, the eldest of the Williams sisters, Yetunde, a registered nurse, was shot to death in 2003 at the beauty salon she owned.

Seeing the temper and purposeful tenacity of the father who raised these five daughters and put both sisters on the road to championship, I can perceive the afterglow of the Black Power movement that once radiated through Mr. Edmond. This may also be said to be a form of great pride on the part of blacks.

Then there is the famous Tiger Woods. Preceding the Williams sisters by three years, Woods bounded to the summit of the U.S. professional golf world by winning the Masters Tournament in 1997. He still maintains the top position, and I can sense black pride in him just as I do with the Williams sisters. It is well known that his brilliant game is the result of the special golf training for gifted children that his father started immediately after Tiger's birth. It is not, however, a mere question of golf. It is evident to me that Woods' accomplishments since first winning the Masters, his calm, confidence-filled movements in the limelight, are unlike those of any other black hero before him. I think it may be safe to call his demeanor the appearance of the honor student of the era of multiracial power.

Woods has earned a great deal of respect, not only for his search for inner truth and his devotion to his Native-American/black father and Chinese-Thai mother, but also for investing huge amounts of money in golf lessons for blacks in the ghetto. At the time of his Masters victory, a comment appeared in a column of the *New York Times* explaining that Americans recognized in the wonderful relationship between Woods and his father the importance of a father's inspiration and influence.

Incidentally, the word "Negro" has not been used for many years in either official remarks or documents by the president, other government officials, or media reports. Blacks are now commonly referred to as "African Americans." This is evidence that the concept of the melting pot is being discarded in favor of a salad bowl multiracial society in which people take pride in their ethnic roots yet live together. Accordingly, Tiger Woods is commonly referred to as an African Asian American.

In September 2002 I returned to Harlem after an absence of ten years. During my visit the popular musical "Harlem Song," a work based on Negro spirituals, a musical genre performed since the days before World War II, was being staged at the Apollo Theater, home to many of the world's renowned black musicians. A full house of white spectators packed the theater.

Harlem Song is an unbiased history of the rise of Harlem. The plot deals with the glory days that gave birth to many musicians and the dream of their rejuvenation. The production I saw made effective use of dynamic gospel music in conjunction with slide shows and exceptional dancing. The audience, which transcended racial boundaries, reacted with a long and frenzied standing ovation.

I first visited with Mr. Edmond two years after Harlem had fallen into ruin as a result of the riots of 1963. A place known as the "Republic of Harlem" before World War II, in 1963 it had the atmosphere of a black liberation zone. When I revisited the area about ten years ago, the flow of middle-class blacks out of Harlem had been accelerated by repeated riots, and I was astonished by the severely rough character of the neighborhood. At that time, not even the *New York Times* paid any heed to the now-extolled Apollo Theater.

As I stood on the "Ginza" of Harlem near the corner of 125th Street and Lenox Avenue, I looked for Micheaux's Bookstore, but it was no longer there. The ruined buildings were conspicuous and far from rehabilitation.

The crowds had returned, however, and there was life in the shopping district. There were also signs for Martin Luther King, Jr. Street and Malcolm X Street, the latter unique to Harlem, where the red, black, and green Africa Flags (as they are known in Harlem) flew alongside the Stars and Stripes. New black immigrants from various African countries stood out from the crowd. For me, who had followed the Black Power movement that openly declared its hate for whites in the 1960s, it was a deeply emotional change. Former President Clinton was establishing an office in one corner of this new, revitalized Harlem.

Considering Matsui and Ichiro

From my visit to Harlem I moved on to Washington, D.C. where the annual meeting of the International Monetary Fund and World Bank was being held. Tight security was deployed throughout the city, and the air was filled with the shrill sirens of patrol cars that were accompanying the movements of the delegations. There, I recalled again covering the intense black riots immediately following the assassination of Dr. King in April 1968, and I was deeply moved.

I was impressed that most of the Washington police, riot squad, and National Park Police commanders that deployed the elaborate security equipment were black. In 1968, there were no black members among the police and National Guard that fired tear gas into the crowds. Most of the police officials that appear and comment now on television news broadcasts when atrocious crimes occur are black. Moreover, one-fourth of all National Guardsmen today are black.

In Los Angeles, my last stop on this trip, the Mexican taco stands that had conspicuously dotted the landscape seven years earlier were hardly noticeable. When I asked the Japanese living in Los Angeles about this, they said that the standard of living of the Hispanic residents had risen, and tacos had now become just another item on restaurant menus. At the same time, the major franchise chain of Americanized taco restaurants known as Taco Bell had spread across the United States.

California maki and other American sushi that differs from original

Japanese-style sushi have also proliferated. On public telephones, English explanations are automatically followed by Spanish, and the voices that for a time had called for the establishment of Spanish as a second language have all but vanished.

Beginning with the new blacks from Africa, the energy and competition of the immigrants who still assemble here from all over the world are a hidden power behind the barely increasing labor costs of the U.S. economy. The Internet revolution, which has made faceless business possible, has become the ultimate platter for serving up multiracial power.

Ichiro Suzuki, Hideki Matsui, and other Japanese baseball players have succeeded in the Major Leagues and been absorbed into America's multiracial power. As Japanese, we mustn't forget that there are two sides from which we can view their achievements in America. Are they something we should be happy about or something to lament?

Not all of America's race problems have been solved, of course. A backlash against affirmative action for blacks and other minorities has quietly emerged over the past half-century.

Still, President Bush, who garnered just under 10 percent of the black vote during the 2000 election, gained the support of over 60 percent of blacks at the beginning of the Iraq War. The so-called neoconservative groups also point to the success of multiracial integration as one of the characteristics of the United States as the "Empire of Liberty." At the very least, I believe it is important to recognize the role of multiracial power in supporting the United States as the contemporary sole superpower, ironic though it may be.

I have written only of blacks. To encompass the entirety of multiracial power, I would have to rewrite this manuscript. In the end, however, I think the existence of the Jewish community should also be regarded over the long term as a part of this multiracial power.

Although a minority of 6.2 million Jews accounted for only 2 percent of the total U.S. population as of 2003, they have excelled in such achievements as nuclear bomb development, motion pictures, department stores, cutting-edge medical treatment, cosmetics, fashion, and finance, not to mention capturing 40 percent of the nation's Nobel Prizes in science and economics. This disproportionate power naturally gives rise to concerns that their contributions to the main facets of American civilization add up to a conspiracy.

Their turbulent history and support for Israel, a global flashpoint, also perhaps serve as causes for this wariness.

In my own experience, however, their assimilation into American society has progressed with the changes in generations, and one Jewish friend of mine once remarked with humor that the "assimilation has progressed completely." Considering that the first Jewish immigrants arrived in New York in 1654 and Jewish citizens were counted among the dead at the Alamo and on both sides of the Civil War, I think they should be regarded as multiracial power "pioneers." It is said that the happy endings with which most Hollywood movies conclude are an expression of gratitude and loyalty by the large number of Jewish citizens in the motion picture industry. These Jewish Hollywood pioneers were grateful both to the United States that took them in and to the American way of life. In a similar vein, it is easy to understand why neoconservative groups with their many Jewish intellectuals have taken the lead in arguing that the prosecution of the Iraq War and the democratization of the Middle East are the responsibilities of the "empire of liberty."

EIGHT

The 1968 Watershed

Johnson's Tragedy

At this point I'd like to take us back to the year 1968, because I think the frustrations and changes taking place in the United States—epitomized by the events of that year—are worth describing.

Above all it was a year of upheaval. Despite eventually having poured a force of 543,000 troops into Vietnam, the United States saw impending defeat before its eyes. That year opened the curtain of defeat abroad for the first time for the United States, which from the time of its founding had expanded from the Atlantic to the Pacific supported by the DNA of the use of force and faith in Manifest Destiny.

President Richard Nixon, who was elected to the White House that year, would transform the nation from the world's police force into a country pursuing its national security interests among several competitors. He would change the world by taking advantage of the confrontation between China and the Soviet Union and establish a reconciliation with China. This planted the seeds of the eventual end of the Cold War. Promoting the Nixon Doctrine, Nixon stated that there would be no more American blood spilled and that "Vietnamization" was to be implemented. This set the stage for an orderly American exit from Indochina.

Although the George W. Bush administration succeeded in expelling the government of Saddam Hussein in what was termed "regime change,"

I believe the abundant lessons learned in 1968 still apply in the present situation of stumbling through nation-building and guerrilla war. After emerging as the sole victor of the Cold War and proclaiming itself the empire of liberty, the United States under the younger President Bush was pushed into the invasion of Iraq by the neoconservatives, whose actions suggest a wish to compensate for the old wounds inflicted by the Vietnam experience.

I want to start with the tragedy of President Lyndon Johnson, who was the leading figure of that year and, like President Bush, hailed from Texas.

Johnson was at the height of his powers when I arrived at my post as Kyodo News's New York special correspondent, about one year after he became president following the Kennedy assassination. His ability to move legislation through Congress, which was fully demonstrated for many years as Senate majority leader, but had become stagnant under Kennedy, was again displayed when he became president. He signed numerous bills into law, including the Civil Rights Act and a new Voting Rights Act that are still hailed as historical achievements. Due in part to the popularity of his domestic policy plan dubbed "The Great Society," he defeated his Republican opponent Barry Goldwater by a margin of 15 million votes, receiving a larger percentage of the popular vote than any other Presidential candidate before or since. The 1965 New Year editions of *Time* and *Newsweek* magazines carried articles reporting that Johnson had ordered his staff to draw up a blueprint for utopia in the United States.

Unlike the current President Bush, who goes to bed at 9:30 p.m. and wakes up at 5:30 in the morning, Johnson in the late 1960s would sit up all night in the White House—long after the exterior lights had been shut off to save energy—to discuss ways out of the Vietnam War. In those days journalists were still quite free to roam the White House and often interacted closely with Johnson. There were many instances when the press corps would assemble in the Oval Office and interview Johnson at his desk. A large, tall man, his eyes were always swollen, and it was obvious to everyone that he hadn't had enough sleep. Nevertheless, he always stood ready to address the press corps.

President Bush received his education from elite schools in the East, but Johnson worked hard and graduated from a teacher's college in west Texas. Robert McNamara, who bore the brunt of the Vietnam policy failure as secretary of defense, commented in his memoirs:

Lyndon Baines Johnson was one of the most complex, intelligent, and hardworking individuals I have ever known. He possessed a kaleidoscopic personality: by turns open and devious, loving and mean, compassionate and tough, gentle and cruel. He was a towering, powerful, paradoxical figure, reminding me of a verse from Whitman's "Song of Myself":

> Do I contradict myself?
> Very well then I contradict myself;
> I am large, I contain multitudes.[1]

He possessed a grim personality and was known for his considerable secretiveness.

In 1937, he rode the waves of the New Deal into Congress as a twenty-nine-year-old Democratic representative. After serving six terms in the House, he went to the Senate. His flexibility led to his selection in 1953 as the youngest Senate majority leader in the history of the United States. On losing the contest for his party's presidential nomination to Kennedy in 1960, his vote-garnering power in the South gave rise to his selection as the vice-presidential candidate. With the Kennedy assassination, Johnson assumed the task of seeing the former president's policies to fruition. His strong influence on Congress turned into both an asset and a liability.

Above all, Johnson inherited Kennedy's Vietnam policy. Shortly before Kennedy's death, Ngo Dinh Diem was overthrown in a coup d'etat with the president's consent. Moreover, Kennedy had decided to make greater use of the U.S. military in South Vietnam. Even so, he was groping in the dark, and McNamara considered it a "god-awful mess eminently more dangerous than the one Kennedy had inherited from Eisenhower."

It was at this time that Johnson put himself on the road to quagmire. He believed that losing South Vietnam would result in the spread of communism throughout the entire Third World. He further thought that the United States must not only prevent this from happening but show the world it was not a paper tiger. Finally, he declared that "America is the world's policeman," demonstrating a true Texan style in his sense of mission.

The Emergence of the "Best and the Brightest"

In eulogizing the souls of those who fought the Mexican Army at the Alamo, which is located in San Antonio near his birthplace, Lyndon Johnson often remarked that America had not been sold for the sake of peace. For Johnson, the mere thought of losing face before the world by withdrawing U.S. troops from Vietnam gave him cause to shudder.

Thus, the fear of a loss of Vietnam was less politically desirable than the risk of expanding the direct deployment of U.S. forces. On top of this, he wanted to maintain support for the Great Society and his domestic policies.

On the other hand, the Johnson administration was keenly aware of the foreign-policy priority that had concerned Kennedy: that, at all costs, developments that could lead to all-out nuclear conflict with the Soviet Union—and by Johnson's time, China—had to be avoided. After the Cuban Missile Crisis that had brought the two superpowers to the brink of catastrophe, the need for peaceful coexistence, a term that Khrushchev used repeatedly, had become ever clearer.

But the path that confronted Johnson in Vietnam led him to wage a painful, prolonged, conventional war with non-nuclear weaponry against guerilla adversaries, to prove to the world that the United States was not a paper tiger. McNamara's so-called "flexible response" strategy became the administration's key hope in the conflict. With the premise of avoiding nuclear war through a policy of mutual deterrence, McNamara advocated stamping out fires in any world conflict with complete military superiority. Thus, the Special Operations forces, whose capacities are again being tested in the current war on terror, were touted as the main players on a grand scale.

Of course, behind Johnson's decisions were the Kennedy-appointed power elite who had studied at England's Oxford University through Rhodes Scholarships and at prestigious East Coast universities and who were later branded by David Halberstam as "the best and the brightest." Such figures included McNamara, Secretary of State Dean Rusk, National Security Advisor McGeorge Bundy, and soon-to-be Bundy successor Walt Rostow. These powerful officials undercut the hesitation of the uniformed forces and the prudence of the CIA.

In his classic book *The Best and the Brightest*, Halberstam tells of the exuberance of those days:

So they carried with them an exciting sense of American elit-
ism, a sense that the best men had been summoned forth from
the country to harness this dream to a new American nationalism, bringing a new, strong, dynamic spirit to our historic role
in world affairs, not necessarily to bring the American dream to
reality here at home, but to bring it to reality elsewhere in the
world. . . .

A remarkable hubris permeated this time . . . the Kennedy
group regarded the Eisenhower people as having shrunk from
the challenge set before them. Walt Rostow, Bundy's deputy,
thought the old Administration had overlooked the possibilities
in the underdeveloped world, the rich potential for conflict and
thus a rich potential for victory. . . .

But this new Administration understood ideas and understood the historic link-up between our traditions and those in
the underdeveloped world; we too were heirs to a great revolution, we too had fought a great colonial power. Were we much
richer than they, and more technological? No problem, no gap
in outlook, we would use our technology for them. . . . Rostow
in particular was fascinated by the possibility of television sets
in the thatch hutches of the world, believing that somehow this
could be the breakthrough.[2]

Today, the neoconservatives have truly become the successors of "the
best and the brightest." I will analyze them in the next chapter.

At the time of the Gulf of Tonkin Resolution in Congress in August
1964, the commencement of the bombings of North Vietnam in February
1965, and the Marine Corps landing at Da Nang, the path taken by Johnson
and McNamara had the support of the public and Congress. Even the great
liberal commentator Walter Lippman, who later harshly criticized Johnson and his Vietnam policy and who was surprised by the public support of
Nixon during the presidential election of 1968, encouraged Johnson by saying
that although the U.S. could not win a guerilla war, it should use its powerful navy and air force to demonstrate to China in no uncertain terms that it
would never be a paper tiger.

Because Johnson had a tendency for secretiveness while wanting to save
face, he hesitated to reveal the difficulties of this guerilla war to the public.

Nevertheless, the number of casualties began to climb rapidly bringing into vogue the term "credibility gap." The antiwar movement began with the burning of draft cards as its most powerful symbol. While burning a draft card was punishable by a maximum of five years in prison, antiwar movements of various forms quickly spread across the country.

On November 6, 1965, I covered an antiwar rally at New York's Union Square sponsored by the pacifist Catholic War Resistance League, the Committee for Nonviolent Action, and the New York Workshop in Nonviolence. Five young men took the stage one after another to deliver antiwar speeches. Everyone was tense, and their faces were pale. After having a *New York Times* journalist verify the genuine articles, the five together set fire to their cards with lighters. At that moment, a shout of "Queers!" flew out from the crowd. A man in front of me took out a fire extinguisher hidden under his coat and sprayed the men. He was arrested.

As the light-brown draft cards, about the size of a Japanese commuter pass, began to burn eerily with a white smoke, a large chorus of "We shall overcome!" rang out and filled the square. Both the thronging crowd and the police held their breath as they watched the orange flames. There was gloom on every face.

A week later the five men were arrested by the FBI. I still have my notes of my coverage of that event. Around this time Senate Foreign Relations Committee Chairman Fulbright opened public hearings on Vietnam and began to challenge Johnson openly. In late 1966, *New York Times* journalist Harrison Salisbury sent a direct telegram from Hanoi describing the ineffectiveness and inhumanity of the bombings of that city. A week when the number of U.S. casualties surpassed those of the South Vietnamese was also soon to come.

The Shrewdness of Ho Chi Minh

At this point a discussion is warranted regarding the shrewd strategy employed by the Vietnamese Communist Party (VCP) Central Committee commanded by Ho Chi Minh.

Journalists and representatives from various peace groups in the United States were invited to Hanoi, helping to drive a wedge into U.S. public opinion and igniting another war inside the United States. As for the People's Liberation Front, or Viet Cong (VC), in South Vietnam, even though they were under the command of the VCP, or more accurately, a part of it, the outward myth of the VC as the standard-bearers of the national liberation movement persisted, ultimately resulting in the presence of VC representatives at the Paris Peace Accords.

Ignoring opposition within the VC, the Hanoi leadership forced them to conduct the Tet Offensive of February 1968. Despite its military failure, the Tet Offensive received wide coverage in the American media where it was often perceived as a U.S. defeat, effectively giving President Johnson his political walking papers.[3] Ho Chin Minh skillfully manipulated its allies, the Soviet Union and China, into providing North Vietnam with the support it needed to draw the nuclear-superpower United States hand and foot into the quagmire of guerrilla war, successfully achieving his goal of depicting the United States as a "paper tiger."

The tragedy of Johnson's Vietnam policy can also be regarded as a drama initiated and directed by Hanoi.

One year earlier, in October 1967, the same Pentagon that was later hit by the 9/11 terrorist attack became the stage for another war as called for in Hanoi's intended scenario. White radical students from an antiwar demonstration rushed toward the main entrance and collided with a mobilized army platoon, leading to injuries on both sides. Meanwhile, as a journalist I followed this skirmish from inside the Pentagon. Red fire licked from burning draft cards while the red and blue flag of the VC waved before the bayonets of the soldiers, including Vietnam veterans, a spectacle of a kind not seen since the creation of the national capital. It seemed that I was gazing upon the graveyard of the military intervention in Vietnam.

While school lunch subsidies, a lynchpin of the Great Society, were cut by one-fifth due to the increased cost of the war in Vietnam, fires and riots flared in the black ghettos of major cities. This was truly a long, hot summer. Proposals for tax increases to fund the war again inflamed animosity, and in that October the person responsible for the war's prosecution since the Kennedy era, Secretary of Defense McNamara, resigned to become President of the World Bank.

That same month Senator Eugene McCarthy—a little-known figure nationally but regarded in Washington as a pretty boy of witty though cynical speech, and sometimes opportunistic conduct—announced his candidacy for the Democratic nomination for president. His platform rested on the early conclusion of the Vietnam War. Lacking television coverage or public relations arrangements, he had really been chosen for this candidacy by Allard Lowenstein, a skilled behind-the-scenes figure in liberal Democratic politics. His race for the White House was at first perceived as simply one person's rebellion against Johnson, who still believed his reelection was certain.

A Pale Victory

The year of upheaval that ended with the election of Nixon to the White House began with McCarthy assuming a leading role.

The Tet Offensive throughout South Vietnam from January through early February publicly exposed the lack of progress of Johnson's war. Meanwhile, the McCarthy campaign was bringing together the support of disparate elements from the Students for a Democratic Society (SDS) to straight-A students from elite eastern schools like Harvard. The latter had until this time kept their distance from the radical student antiwar movements that had snowballed on large public campuses such as Berkeley and Wisconsin. In March, the "Get clean for Gene" volunteers saw their efforts rewarded as McCarthy garnered more than 40 percent of the vote in the New Hampshire primary. It was a political defeat for Johnson.

With the entry of Robert Kennedy into the Democratic race, Johnson decided to drop out of the reelection campaign while at the same time announcing a partial suspension of the bombing of North Vietnam and accepting the North Vietnamese offer of peace negotiations.

A few days after this startling news, a bloody incident occurred that shook every corner of American society. The Reverend Martin Luther King, Jr. was assassinated, and black riots raged near the White House.

In May, peace negotiations with Vietnam finally began in Paris as the blossoms were falling from its beautiful chestnut trees. The small North Vietnamese delegation that had arrived in a Citroen shook hands with U.S. delegate Averell Harriman, who rode up in a Cadillac. As if waiting for the decline of the United States, the May Revolution flared up in the streets of Paris. However, the Vietnam peace negotiations proceeded slowly.

With Johnson having abdicated his throne, Robert Kennedy, who had been eclipsed by McCarthy, was assassinated just after the hard-fought California primary. During a televised debate, the enraged eyes of the Arab immigrant, Sirhan Bishara Sirhan, had watched as Kennedy announced his support of Israel in its conflict with Lebanon, in a bid for the Jewish and labor vote.

It was the fourth major political assassination (if the death of Malcolm X is included) in five years, and the televised coverage of the funeral procession continued for a lengthy time. One American journalist watching television at the Senate press gallery suddenly shouted "No more funerals!" and left.

The dissident movement known later as the counterculture appeared in full bloom in the Washington streets later during the Nixon years. Impoverished groups set up tent cities in Washington and were subsequently arrested, setting off riots once again in cities around the country. The Democratic National Convention in Chicago turned into a huge melee that was televised nationwide. At the Mexico City Olympics in October, black athletes who won medals refused to acknowledge the U.S. flag or the national anthem. Students began to stage sit-down strikes at universities.

Thus eight years of rule by Democratic presidents ended in the midst of violence and disorder.

Nixon rode the tempest of 1968 straight into the White House. With the split in the Democratic Party and the cycle of self-denial near at hand, the only thing necessary for Nixon was to sell the notion of "law and order." For Hubert Humphrey, the Democratic candidate, the only breakthrough would be the unconditional cessation of the bombing of North Vietnam. Johnson, however, who was beginning to become conscious of how history would judge him, did not respond so easily.

Ironically, the 1968 election was decided with Nixon's victory in Illinois, the state that had cost him the presidency eight years before. A columnist at the *Washington Evening Star* commented at the time that it was "a pale victory." But, pale or not, this victory marked the birth of "Nixon's America."

The Self-Destruction of the Liberals

It is important to grasp the historical facts surrounding the election of Nixon, who lost to Kennedy by a narrow margin in 1960 but rose to victory in 1968 as a result of Johnson's self-destruction.

The collapse of Johnson's presidency in 1968 meant that the "big government" politics of the Democratic liberals, which had become the mainstream philosophy of American government since 1933, fell from favor. In

1960 the liberals concentrated all their efforts on supporting the Kennedy administration. But Johnson's effort to consolidate the achievements of liberalism with his Great Society programs failed and put the Democratic Party on the defensive, a situation that remains today.

The new "best and the brightest," the present-day neoconservatives, arose from the ashes of this liberal self-immolation; some, indeed, were liberals who moved to the right around this time. For Irving Kristol, the godfather of the neoconservatives and father of William Kristol, editor-in-chief of the *Weekly Standard*, this was his second change of direction, having first turned from the Trotskyites to follow the liberals in the 1930s.

In order to understand contemporary America, a grasp of these causal relationships going back as early as the Kennedy victory of 1960 is important.

In 1968 Walter Lippman, who for years had written progressive columns from his corner in the dominant eastern establishment, shocked the public by announcing his support not for the Democratic Humphrey but rather the Republican Nixon. In a contribution to the *New York Herald Tribune* he described his disillusionment with the liberals as follows:

1. Although liberal Democrats had sold the dreams of Kennedy's New Frontier and Johnson's Great Society at huge bargains with showy slogans, what they had actually produced were a deepening of racial tensions, the assassinations of the Kennedy brothers and Reverend King, and black riots throughout the country.

2. America's excessive interference in the affairs of foreign nations, typified by the Vietnam intervention, planted the seed of division by the domestic antiwar movements and further reduced the value of the dollar and weakened the economy.

3. The "inflation politics" that the Democrats had developed in all aspects of politics, diplomacy, finance, and society, threatened the United States with ruination.

Lippman called for an end to the wild merrymaking politics of the liberals and announced his decision to back Nixon in the 1968 election.

To be sure, Nixon's election was a product of America's tiring of Kennedy's and Johnson's grandiose "inflation politics" as described by Lippman. Certainly, the administrations of Kennedy and Johnson attempted to call the shots with a sharp heroic image and sense of mission, but their grandiose proclamations resulted in self-destruction as Lippman had predicted.

Following eight years of Eisenhower, the Kennedy administration's high rhetoric was intended to replace talk of the decline and fall of the United States. Toward the end of the Eisenhower years the Soviet Union began to catch up to the United States militarily (symbolized by the startling launch of Sputnik). At the same time the growth rate of the U.S. economy began to slow down, the dollar fell into a chronic state of crisis, and U.S. influence in the Third World began to wane. When Kennedy proclaimed that democracy must not hesitate to stand up and take the lead in revolutions around the world, the sense of mission of the New Frontier was born, leading inexorably to intervention in Vietnam.

Through incidents such as the Cuban Missile Crisis, the United States was able, over time, to build a realistic relationship of peaceful coexistence with the Soviet Union centering on the common interests of the two nuclear powers. Ultimately, however, in its ceding of the pacemaker role to the Soviet Union, enmity toward China, continuation of the containment policy, and opposition to Third World liberation efforts, the path to intervention in Vietnam was paved.

Some experts still believe that had he not been assassinated, Kennedy in his second term of office would have undertaken the same kind of opening to China that Nixon so spectacularly achieved. Robert McNamara, who served as secretary of defense under both Kennedy and Johnson, holds this view.

I believe, however, that finding a solution to the China problem was shelved in order to placate the dissatisfaction of the military leaders and congressional conservatives opposed to the policy of peaceful coexistence with the Soviet Union, and to prevent a repeat of the "Loss of China" syndrome. During his first summit talks with Khrushchev in Vienna in June 1961, Kennedy had even tried to work out a deal to maintain the status quo in Southeast Asia, keeping the influence of the United States and the Soviet Union excluding China, and simultaneously by staying out of the Laos crisis.

Kennedy's War

The first military intervention in Vietnam was launched by Kennedy in February 1962. He disregarded the 685-person limitation specified by the Geneva Agreement of 1954, which accepted the separation of South and North Vietnam, opted to reinforce the team of U.S. military advisors already in Vietnam, and established the Headquarters Military Assistance Command Vietnam (MACV) in Saigon. Just twenty-two days before his assassination, he gave tacit support to preparations for fighting the Viet Cong and effectively ignored the coup d'etat that overthrew and killed Ngo Dinh Diem. Kennedy had rejected a CIA report asserting that as long as the United States maintained bases in Okinawa, Guam, the Philippines, Japan, and elsewhere, American military strength would likely be sufficient to prevent China and North Vietnam from invading Southeast Asia. Instead, he opted for a course of action to reinforce perceptions of America as the world's policeman and placate critics who accused him of being soft on Communism.

According to former special adviser Theodore Sorenson, Kennedy recognized that Vietnam could not be rescued by military action alone.[4] If this is true, he might have avoided a quagmire and deserved the unending praise of his close aides, had he been able to complete his term.

A contradictory view, however, is expressed in the masterpiece of historical journalism, *Vietnam: A History*, by Stanley Karnow, the renowned Vietnam and China correspondent whose work became the basis for a famous PBS documentary[5] and who covered Washington around the same time as me. Karnow reports that Kennedy revealed a less peaceful side of his nature to *New York Times* journalist James Reston immediately following some intense exchanges with Khrushchev in Vienna in June 1961. This had come even as he was still reeling from the Bay of Pigs fiasco that greeted him soon after assuming office. He told Reston that in the wake of recent events, "we have a problem in making our power credible, and Vietnam is the place" to overcome that problem.

Robert Bartley, editor emeritus of the *Wall Street Journal*, who passed away in November 2003, wrote:

> [Eisenhower] favored American intervention in Laos, predicting that unless the U.S. resisted there South Vietnam and Cambodia would also fall.

In the event, President Kennedy negotiated the Laos accords, a coalition arrangement that gave the Communists de facto control of the Ho Chi Minh trail vital to infiltration into South Vietnam. . . .

. . . The reasons JFK was reluctant to withdraw from Vietnam: failure at the Bay of Pigs, the Vienna summit with Khrushchev, defending Laos, the Berlin Wall, the Soviet resumption of nuclear testing. He feared the international and domestic reaction to another defeat. . . .

[Bartley quotes JFK] "Withdraw? . . . Give me a break."[6]

Four months after the Kennedy-Khrushchev talks, General Maxwell Taylor and Walt Rostow were sent to Vietnam and submitted a report to Kennedy titled "The Last Great Confrontation with Communism." The U.S. military dispatched its first helicopters, and the plan for commencing de facto military intervention was decided.

The phrase "nation-building" now being used in Iraq appeared in the early 1960s as the name of the support policy for South Vietnam. Included under this rubric was the notorious Pacification Plan that forcibly relocated approximately 33 percent of South Vietnam's population, or about 4.3 million people, from their traditional ancestral homes to "strategic villages."

A key figure in all this was Walt Rostow, a Yale graduate who had studied at Oxford on a Rhodes scholarship. Hired by MIT as a professor of economics at the age of thirty-four, he developed a strong taste for politics after the Eisenhower era. He gave the name "The New Frontier" to the numerous policies of the new Kennedy administration.

Rostow constantly advocated a hard-line position favoring military intervention in Vietnam. Even after the fall of Saigon, he insisted that "the Vietnam War delayed the Communist take-over by a period long enough so that the whole of Southeast Asia was able to grow economically." He also added, "and I don't for a moment deny that we got sick of the war." He continued to voice this opinion until his death in February 2003 at the age of eighty-six. These same sentiments were voiced by Dean Rusk, another Rhodes Scholar who served for eight years as secretary of state in both the Kennedy and Johnson administrations and who joined Rostow and other hard-liners in defending the Vietnam War. Like Rostow, Rusk also died at the age of eighty-six. Among these veteran "best and brightest," the saga of McNamara's confession, described in chapter 1, stands out.

In a television interview with Walter Cronkite in September 1963, about two months before being killed by an assassin's bullet, Kennedy strongly criticized Ngo Dinh Diem's alienation from the public while simultaneously declaring:

> I don't agree with those who say we should withdraw. That would be a great mistake. I know people don't like Americans to be engaged in this kind of an effort. Forty-seven Americans have been killed in combat with the enemy, but this is a very important struggle even though it is far away.

After Kennedy, Johnson took up the banner of "Kennedy's War" in a more expansive, archetypal Texan fashion, and stepped up the war by sending in more than five hundred thousand U.S. troops.

For Johnson, the Vietnam War had at some point become a crusade by which he could take his Great Society to Asia. The large-scale deployment of American forces temporarily restructured the government of Saigon prior to its collapse. There was also the growing Sino-Soviet confrontation, and China's confusion under the Cultural Revolution. Rostow saw trends of hope while the United States was sacrificing its blood in South Vietnam. In Asia the wind of change was beginning to blow, signaling progress in building stable nations and regional cooperation. Although China had developed nuclear weapons, it had no missile systems with which to launch them and was effectively contained as a threat. It was through such rose-colored glasses that Rostow viewed the world, but the Tet offensive shattered that illusion.

At this point, let's take a look at the Kennedy myth. The Kennedy family used its wealth to develop new means to take over the White House—the political use of television and opinion polls, and the systematic courting of the black vote—that certainly opened a new page in U.S. politics. Kennedy himself was handsome, eloquent, and overflowing with charm. He was the first Irish-American and Catholic president in the history of the United States. For many ethnic and blue-collar Americans his achievement of the presidency represented the summit of the American dream.

On the other hand, this forced, artificial victory lit the flames of racial, regional, and ideological confrontation. The heroic image of "The New Frontier," which Kennedy successfully sold to the public by means of television appearances, diminished his power to compromise with Congress and in diplomatic negotiations. As a result, the seeds of discontent were scattered about in all directions.

The November 1963 Dallas visit was itself a political venture to restore relations with the hostile territory of the South.

In the final analysis, I believe the Kennedy assassination itself was related to the social tensions produced in American society by the ambitious achievements of this Irish-American, whose people had once ranked low in the racial class structure.

Opening the Door to China—The Kansas City Speech

At this point I'd like to summarize the five years of the Nixon era after the 1968 presidential election. Because of its sensationalism, Nixon's post-Watergate resignation, the first in history by a U.S. president, has tended to overshadow the story of his real achievements in office.

Without correctly understanding the legacy of the Nixon era, however, I don't think one can grasp Bush's America and one neoconservative heavy hitter in particular who plays a major role. I believe that an understanding of this continuity is important.

The Nixon years were a time when the United States was transformed from the world's policeman into an indifferent competitor whose greatest accomplishment was reconciliation with China.

On July 6, 1971, immediately after secretly dispatching Henry Kissinger to Beijing, Nixon delivered a speech in Kansas City, Missouri, to news media executives from thirteen Midwestern states. As Nixon himself notes in his memoirs, this speech attracted little attention except in Beijing where the Chinese showed great interest in it as they prepared to welcome Kissinger.[7]

China did not miss the point of the message that Nixon had delivered nonchalantly from Kansas City in the Midwest, a city in the heart of Nixon's America. When Kissinger arrived in Beijing on July 9, Chinese leaders reportedly first asked him what the president meant by the Kansas City speech. When Kissinger responded that he hadn't read it yet, they reportedly delivered the text of the speech to him with an attached memo requesting that he return it to them when finished because they only had one copy. It was one of the few episodes revealed to reporters after Kissinger returned to the United States from his historic visit.

For China, the contents of this speech were certainly important as the determination to normalize relations with China was presented as a part of America's desire to act as a competitor. A series of excerpts from the speech reveal Nixon's logic:

1. We were number one in the world militarily. . . . We also at that point were number one economically by all odds. . . . That was just twenty-five years ago. . . . Now, twenty-five years have passed, let's look at the situation today and what it may be five years from now or ten years from now.

2. When we think in economic terms and economic poten-tialities, there are five great power centers in the world today. . . . There is, of course, the United States of America. There is, second, Western Europe . . . we have a resurgent Japan. . . . Now we turn to the other two superpowers, eco-nomic superpowers I will say for the moment. The Soviet Union, of course, first comes to mind . . . and this is also true of Mainland China.

3. In terms of economic capacity at the present time, a pretty good indication of where it is is that Japan, with 100 million people, produces more than Mainland China, with 800 mil-lion people. But that should not mislead us. . . . Because when we see the Chinese as people . . . they are one of the most capable people in the world. And 800 million Chinese are going to be, inevitably, an enormous economic power, with all that that means in terms of what they could be in other areas if they move in that direction.

4. That is the reason why I felt that it was essential that this Administration take the first steps toward ending the isola-tion of Mainland China from the world community. We had to take these steps because the Soviet Union could not. . . . We were the only other power that could take these steps.

5. What we have done is simply opened the door—opened the

door for travel, opened the door for trade. Now the question is whether there will be other doors opened on their part. But the doors must be opened, and the goal of U.S. policy must be, in the long term, ending the isolation of Mainland China because . . . the United States could have a perfectly effective agreement with the Soviet Union for limitation of arms; there danger of any confrontation there might have been almost totally removed. But Mainland China, outside the world community, completely isolated, with its leaders not in communication with world leaders, would be a danger to the whole world that would be unacceptable, unacceptable to us and unacceptable to others as well.

6. So consequently, this step must be taken now. Others must be taken, very precisely, very deliberately, as there is reciprocation on the other side.

7. The United States, as compared with that position we found ourselves in immediately after World War II, has a challenge such as we did not even dream of. . . . Then we were talking about the necessity of—putting it in terms of a poker game—that the United States had all the chips and we had to spread a few of the chips around so that others could play. . . . The United States no longer is in the position of complete preeminence or predominance. . . . The United States, let us understand, is still the strongest nation in the world; it is still the richest nation in the world. But now we face a situation where four other potential economic powers have the capacity, have the kind of people . . . who can challenge us on every front. (That) brings us back home for a hard look at what America needs to do if we are going to run this race economically and run it effectively and maintain the position of world leadership, a position that can only be maintained if the United States retains its preeminent position in the economic field . . . because five years from July 4 of this year we will celebrate the 200th anniversary of the United States of America. . . . I think of what happened to Greece and to Rome and, as you see, what is left—only the pillars. . . . The

United States is now reaching that period. I am convinced, however, that we have the vitality, I believe we have the courage, I believe we have the strength cut through this heartland and across this Nation that will see to it that America not only is rich and strong, but that it is healthy in terms of moral strength and spiritual strength.

The speech made an appeal for a change of course not only in U.S. foreign policy but also in the American way of life itself. It contained not even an echo of Kennedy's grandiloquent sense of mission. Instead, it was a renunciation of America's self-proclaimed duties as the guardian of democracy, the leading advocate of anti-Communist ideology, and the world's policeman. It was an acknowledgement of America's transformation into a realistic and self-centered competitor committed to putting its national interest first.

The address was, furthermore, a provocative declaration that pluralistic competition, which was brought to a standstill by the Cold War confrontation between the United States and the Soviet Union, should be reinvigorated; that is, an attitude should be set for prevailing in a competition between the "five great power centers." The bold reconciliation initiative with China, an adversary for the twenty-one years since the Korean War, was presented as a unique opportunity in which only the United States could dominate the competition.

The Vietnamization Exit

Nixon had been groping for a solution to the problem of reconciliation with China ever since assuming office. He had been espousing the merits of approaching China as a lever to check the Soviet Union since 1970. In a 1970 television interview Nixon stated that the Soviet Union sought to catch up to and pass the United States in missile production at the same time that its navy was moving into the Mediterranean and the Indian Ocean. The number of Soviet troops stationed in Europe in peacetime was now at an all time high, yet the Soviet Union's weakest point was its border with China. To prevent the Soviet Union from tipping the balance of power in the world toward its own favor, it was essential that the United States embark on improving its relations with China.

Nixon's new policy meant adopting classic power politics, using Kissinger's secret diplomacy to take advantage of the Sino-Soviet confrontation. The transformation of the policy toward China signified a turn toward realism based on the concept of competing interests.

It must be understood that this sudden road to realism did not make its appearance solely with respect to China. There was also the policy known as the Nixon Doctrine, which the president had promoted since assuming office to reduce foreign obligations.

Against this background was the "Southern Strategy," a basic domestic game plan aimed at creating a new pro-Nixon majority by exploiting the dissatisfaction of a number of groups: blue-collar workers angered at long-haired radicals; formerly Democratic Southerners annoyed by the pro-busing decisions of federal judges; middle-Americans from the so-called "silent majority" who felt alienated by the changes of the 1960s; and, indeed, the formerly liberal intellectuals who had begun to embrace the term "neoconservatism" to describe their views.

Conversely, the Nixon Doctrine was hammered out as a foreign policy to indulge the realism, egoism, and honor of this silent majority. This was a policy designed to find an exit from Vietnam in accordance with a policy of Vietnamization and the catchphrase "no more American blood."

In this way, Nixon set the stage for a peace with honor despite the reality of a defeat in Vietnam that he had inherited from a Democratic administration. Thus, he could announce that the invasion had been repelled, the United States had kept its pledge, no more American blood would be shed, and the baton had been passed to a government capable of defending itself. America's troops were not returning home in defeat. Through this approach he succeeded in checking the antiwar movement.

The considerable escalation of attacks in the form of stepped-up bombings of North Vietnam, Laos, and Cambodia was put into execution in order to produce the conditions for preserving American blood. That the blood of 27,623 Americans was shed after the implementation of Vietnamization under the Nixon administration—accounting for almost half of all the war deaths in Vietnam—demonstrates the frightful egoism of this concept. It is a precedent that the United States must not forget when looking for an exit from the Iraq War.

A change in policy toward China was possible only by extending this very intense realism and egoism. The "competitor" declaration of the Kansas

City speech was both an assertion and a challenge. It was no wonder that Japan was somewhat traumatized by this "Nixon Shock."

The pace of transformation was quick. Kissinger arrived in Beijing three days after the Kansas City speech. Nine days later, Nixon himself delivered the historic announcement of his decision to visit China. Only one month later came the unabashed defense of the dollar by the elimination of the gold standard.

If reconciliation with China was proof of America's abandonment of its role as the world's policeman, the elimination of the gold was the abdication of the dollar from its reign among the world's currencies. It was the prelude to further cuts in the dollar's value at the Smithsonian Agreement five months later in December 1971. History must record this transformation of the United States to competitor status as important as Nixon's resignation following the Watergate incident. Now it's time to look at the era's egoism.

The "Southern Strategy" Scenario

At this point an account of the Southern Strategy is warranted. It is especially helpful in comparing Nixon's peace-with-honor road out of Vietnam under the Vietnamization Plan with the situation in Iraq.

A product of Attorney General John Mitchell and presidential advisor Kevin P. Phillips, Mitchell's executive assistant, the concept of the Southern Strategy was proudly introduced in Phillips's 1969 book, *The Emerging Republican Majority*.

It was aimed at creating new supporters for the Republican administration among those who were richly patriotic, hard-working, deeply religious, and moralistic, who dreamed of a life out of the Sears & Roebuck mail-order catalogs, and whose tastes ran to new cars, cottage cheese, apple pie, and bourbon; in other words, the late-1960s white middle class designated by Nixon as the Silent Majority.

The South, which had consistently served as the base of the Democratic Party since the days of slavery, had been reborn as a new industrial region. The Republicans took notice of the new middle class that was flowing in from all over the country and ambitiously calculated them into their plans to undercut the Democrats. The Nixon Doctrine, which called for the withdrawal of U.S. forces even as the war and bloodshed continued to spread in Indochina, was a part of this Southern Strategy, targeting the self-centeredness of the Silent Majority.

Phillips named this region, which became a fertile platform for industrial energy spreading from the new South through the semi-desert regions of New Mexico and Colorado to Southern California, the "Sunbelt."

The Southern Strategy succeeded as a Republican strategy in part because it represented a shift in population and political power to the South and West, a phenomenon that can be seen to this day. The Internet industrial revolution sprang from Silicon Valley, which derived its own energy from that which was first born in the Sunbelt, and it has become a pillar of American triumph in the international marketplace.

The Nixon administration started to severely criticize the permanent federal bureaucracy and the eastern establishment, the so-called loud minority consisting of liberal intellectuals, labor unions, black organizations, the three major television networks, the *New York Times*, and the *Washington Post*. Vice President Agnew, whose popularity grew with garish speeches attacking the eastern media and eastern establishment, acted as the advance guard of this attack.

It must not be forgotten, however, that both the Southern Strategy and the Nixon Doctrine were made possible through the existence of a serious crack in American society.

In other words, the more the counterculture movement brought black riots, long hair and student demonstrations, collisions with police forces, flag trampling, draft card burning, marijuana smoking, free sex, legalized pornography, and admissions of homosexuality into American society, the more law and order became a watchword for the conservative white middle-class, a development that the Nixon camp coldly capitalized upon. The existence of the black, student, and antiwar movements certainly provided leverage for the administration to maintain its power.

In fact, the SDS (Students for a Democratic Society), which at one time stood at the center of the student movement, experienced a division by the more extreme Weatherman faction. This breakaway group steadily gravitated to more radical dissident activities such as bombings, sometimes under the influence of FBI-associated infiltrators and provocateurs acting under the auspices of J. Edgar Hoover and, many argue, with the implicit approval of the Nixon administration.

While the truth of the Nixon connection is debatable, the continuation of black and student riots was a plus for Nixon. The left-wing magazine the *Nation* asked at the time if the Nixon administration in its heart hadn't actually chuckled at the daily deterioration of social, political, and economic conditions, as evidenced by the rise in crime, race riots, inflation, drugs, the appearance of extremists, women's liberation, and the generation gap.

Digging His Own Grave

Nevertheless, with each success in the political arena, Nixon dug his own grave. Such is the drama of this president whose career swung back and forth between glory and catastrophe.

After working his way through school and becoming a lawyer, Nixon served in the navy during World War II. In 1946, immediately after leaving the service as a Lieutenant Commander he ran for the House of Representatives as a Republican from his home state of California. Recommended as a candidate by a friend of his mother, he won the election by skillfully riding a wave of criticism of the Roosevelt's New Deal and a mood of generational change after the war. He later ascended to the Senate and then, at the age of thirty-nine, just six years after entering politics, he was elected as Eisenhower's vice president. His success coincided with an intensified Cold War, anti-Communist witch hunts, and the rise of political influence by the Western states.

The first act of this success story was short-lived, however, when Nixon was beaten in the presidential election of 1960 by the Democratic candidate John F. Kennedy. Kennedy, who had been Nixon's colleague during his first two terms in Congress was an Irish-American like Nixon, but he had received an elite education in the East as the son of a successful Wall Street magnate. With his father's sponsorship, he had risen steadily from the House to the Senate. He defeated Nixon by a slim margin in part through his abundant wealth, and by making full use of new political technology such as television and opinion polls. The dominance of Kennedy in the first presidential debate in history to be televised is recognized as a conclusive factor in the election.

Nixon also lost the California state gubernatorial election in 1962, but he never gave up, tirelessly making the rounds of Republican grassroots organizations nationwide. The second act of his glory opened with the coming of 1968, the year of upheaval. Nixon arrived in Washington as the first president in history to hail from California, and, indeed, the first president from any state west of the Rocky Mountains. What made him stand out, however, was his excessive rivalry and obsession with the eastern Democratic (and also Republican) establishment from which he had been estranged ever since his defeat by Kennedy.

In order to protect itself from what it perceived as attacks from the Democrats, the Nixon administration began to bug government offices, eventually organizing a covert group known as "the plumbers," an outfit assembled just two days after the historical announcement of Nixon's visit to China. It was around this time that the decisive recordings of the White House's internal conversations began. As correspondent Dan Rather once noted, history would "accurately record President Nixon's strengths and weaknesses, both as a person and as a president."

Despite the overwhelming support that led to his reelection in 1972, the stress of being the first president from the West soon gave way to arrogance toward the eastern establishment and accelerated his road to catastrophe.

After Nixon, "non-eastern" presidents—Carter, Reagan, Bush senior, and Clinton—from the South and West became the rule rather than the exception. This means that Nixon's life, which was filled with so much drama and irony, was one part of the profound transformation of an America that continues to develop day by day in diversity through multiracial power.

Nixon wrote eight books after resigning from the presidency, and the awareness he displayed toward Yeltsin's Russia earned him the distinction of serving as a diplomatic mentor in the construction of post–Cold War U.S. diplomacy. Nixon's life ended with a splendid funeral after he passed away from a cerebral hemorrhage at the age of eighty-one on April 22, 1994. With President Clinton at the head, the surviving presidents, their wives, and most of the leaders of the U.S. political world assembled together. The media, which had been so hostile toward Nixon during his tenure, recounted not only Watergate but his entire life's accomplishments, and for once treated his career fairly from beginning to end.

The Wounds in the Democratic Party

After 1968 the United States continued to change. Nixon's America built the Vietnam withdrawal on the self-centered phrase "no more American blood," and it created a reconciliation with China. The results of tearing down the framework of the Cold War remain in the nation's infrastructure to this day with the loss of the liberals' leadership in domestic politics and the emergence of the United States as the sole superpower.

The Bush administration's decision to react with preemptive strikes against Afghanistan and Iraq in response to 9/11 was also a product of this self-centeredness. Bush's America unmistakably stands as an extension of Nixon's America, which was born of the Vietnam War led by Kennedy and Johnson.

In this context, I believe the still-lingering Kennedy myth must be considered in light of the subsequent self-destructiveness of the Kennedy dynasty.

I have been fortunate to have had the opportunity to discuss in depth the problems of the Democratic Party with David Riesman, professor of sociology at Harvard University, author of the famed book *The Lonely Crowd*, and a liberal opinion leader of the same school as Walter Lippman.

The first time I interviewed him was in Cambridge, Massachusetts in August 1967. This was three months before Eugene McCarthy, the obscure liberal senator, triggered the Democratic Party's implosion by opposing the war and declaring his candidacy for the presidential nomination in 1968. This started a chain of events that brought down the Johnson White House. In Washington, this was the time of the "long, hot summer" when pundits steadily predicted that something was about to happen. The second time I met Professor Riesman was about a year and a half later in March 1969 in the San Francisco suburb of Palo Alto. I had finished five years of coverage of the Nixon administration as a foreign correspondent and was returning home to Japan.

My Time with Professor Riesman

After my return I compiled a report about this remarkable encounter, which was distributed from the Cultural Affairs Department of Kyodo News to the fine arts and literature column of an affiliated newspaper. As I read it again today, I find myself contemplating the goodwill of the Cultural Affairs Department that distributed this long piece. Since I believe Professor Riesman's sharp insight illuminates those times so vividly, the original text is presented here in its entirety. This is my manuscript dated July 21, 1969.

In Pursuit of a Changing America: My Time with Professor Riesman
By Fumio Matsuo, former Washington Correspondent
(Distributed by Kyodo News on July 21, 1969)

While the "failure" of the Vietnam War becomes reality with each passing day, the United States is presently undergoing a significant degree of change. "The rise of the new isolationism," "the revival of apathetic egoism," "the transformation from idealism to realism," "the return to the normalcy of law and order"—these various catchphrases clearly reveal a thick line of discontinuity. Even New York's reformist mayor Lindsey, who celebrated his victory four years ago as the "Republican Kennedy," has now had to accept defeat by conservative candidates of "law and order" during the recent Republican primary.

The nature of change in the U.S. is kaleidoscopic—as fully inconsistent as a zigzag, secret and difficult to grasp, much the same as the politics of the chameleon-like Nixon. The tales of the "good old days" of American politics, in which all the Democratic and Republican changes in the White House were laid bare and open, were abandoned long ago.

So, having completed my four year and three month tenure as a foreign correspondent in New York and Washington, the strongest impression that remains with me now are the handful of people I encountered who suddenly opened my eyes to the subterranean changes taking place in this absurdly large, vast, rich, diverse, and pluralistic "monster" known as the United States. It is still as fresh an experience as a quiet, gentle lagoon suddenly stumbled upon, after one has struggled with the waves of news that come crashing in day after day.

A Visit to Cambridge
One of these encounters was with Harvard University Professor David Riesman. His pregnant predictions and their implications are not easily forgotten.

The first time I encountered this famous don of American

sociology was on a hot and sultry evening in late August 1967 at
the professor's home in the Harvard University town of Cambridge in the Boston suburbs. After passing through the small
business district of Harvard Square, where European fashions
were all the rage even before reaching New York, I turned at the
old Continental Hotel across from Radcliff College, Harvard's
women's school, and proceeded straight for several blocks until
I came to the modern Radcliff student dormitories. Across the
street from the dormitories, I found the professor and his wife,
Evelyn, waiting for me at their two-story home painted in a
uniquely New England scheme.

I spent a full three hours with him in his spacious living room, where there was an old grand piano once used by a
musician's son. Snacking on homemade cookies and iced tea,
they began with an account of their trip to Japan in September
to December 1961, which they wrote about the following spring
in a book titled *Conversations in Japan*. They spoke of the many
Japanese with whom they had become acquainted, the Vietnam
War, the presidential election, China's Cultural Revolution and
Red Guard Movement, and the future of Sino-Soviet relations,
which at the time had drawn the attention of the world. Our
conversation continued on until the summer dusk had finally
blanketed the interior of the room.

For this journalist who had just met him for the first time,
it seemed as though I was taking an oral examination under the
professor's continuous sharp questioning.

Although my armpits were drenched with cold sweat, I was
able to toss out the one question I wanted to ask of him, "Do you
think the Johnson administration will fall?"

An Unexpected Prediction

Taking a little time to gather his thoughts, Professor Riesman
declared:

> I can't say yet, but the popular sentiment in the U.S. will
> absolutely turn conservative in the next election, because
> everyone is tired of Vietnam, tired of the race riots, and

tired of the liberal image since Kennedy. I can say that for certain. The liberal parties have yet to notice this trend.

Sensing the journalist's bewilderment, the professor continued on.

What must not be forgotten is that the new-type leaders riding on this mood of conservatism were born from among the traditional conservatives. Governor Reagan of California and Governor Kirk of Florida are of this type. They would calmly go into a black demonstration and conversely begin to get caught up in the speeches. They are a completely different breed apart from Goldwater in the way they have assimilated the new political technologies of mass manipulation. The liberals have a lot to learn about this reality. If they basically haven't gotten over the stage that began with the Kennedy movement of 1960, I can also say that they have begun to take one step forward. The new conservatives differ from their predecessors who have been caught up in the framework of the so-called old Eastern Establishment. The difference is that where the old conservatives looked to the Navy, the Air Force and missiles are the symbols of the new conservatives in the West and South.

The United States Is a Complicated Country

At the time, the congressional dove movement in the Fulbright Senate Foreign Relations Committee, which became the starting point of the Vietnam War opposition, began to spread until it ultimately achieved the participation of Robert Kennedy. The antiwar opinions spearheaded by the *New York Times* had finally run aground when the rise of the liberal anti-Johnson movement gained momentum. Therefore, I started to feel a sense of evasiveness. I couldn't precisely define the meaning of the word "conservatization." When it was time for me to leave, the professor said to me as he walked me to my car hand-in-hand with his wife, "You are fortunate to be working in Washington from now on. There will be a lot going on. Anyway, the United States is a complicated country," and, parting, he firmly shook my hand.

When I returned to Washington, a huge wave of news awaited. In the autumn of 1967, the curtain had opened on the negotiations between the United States and Japan for the return of Okinawa. I spent many months covering a wide variety of U.S.-Japan negotiations in addition to my regular coverage of the White House, State Department, and Congress. Professor Riesman's prediction of "conservatization," however, has always stuck firmly in my mind.

A Blow Dealt to Johnson

But the tide was increasingly running in the opposite direction. President Johnson's bold policy of continuing the bombings of North Vietnam was not at all perceived as a victory, and the possibility of a serious dollar crisis had surfaced in parallel to declines in the British pound. Then, just when the underpinning of the Johnson administration began to shake at last with the resignation of Defense Secretary and Vietnam War promoter McNamara, Senator McCarthy, who had overnight become the liberals' darling, began hurtling anti-Johnson slogans and dropped the bomb of announcing his Democratic candidacy in the 1968 presidential election. The liberals in and out of the Democratic Party respected McCarthy as an intellectual senator who loved poetry, even while feeling some distance from the none-too-presidential "courage" of the "Don Quixote-like" candidate. But they began to bubble with the possibility of the sudden overthrow of the once seemingly immovable President Johnson.

A Superficial Rebellion

It is now clear, looking back at the opening months of 1968, that as the New Hampshire primary approached that March, the nation was still reeling from the shock of the Tet Offensive that eventually came to be seen as the beginning of the end of the Vietnam War. With that primary came McCarthy's *de facto* victory over Johnson. Through this "miracle" and despite McCarthy's obviously amateurish maneuvers, the Johnson juggernaut began to wobble visibly, then came to a crashing halt when Robert Kennedy, at the time regarded as Johnson's favored rival candidate, finally climbed into the presidential ring after a long hesitation. At first glance, it seemed as though an intense mood of rebellion far from "conservatization" had blanketed Washington.

I had thought that, by chance, perhaps Professor Riesman's strong premonition of "conservatization" may have been due to his frustrations and to his work on the newsletter the *Correspondent*, in which he continued to play a central role. This newsletter took its name from the Committees of Correspondence, the famed organizations of militants from the days of the U.S. independence movement, and was known even in Japan for its unique policy criticisms from the liberal standpoint and as a vehicle for exchanging information. In 1965, however, it ceased publication due to a shortage of staff, and in our letter exchanges prior to meeting, the professor had become very disappointed and jaded about this.

Enough Funerals

This, however, was just a superficial observation that looked only at the limited aspect of affairs. Johnson's speech of March 31, 1968, announcing the partial cessation of the North Vietnam bombings and his own retirement, marked the moment when Professor Riesman's "prediction" became increasingly true with each passing day. Once the shock of Johnson's "final great stage" subsided, the serious struggle for succession in the Democratic Party ironically also led to quarrels among his "liberal colleagues" McCarthy, Kennedy, and also with Vice President Humphrey. This allowed a strengthening of the Republican position blaming Johnson's adjusted Vietnam policy as a failure of the Democratic administration. Furthermore, the aversion the Johnson White House had to the idea of acknowledging defeat in Vietnam became evident. "Conservatization," paradoxically, gained momentum on the steep hill of deep frustration evident in U.S. public opinion and in the egoistic trends in popular sentiment.

The decisive blow came earlier than expected. On the night of April 4, less than a week after Johnson's speech, black leader Martin Luther King, Jr. was suddenly assassinated, and black riots broke out in cities nationwide, starting with Washington. About two months later, on June 6, TV screens across the United States chronicled the assassination of Senator Robert Kennedy. At the Senate press gallery, an American journalist friend of mine, watching the funeral procession on TV, was heard to lament, "No more funerals, and enough of heroes."

Reunion at Stanford

The long, dark, intense year of 1968 closed with the sudden good news of Apollo 8's successful moon orbit, and the new year opened with Nixon's inauguration.

On a cloudy day hovering around 32 degrees, as the new president took the oath of office on a specially built stage in front of the Capitol building, the overall mood was subdued except for Mrs. Nixon's bright salmon-pink overcoat. The new president's first words after inauguration, spelling out the "road to peace" were interrupted by polite applause only nine times, making the whole affair seem rather indifferent and lacking in excitement. In that moment, the leadership of the "world's greatest power" was changed to a more "businesslike" manner.

When the ceremony had finished, while filing out of the boarded press gallery to the exit just below the platform that was surrounded with bulletproof glass, I was thinking how this day had fulfilled Professor Riesman's prediction of "conservatization." Wondering what his take was on America's future from this point, I suddenly found myself wanting to meet him again. After that first meeting, I had not been blessed with much opportunity to fly to Boston, and had only talked with him over the telephone two or three times. In the autumn of 1968, Riesman moved with his wife to the Center for Advanced Studies in the Behavioral Sciences at Stanford University for one year as a visiting professor. As my five-year assignment as a U.S.-based foreign correspondent was coming to a close, it occurred to me that I could wind up my assignment with a stopover in San Francisco to talk with the professor.

When February rolled around, I wrote to Professor Riesman asking for an appointment. To this letter I added a postscript that said, "In the past year I covered events from New Hampshire to Houston, and although I have been blessed with the chance to get to know the United States further, it seems that the more I know about the United States, the more difficult it becomes to write about it." Not a week later, I received a brief but exquisitely kind reply stating, "I am gladly waiting. Will you come by train or by car? If you take the train, I can come pick you up at the station." The letter concluded with:

> I agree with you completely that the more you know the U.S., the more difficult it becomes to write about it. The same problem bothers me now. I have been told to write the preface to the Japanese edition of my book *The Academic Revolution*, which Japan's Simul Press is now translating, but how can I sum up the universities of a country with such infinite variety and diverse sides so concisely to the people of Japan, who live in a completely different environment? It really has me worried.

The Weighty Black Problem

On March 1, when Washington was once again shut in by heavy snow, I flew with my wife and daughters to the West Coast, which was overflowing with dazzling sunlight. The Center for Advanced Studies in the Behavioral Sciences of Stanford University was wrapped in deep green at the top of a slightly elevated hill in the San Francisco suburb of Palo Alto, and rested in tranquility amidst the chirping of various birds. Appearing from behind the Center, Professor Riesman remarked, "You're lucky. It was pouring rain up until yesterday." He seemed to be quite well, but appeared to have aged considerably and unwittingly walked bent over. As he drove me and my family down the hill in an old British car he had brought from Cambridge, the professor murmured, "I want to meet Nathan Hare, but I'm not able to."

Nathan Hare is a black sociologist hailing from Professor Riesman's alma mater of the University of Chicago and is a professor at San Francisco State University. He is a Black

Power leader who continues having trouble with his requests to
establish a course dealing with black issues, and is known for his
confrontations with Japanese language scholar and university
president Hayakawa. He was in Washington, where he was inti-
mate with journalists, until 1968.

During that spring, black students were stepping up their
demands for school reform, starting at San Francisco State and
spreading to Berkeley and Stanford, and it seemed that the
professor had been worrying about how to fend this off. He
seemed lonely as he said:

> I've had a lot of support since talking about taking on the
> building of a Third World lecture beginning with research
> on black, Asia, and Africa issues at a gathering of blacks.
> When I said we also need scholars from Japan, they refused
> and said the Japanese aren't qualified to talk about the
> Third World. They are becoming more radical each day.

Then he laughed, "Washington is so far away."

Nixon the Opportunist

However, after I dropped my family off at home where his wife
was waiting, the professor and I began to talk while enjoying a
delicious lunch at the Stanford Faculty Club, and soon Washington started to seem not such a far-away place. When I opened
the conversation by remarking, "It looks like what you said two
years ago was right after all," Professor Riesman nodded and said:

> The problem is that everybody has become much too
> selfish and conservative. Even the New Left radicals are
> satisfied with the four-way talks in Paris, and they have
> forgotten that the Vietnam War is still going on. But even
> so, it would be a mistake to underestimate Nixon.
>
> I thought that Nixon would win the election from
> the beginning, but he might also go down in history as a
> good president. What I'm saying is, he has the ability as
> a first-class opportunist. For example, in order to stop the

Vietnam War, the man compromised smartly by okaying ABMs (antiballistic missiles) as compensation for the military. So in the end, won't we have eight years of Nixon administration?

His logic and reading of the situation were sharp and without hesitation.

A United States Oblivious of the West

For me, this was a skillfully organized summary of my one-and-a-half-month's experiences in Washington under Nixon. The professor continued to impress me further by lamenting:

> This is the first time in American history that a president has come from the West Coast. Nobody expected this. Americans, or rather American politics itself, doesn't know anything yet about the individual vitality and capabilities of Californians. Of course, I don't know anything, either.
>
> Americans don't know America. . . . The problems that have arisen in America have not been answered fundamentally.

These observations on U.S. politics and society impressed upon me Professor Riesman's strong love of his country and his modesty in not claiming to understand its unlimited potential.

Whether the Japanese can understand American diversity, which Professor Riesman himself has given up trying to understand, remains to be seen. After spending almost five years as a foreign correspondent, I must question whether I have been able to fulfill my duty of portraying the United States accurately, or what kind of effort I must put forth upon my return to Japan.

"I'd like to go to Expo '70 in Osaka, but I don't think I'll have the time," Professor Riesman remarked. He continued, "I'd like for the Japanese to be romanticists when it comes to China."

As I parted ways with the professor, who still didn't conceal his yearning for Japan, I became overwhelmed with a desire to reexamine the deep gulf in U.S.-Japanese relations.   (End)

Proof of the Watershed

Professor Riesman did not foresee Nixon's downfall. But by then, Nixon, who the professor said "has the ability as a first-class opportunist," had finished his great task of reconciling the United States with China.

I was surprised to find Professor Riesman mentioning Governor Reagan of California in August 1967 as one of the "new-type leaders born from among the old conservatives riding on this mood of conservatism." The pluralism inherent in the phrase "Americans don't know America" was explained again by Professor Riesman, and although I met him only twice, I find myself contemplating his enormous graciousness in imparting his knowledge to me.

In seminars delivered in Cambridge circles toward the end of the 1950s, Riesman became known as an antagonist of MIT professor and later presidential adviser Walter Rostow, of whom he said, "That guy's a hillbilly. He's crazy. But he's only a hillbilly who knows the Atlantic." I later came to understand why he had made such a comment, after reading Halberstam's *The Best and the Brightest*. Professor Riesman passed away in May 2002 at the age of ninety-two. I regret that I failed to correspond with him during his later years.

Since meeting him in 1969, U.S. politics have continued to develop within this framework of conservatization even to this day. Though the Democratic Party, particularly the liberals, has forsaken giants like Lippman and Riesman, they have not slipped out of their pathology even after thirty-six years. They have not escaped from the defensive, not even in the election of 2004.

Now I'd like to report the results of a recent poll. A survey by Louis Harris concludes that the differences between the voters who regard themselves as members of the Democratic Party and those who regard themselves as Republicans have lessened over the past thirty years, with the two groups approaching commonality. According to this poll, which was carried in the *Los Angeles Times* on July 21, 2003, during President Nixon's second term in 1973, only 26 percent of voters considered themselves Republican as opposed to 48 percent Democrats and 26 percent independents. During President Reagan's second term in 1988, however, Republicans were catching up, with 31 percent Republicans, 39 percent Democrats, and 25 percent independents. In the year 2002 under President Bush, 31 percent were Republican, 34 percent

Democrats, and 24 percent independents, a difference of three percentage points between Republicans and Democrats.

I believe that the conclusion that American politics reached its watershed in 1968 is inevitable.

Finally, I'd like to touch upon an episode that illustrates the defensiveness of the Democratic Party. It is a fact that, after Hillary Clinton won the senatorial election from New York State in 2002, she strongly and successfully asserted her desire to join the Senate Armed Services Committee and build a close working relationship with military authorities.

In the autumn of 2002 the House and Senate approved a resolution recognizing the need for the use of force in Iraq, and soon afterward, in March 2003, the Iraq War commenced. When America's military strategy came to a temporary standstill because of a sandstorm, Defense Secretary Rumsfeld found himself in the hot seat responding to criticism by the domestic mass media and his own friends among retired officers.

Senator Clinton reportedly supported and encouraged Rumsfeld in secret meetings of the Senate Armed Services Committee. In November 2003, she didn't miss a public relations beat, visiting both Afghanistan and Baghdad to inquire about the health of the soldiers and to share meals with them. Regarding the U.S. policy toward Iraq itself, although the Bush administration had affirmed its cooperation with the United Nations, she maneuvered toward the broad and popular spectrum of patriotic public opinion after 9/11 by going after the hearts and minds of the senior military officials and soldiers over which the Republican Party and Bush administration have demonstrated overwhelming influence. Through such actions she also made a point of erasing the liberal tint of the Democratic Party.

I believe an attitude of defensiveness would have been the hallmark of the Democratic Party even had Senator Clinton chosen to run in 2004, for the party simply has not yet closed its wounds from 1968.

To add one further piece of data, the percentage of workers belonging to labor unions, which normally support the Democratic Party, has continued to decline every year. Union membership peaked at 35.5 percent in 1945, fell between 18 and 20 percent in 1985, dropped to 16.1 percent in 1990, and further dropped to 13.5 percent in 2000.

NINE

The Real Neoconservatives

A Test in Nation-Building

About the time I began writing about LeMay's scorched-earth strategy against Japan and tracing the DNA of the American use of force, the Bush administration, in cooperation with the British government under Tony Blair, began conducting preemptive strikes on Iraq. Were LeMay living, he likely would have envied these strikes. With them, the mightiest standing military in the history of the world, the United States Armed Forces, made maximum use of high-tech weaponry to instantly topple the Hussein regime in "Rumsfeld's War."

This happened without obtaining the consent of the United Nations and by overcoming the opposition of France, Germany, and Russia. This war was fought under the premise that Hussein had used biological and chemical weapons in the past and was hiding weapons of mass destruction. The Bush administration contended that eliminating him would prevent a 9/11-like terrorist attack on the U.S. mainland and light the torch of hope for democratization in the Middle East. U.S. actions constituted the democracy with a gun faithful to the DNA of the use of force.

However, the nation-building that followed the success of regime change became a protracted miscalculation for the Bush administration. I raise the main points of this as follows:

1. The failures of the initial U.S. occupation administration caused delays in handing over power to the new Iraqi government.

2. The restoration of the utility infrastructure such as electric power and water service, destroyed by Rumsfeld's War, was protracted beyond expectation.

3. The forced, complete reorganization of military and police organizations resulted in widespread unemployment primarily among veteran soldiers and civil servants. This, in turn, resulted in a deterioration of security.

4. The former Iraqi Army did not surrender by unit, and the full destruction or confiscation of weapons failed.

5. Guerrilla attacks by approximately five thousand remaining Hussein loyalists and foreign terrorist organizations have increased against U.S., British, and other deployed military forces and Iraqi occupation collaborators.

Since before the outbreak of the war there was continuous disagreement on the basic question of how to deal with the confrontation between the Shiite and Sunni Muslims. Even Deputy Secretary of Defense Wolfowitz, after a visit to Iraq in August 2003, frankly accepted that "the fundamental point was that terrorism had reached a scale completely different from what we had expected up until then." It might also be said that the war had exposed the naiveté in thinking that Rumsfeld's War could be wrapped up with high-tech weapons.

A report compiled in November 2003 by specialists at a leading think-tank, the Rand Corporation, titled *America's Role in Nation-Building: From Germany to Iraq*, points to the inadequate nation-building preparations in Iraq and serves as an example of American self-criticism.[1]

The report cites Japan as a successful example of U.S. occupation, which included cooperation by existing organizations in the country with the Allied occupation resulting in the granting of special Korean War procurements that accelerated Japan's economic recovery.

The overall tone of the report is harsh. The report states that, although the United States was engaged in nation-building six times over the past dozen years (four times under Clinton: Somalia (1992), Haiti (1994), Bosnia (1995), and Kosovo (1998); and twice under Bush: Afghanistan and Iraq), there was institutional resistance within the State Department and the Pentagon. Therefore, these missions were not treated as core business, and the necessary expenditures were not budgeted over the course of the two administrations.

The Rand report concludes that each case of nation-building must always be treated as the first and final task. As the only superpower in the world today, the United States needs to accept nation-building as an inescapable responsibility, and once it recognizes this fact, it can competently prepare for and execute this duty well. Certainly, the United States is being made to pay the price of its insufficient preparation.

A government council of the Iraqi people was installed and power shifted from the Coalition Provisional Authority in July 2004. The United Nations passed a new resolution, and at an Iraq Humanitarian and Reconstruction Assistance meeting, seventy-seven nations elected to donate $37.5 billion. The U.S. Congress also approved a supplementary budget for Iraq amounting to a total of $8.75 billion, almost as much as President Bush had proposed. Later that year Saddam Hussein was captured at last.

Nevertheless, peace has not come. The U.S. forces that were supposed to have been welcomed as liberators became the objects of anti-American demonstrations, and in order to fight the guerrilla war, it became necessary to station more than one hundred thousand U.S. troops long-term. The number of American servicemen killed during the occupation has passed the number killed during the war leading up to it, drawing negative publicity to President Bush's arrival on the deck of the aircraft carrier USS *Lincoln* in a flight jacket on May 1, 2003, and his declaration of victory as he stood there.

Weapons of mass destruction were never found, and it turned out that Bush's sworn friend Prime Minister Blair had used suspicious intelligence before the war began. A rift appeared in the public's support of the Bush administration.

The restoration of Iraqi oil resources has not gotten off the ground, and the cost has exceeded prior expectations. A war budget of $20 billion disappears every year and the reconstruction fund has reached a total of $130 billion. The U.S. government budget deficit was expected to pass $500 billion for fiscal year 2004, approaching the maximum GDP ratio of 5 percent that Bush himself proposed.

The U.S. economy has been bearing the heavy brunt of twin deficits once again. Moreover, in the blink of an eye, the dream of an Israeli and Palestinian roadmap to peace—constructed as a special feature of the new Middle East order following the democratization of Iraq—has also stalled. The price of acting without the United Nations has proved too heavy, and the participation of multinational forces has been limited.

The Democratic presidential candidates running against Bush in 2004 almost uniformly compared the Iraq War to Vietnam, used the word "quagmire," and began to conduct inquiries into the president's responsibility. For the Bush administration, the practice of democracy with a gun has become a burden.

Will Iraq become a second Vietnam? Will the deserts of Iraq become the second Mekong Delta? Despite the lessons taught by the fall of Saigon twenty-eight years ago, will the United States fail in nation-building after its success with regime change? Will the same exit policy that existed in Vietnamization soon be found and the country abandoned? Did President Bush narrowly escape through the same low-altitude flight in his 2004 reelection as he did in 2000? These are the questions thrust upon the United States at present.

As a journalist who witnessed the start and finish of the escalation of the Vietnam War, the defeat that was termed an exit under Vietnamization, the transformation of Nixon as he shook hands with Mao Zedong himself, and the true face of Reagan's strong America, I will try to answer these questions by clarifying the similarities and differences.

Since returning to journalism in May 2002, I have continued to watch the neoconservative groups that have influenced President Bush's Iraq policies since the shock of 9/11, and I have maintained contact with some of them. I will begin with what I have learned from my observations.

Exuberance Revisited

In May 2002 when I visited the United States after an absence of about a year and for the first time since 9/11, the country was experiencing a state of exuberance. I wondered inside whether the nation would be tingling with fear and insecurity, but it had assumed a defiant attitude toward the danger of a second and third terrorist attack, and I felt an air of bracing for the inevitability that further victims would be sacrificed.

People were praising the courage of the passengers who were said to have prevented the fourth suicide terrorist attack, plunging into the cockpit with the immortal words, "Let's roll." The citizens with whom I came in contact at airports, stations, hotels, and restaurants were kinder compared to the year before. I often encountered the goodness of heart I had experienced when I lived in the United States a year before the rifts of the Vietnam War spread across the country. American society seemed to have regained its unity through the traditional spirit of mutual assistance.

In order to tighten security, the government instituted the Patriot Act, allowing arrests on minor unrelated charges and preventative detention—that infringed upon human rights in a manner not seen even during World War II. Those who protested this legislation as unconstitutional were not strong enough to influence Congress and the media.

Bush's policy of using force to confront the foreign ringleaders of terrorist attacks and his confrontation with the so-called "axis of evil" to prevent the development and possession of weapons of mass destruction garnered an unusually high support rate of nearly 70 percent.

An old American journalist colleague of mine since Saigon said, "I want you to know that the use of force to retaliate against terrorism has become a part of daily life in the United States." Aside from Iran and North Korea, one could say that the national consensus toward the elimination of the Hussein regime in Iraq had already exceeded the norm and reached a stage where opinions were divided only with respect to the methods to be employed.

While Russian President Putin had met U.S. expectations by agreeing to a reduction in strategic nuclear weapons, America's victory in the Cold War needed to be confirmed anew. An upsurge in the sentiments that the United States must now bear the burdens of the whole world sprang up everywhere with only differences in shading.

It was a revisit to the starting point of my coverage of the United States exactly thirty-nine years earlier. In December 1964, when I first set foot upon American soil, President Johnson was at the peak of his power. The country was full of exuberance, believing in its ability to serve as the world's policeman. Just two months later Johnson pushed the button of expanding intervention in Vietnam, as has already been described in detail in chapter 8.

In any event, the exuberance that was displayed in openly discussing the option of using force against Iraq was exactly as it had been in the months before the massive American intervention in Vietnam. The sense of mission displayed by President Bush in his 2002 State of the Union Address was almost an exact reincarnation of the rhetoric used by Kennedy and Johnson when Bush declared, "History has called America and our allies to action, and it is both our responsibility and our privilege to fight freedom's fight."

And then there were the new "best and brightest," declaring themselves neoconservatives and even new imperialists. These hawks, based at such magazines as the *Weekly Standard*, *National Review*, and *Commentary*, loudly called for the immediate elimination of Hussein by means of a clean-cut coup d'etat or preemptive strikes including the use of tactical nuclear weapons.

Unlike the Bundy brothers, Rostow, and others who in that time moved Kennedy and Johnson through means of individual persuasion, these people exercise their influence as a group. They are numerous and scattered widely.

The undisputed godfather of neoconservatism, Irving Kristol, noted in the 2003 Summer issue of the *Weekly Standard* that neoconservatism was "not a movement."[2] Certainly, their remarks do not constitute a monolith.

Still, the exuberance in voicing America's responsibility is exactly the same as it was in the 1960s. To me, they appear to be the successors of the "best and brightest."

An Encounter with the Project for the New American Century

The fact is, I had been observing the exuberance of this group since the December 9, 2001 edition of the Sunday *New York Times Magazine*. Under the sardonically titled issue, "*The Year in Ideas: An Encyclopedia of Innovations, Conceptual Leaps, Harebrained Schemes, Cultural Tremors & Hindsight Reckonings That Made a Difference in 2001*," there was a discussion of the activities of a new pro-imperialist organization called the Project for the New American Century (PNAC).

A section titled "American Imperialism, Embraced" describes the PNAC in this way:

> "As we have grown more powerful, we have extended rights to women, to racial minorities, to everyone." These are the values— along with free-market capitalism—that the American empire should stand for, the new imperialists maintain.

The article makes the following four points that further describe the beliefs of the PNAC:

1. The United States does not seek territorial rule but is a new form of liberal imperialism, accepting the creation of a post–Cold War new world order as a positive responsibility as its new "manifest destiny."

2. The national defense budget reduced in the Clinton era needs to be increased, and a motion for a new Marshall Plan should be considered for the future.

3. The United States and its military forces should play an extensive role in the planning of the deployment of U.N. multinational forces and the administration of nation-building in Afghanistan.

4. The Hussein regime in Iraq must be targeted for overthrow.

PNAC Chairman William Kristol responded to the magazine's coverage by commenting that American power today is "the real thing," and that the greatest issue from this point forward is whether this power will be used to fulfill its obligations.

Upon further investigation, I found the PNAC had issued the following main points in a *Statement of Principles* on June 3, 1997, during the Clinton administration:

1. American foreign and defense policy is adrift. Conservatives have criticized the incoherent policies of the Clinton administration. They have also resisted isolationist impulses from within their own ranks. But conservatives have not confidently advanced a strategic vision of America's role in the world. They have not set forth guiding principles for American foreign policy. They have allowed differences over tactics to obscure potential agreement on strategic objectives. And they have not fought for a defense budget that would maintain American security and advance American interests in the new century.

2. Cuts in foreign affairs and defense spending, inattention to the tools of statecraft, and inconstant leadership are making it increasingly difficult to sustain American influence around the world ... We seem to have forgotten the essential elements of the Reagan administration's success: a military that is strong and ready to meet both present and future challenges; a foreign policy that boldly and purposefully promotes American principles abroad; and national leadership that accepts the United States' global responsibilities.

3. Of course, the United States must be prudent in how it exercises its power. But we cannot safely avoid the responsibilities of global leadership or the costs that are associated with its exercise ... The history of the 20th century should have taught us that it is important to shape circumstances before crises emerge, and to meet threats before they become dire.

The 9/11 terrorist attacks of 2001, the Afghan War of 2002, the Iraq War of 2003—it might be said that the neoconservative logic that has moved the Bush administration is displayed here in its entirety. By the end of 2003 twenty-five conservatives including Vice President Dick Cheney, Defense Secretary Rumsfeld, Deputy Defense Secretary Paul Wolfowitz, Vice Presidential Chief of Staff Lewis Libby, and others seated at the center of the Bush administration had lent their signatures to the document.[3]

The PNAC is a nonprofit organization that posts articles by staffers of the *Weekly Standard* and other newspapers every day on its website. It also focuses on influencing general public opinion, the government, and Congress. It also held a seminar titled the "New Citizen Project" that called for strengthening U.S. leadership by reinforcing military might. PNAC was the base for the neoconservatives of the Internet age, the new-edition best and the brightest.

The Responsibilities of the Empire of Liberty

On the first day of my journey, I met the young polemicist Max Boot, whom I introduced in chapter 5. At the time Boot was thirty-three years old and still an opinion page editor at the *Wall Street Journal*. After studying at the

University of California, Berkeley, and later at the University of Chicago, he studied under Paul Kennedy, professor of history at Yale University, historian, and author of the 1987 bestseller *The Rise and Fall of the Great Powers*.

Boot's book, *The Savage Wars of Peace: Small Wars and the Rise of American Power*, begins with an episode in which George Washington decides to establish the U.S. Navy as one of his first acts as president. He does this for the purpose of rescuing American businessmen captured by tribes in North Africa and despite the objections of Congress. Boot explains in full detail the history of America's *small* military actions outside of major wars, including the Boxer Rebellion, the Siberian Intervention, the occupation of Cuba and the Philippines, the Vietnam War, and more recent skirmishes in Bosnia and Kosovo. After identifying successes and failures in which the United States acted in the same manner as the old colonial powers, Boot argues that the United States cannot run away from these small wars that constitute part of its responsibility as the empire of liberty.[4]

The reason I wished to meet Boot was that the PNAC had published a paper of his titled "The Case for American Empire: The most realistic response to terrorism is for America to embrace its imperial role" in the October 15, 2001 website edition of the *Weekly Standard*. I found the following points interesting because they lucidly describe a logic that Americans could easily accept after the shock of 9/11.

1. The imperialistic mission that the contemporary United States has assumed will likely be very different from that of the past. The imperialism of Europe was fought in order to force the "natives" to obey. Americans fight to bring them democracy and rule of law.

2. The United States is independently succeeding in establishing many successful government mechanisms much like the historical successes of General Clay's occupation in Germany and General MacArthur's in Japan. From now on, if the support of the United Nations, several Islamic nations, and important allies is obtained, and if an enlightened international imperialism in which the United States leads the occupation forces is achieved, counterterrorist measures will likely be sharply improved.

3. It would probably be impossible to bury the Hussein regime without an American attack and occupation. Abandoning Iraq after abolishing the Hussein regime would be folly on a par with abandoning Germany after Hitler and Japan after Tojo. The United States ought to honor the same obligations it incurred toward Iraq as it did toward Germany and Japan.

4. The United States has supported tyrannical Arab dictators for many years. However, this is a good opportunity, starting with Iraq, to establish democracy in the Arab world and show that the United States is concerned about the freedoms of the Arab people.

In my interview with him as well, Boot declared that the forced removal of Hussein from power was America's duty.

Of course, he does not know about the Vietnam War. He was clearly optimistic when he stated:

Iraq's military power has fallen, and if the United States shows that it means business, as opposed to the Bush Senior and Clinton administrations that hesitated to attack Baghdad during the Gulf War and later turned a blind eye to the slaughter of the Kurds and the suppression of their uprising, the Iraqi people will also rise up.

And he repeatedly stated:

If the Hussein regime is overthrown, the first democratic Arab state can be established and this would go down in history as lighting the torch of hope in such bases of dictatorial oppression as Saudi Arabia, Jordan, and Mubarak's Egypt. And the Middle East opportunists will start to cooperate so long as the United States doesn't change its decision.

In other words, the overthrow of Hussein was a logical development just as the fight for democracy was during the days of the Vietnam War.

The subject matter was simply the logic of reverse dominos by which the overthrow of communism would be replaced by democracy.

During our meeting, Boot explained to me, a Japanese, that it was America's duty and responsibility to take the post–World War II democratization of Japan as an example and perform the same thing now in the Middle East.

Boot said that it was a grand duty and responsibility of the American empire of liberty as a "liberal, humane empire without territorial ambitions" to produce a new world order in the post-Cold War era and to democratize the entire Middle East and Islamic world. This should even include a preparedness to overthrow the monarchies of Saudi Arabia and Jordan. In this blueprint, Israel was positioned as the only democratic state in the Middle East. Boot also mentioned that the recognition of a Palestinian state was key to the road map hastily hammered out after the Iraq War and conditioned on reform in the Palestinian Authority, excluding Arafat.

The New "Best and the Brightest"

After Boot, I also met with then-PNAC Deputy Director Thomas Donnelly, a research fellow at the American Enterprise Institute for Public Policy Research (AEI). After graduating from American University and continuing his studies at the University of California, Berkeley, and Princeton, Donnelly became an editor of such conservative publications as the *Army Times*, *Defense News*, and the *National Interest*. One of his books mentions the 1987 removal of General Noriega from Panama, his capture by the U.S. Marines and his continuation in custody as an example of the successful achievement of democratization through U.S. military strength.

Donnelly repeated, in essence, what Boot had said. He did mention one thing that concerned me, however: the idea of creating a democratic federation of nations in Asia similar to the North Atlantic Treaty Organization. In his presentation the term "democratic federation" served as the key word. Clearly sympathizing with Taiwan, Donnelly wrote that while Taiwan is a democracy, China is more problematic. Since then, the current Bush administration has drawn a clear line separating itself from the pro-Taiwan position of the neoconservatives. However, it should be recognized that the PNAC is fundamentally pro-Taiwan at its core.

In May 2002, when I inquired about the neoconservative mindset, it was made clear to me that they were still keeping their distance from President Bush. By their logic, 9/11 was the result of the sole-victor United States not executing its responsibilities as an empire. Therefore, they were watching to see if President Bush would take steps toward eliminating Saddam Hussein. This would be taken as a sign that President Bush had reconsidered his statement—made during the presidential campaign of 2000—that a humble posture should be taken in foreign policy and that he opposed taking part in nation-building. It seemed to me that they were cautiously observing President Bush's posture, whether his thinking had been changed by 9/11 or not, and whether he would actually use force or not.

When we met again five months later in October 2002, Boot had changed his opinion of Bush completely. He was now a 100-percent supporter of the president and had moved to the post of Olin Senior Fellow in National Security Studies at the Council on Foreign Relations.

Boot also noted that President Bush had followed the PNAC's recommended path from the time he suggested preemptive strikes in his West Point graduation speech in June. What impressed me were his concerns about the situation after force had been used. He even went so far as to say:

> The biggest issue will be nation-building after the regime
> change. U.S. military participation in Afghanistan is waning, and
> things aren't going well. The problem is that, for some reason,
> the Bush administration adheres to the framework of the United
> Nations in Afghanistan, and furthermore is not growing com-
> petent officials in the military who can perform nation-building
> like Douglas MacArthur in Japan and Lucius Clay in Germany.

Around this time, Boot and the PNAC began to butt heads sharply with the isolationist groups represented by Patrick J. Buchanan. Buchanan was opposed to the PNAC's position from the start, explaining in his 1999 book, *A Republic, Not an Empire*:

> If this Prodigal Nation does not cease its mindless interven-
> tions in quarrels and wars that are not America's concerns, our
> lot will be endless acts of terror until, one day, a weapon of mass
> destruction is detonated on American soil . . . it is a virtual cer-
> tainty that such weapons will be used in an American city if we

do not dump overboard our neo-imperialist foreign policy. . . .
We Americans have been behaving like the Roman Empire. . . .
But if we reject the vision of America as the new Rome, or the
21st century reincarnation of the British Empire, what alternative do we offer? It is this: Foreign policy is the shield of the
republic.

Both conservatives, Boot and Buchanan once joined forces in the fight
against Communism. They shared the belief that the political origins of small
government lie in the nation's traditional values of freedom, equality, and
democracy. But Boot and Buchanan eventually came to butt heads over the
issue of use of force abroad. To me, this clash of approaches manifested itself
in the neoconservatives' rise to prominence in Washington.

In a contribution to the *Wall Street Journal* on December 30, 2002, Boot
dismissed Buchanan and his faction's ideas as "paleoconservatism." He also
noted that realists such as Henry Kissinger, James Baker, and Brent Scowcroft, the traditional advocates of American power and responsibility, had
denounced nation-building as a "mad, hubristic dream," even though they
agreed that Hussein should be fought, removed, and disarmed.

He went on to claim that if America hadn't initiated the occupation
of Iraq and the democratization of the entire Middle East, the fear of 9/11
would never disappear. Moreover, he advocated a return to "Wilsonianism"—the banner of idealism that flew in the post–World War I era with the
establishment of the League of Nations. At the heart of this outlook were
the ideas of racial self-determination and America's policy of championing
its ideals in the world. The United States should not, he said, practice "soft
Wilsonianism," which promotes American ideals without the use of force,
but rather should engage in "hard Wilsonianism." I got the impression that
this exuberance could rise to any height.

Powell's Watchdog

At this point I'd like to introduce a few of the new "best and brightest" men
of the neoconservative groups. Chief among these is former Deputy Secretary of Defense Paul Wolfowitz, the one person who could plausibly be
compared to Bundy and Rostow.

Wolfowitz was born in the home of a Polish Jewish mathematician who taught mathematics at Cornell University. As a student at the University of Chicago, the son was influenced by the teachings of Professor Albert Wohlstetter, who asserted that a nuclear war with the Soviet Union could be won with a missile defense network. In consequence, he became a critic of the U.S.-Soviet détente based on nuclear deterrence. He also studied under Professor Allan Bloom, who is well known for his work *The Closing of the American Mind*. In the Reagan administration Wolfowitz served as head of the Department of State Policy Planning Staff, assistant secretary of state for East Asian and Pacific Affairs. Under George H.W. Bush he served as under secretary of defense for policy and U.S. Ambassador to Indonesia. During the Clinton administration he was Dean and Professor of International Relations at the Paul H. Nitze School of Advanced International Studies (SAIS) of The Johns Hopkins University.

I had attended one of his press conferences at the State Department during the Reagan years. I was surprised at his severe criticism of the Soviet Union, which contrasted with his sober, calm, scholarly appearance. He was in fact an adherent of Reagan's evil empire outlook. He caused much controversy by actually repeatedly proposing a nuclear attack on the Soviet Union in the early 1980s. He continued to build his reputation by arguing that the United States could accomplish its responsibilities as the empire of liberty and build a new world order through the reinforcement of its military strength. It has been said that when President Bush used the term "axis of evil" in his State of the Union Address two decades later in 2002, everyone in Washington recognized Wolfowitz's influence.

Incidentally, while Wolfowitz had criticized the Vietnam War as being too costly, he has also taken the position that Southeast Asia might not have become what it is today had the United States not gone to the lengths it did.[5] The former "best and brightest"—Rusk and Rostow—enunciated this same opinion until the day they died. This, in and of itself, qualifies the new generation as the new "best and brightest."

Having a powerful group of comrades holding important posts within the administration, beginning with Deputy Secretary Wolfowitz, is a special feature of the neoconservative groups. At the forefront of the comrades outside the government is the son of Irving Kristol, PNAC chairman and *Weekly Standard* editor-in-chief William Kristol. A Harvard graduate, he was a former Democratic liberal who taught political science at the John F. Kennedy School of Government and the University of Pennsylvania. In the middle of the 1970s, he joined a group of congressmen, led by the late Washington Senator Henry Jackson, that had become unique in the Democratic Party for its hard-line stance against the Soviet Union. He also met with Richard Perle, who had nurtured these congressmen as close associates and who later became prime members of the present-day PNAC.

After switching to the Republican Party, Kristol served as chief of staff to President Reagan's Secretary of Education, William Bennett. He was also referred to as "Dan Quayle's Brain," at which point he became a weighty figure within neoconservative circles. In 1995 he started the *Weekly Standard* and became a leading player in the PNAC.

While Kristol's photogenic appearance led to his becoming the face of the PNAC, Perle became its behind-the-scenes leader with the nickname "prince of darkness." Perle grew up in Los Angeles. As it happened, the father of one of his high school classmates was Professor Wohlstetter—the proponent of hawkish policies under whom Deputy Defense Secretary Wolfowitz had studied at the University of Chicago—and through this influence he also came to be a staunch hawk.

After earning his master's degree at Princeton, Perle became a member of the American Enterprise Institute and assistant to Senator Jackson. He later became a commanding figure for the neoconservatives and joined the Republican Party. He served as Assistant Secretary of Defense in the Reagan administration. Recently he served as a member of the National Defense Policy Board, a consultative body to Defense Secretary Rumsfeld, and was its chairman until March 2003. He was an early advocate of attacks on Iraq, and to this day he criticizes Secretary of State Powell's restraint in attacking Baghdad during the Persian Gulf War. He declares himself to be Powell's watchdog. Perle has been key in directing President Bush's foreign policy hard line together with Vice President Cheney, Deputy Defense Secretary Wolfowitz, and of course, Rumsfeld.

In addition, Perle's other close associates include: Lewis "Scooter" Libby, chief of staff for the vice president, Eric Edelman, another top assistant to the vice president; National Security Council (NSC) members Elliot Abrams, Robert Joseph, Wayne Downing, and Zalmay Khalilzad; Under Secretary of Defense for Policy Douglas Feith; and Under Secretary of State John Bolton.

As a group, the influence of these neoconservatives in Washington today can be felt more strongly than that of the "best and the brightest" of yesteryear.

A Breakaway Liberal Group

One misses the big picture of the neoconservative groups, however, when looking only at their hard line toward foreign policy. What must not be forgotten is that the neoconservative groups themselves had their origins in the internal debates of the Democratic Party over social policies about forty years ago.

According to the 1993 edition of *Safire's New Political Dictionary*[6] the term "neoconservatism" is defined as "a political philosophy that rejects the utopianism and egalitarianism espoused by liberals, but departs from conservatism by embracing collective insurance and cash payments to the needy; a temperate philosophy, not sharply ideological, that takes modern democratic capitalism to be the best course in most cases."

The term itself was coined by Irving Kristol in an article published in *Public Interest* magazine in 1965. The magazine was edited by Kristol himself and Daniel Bell. It was published by Warren Manshel, with Patrick Moynihan and Seymour Martin Lipset appearing as frequent contributors.

Following are further key points from Safire's description:

> These former liberals were troubled by the failures of Lyndon Johnson's "Great Society" and dismayed at the way political orders throughout the world—especially the social democracies—were becoming statist and simultaneously less stable. When Keynesian economics began to fail to contain inflation, neoconservatives felt the economic basis for social democracy as it has been practiced began to erode.
>
> The last straw for many of the lifelong Democrats was the strident discontent of the youthful counterculture of the sixties, which made liberal elders uncomfortable with the culture that produced it. As it became fashionable all along the political spectrum to be alienated by "big government," that cultural chasm between "new" left and "old" left widened: many of the former liberals could not stomach the permissive attitude toward pornography, homosexuality, and rejection of group responsibility so often espoused by the inheritors of liberalism.
>
> Kristol and "the Public Interest crowd," as the neoconservatives are frequently called, see liberal institutions such as Social

Security to be bulwarks against further socialization. They hope the effect of their movement will be to remove utopian dreams from practical government. To the socialists (who want to center more power in the state), as well as to the "old" conservatives (who want to place more reliance on the individual), the neo-conservatives say that the system the U.S. has now evolved "is certainly not the best of all possible worlds—but the evidence of the twentieth century is quite conclusive that it is the best of all available worlds. That makes it very much worth defending."

The Democratic Party's nomination of George McGovern for president four years after the upheavals of 1968 reportedly became the decisive factor for the breakaway. It is easy to understand why the year of 1968—when the various kinds of counterculture movements peaked along with anti–Vietnam War demonstrations and black protests and riots—turned out to be a watershed for U.S. politics. In short, we have to understand that the neoconservatives reacted against the New Deal big-government liberal politics within the Democratic Party in the late 1960s—that were expressed in Kennedy's New Frontier and Johnson's Great Society—and a process they saw as self-destructive.

Cool Kristol Senior

Irving Kristol was born in 1920 and is still in good health today. Prior to World War II he lived as a young Trotskyite in New York, but he was drafted into the army during the war and afterward became affiliated with the Democratic liberals.

In 1965, however, with the founding of the periodical the *National Interest*, he switched over to the Republican conservatives. He is responsible for converting a large number of former liberal Jewish intellectuals both while teaching economics at New York University and as a fellow at the AEI where he has criticized post–New Deal liberal policies. The tone of his contributions to the opinion page of the *Wall Street Journal* have been characterized as quintessentially neoconservative, and ultimately led to his permanent appointment as a columnist for that paper.

Among the most important liberal Democrat converted to the neoconservative creed by Kristol are Daniel Moynihan—a presidential advisor to

Nixon and Ford and U.S. ambassador to India and the United Nations—and Jeanne Kirkpatrick, President Reagan's ambassador to the United Nations.[7]

Often referred to as the godfather of the neoconservatives, Kristol built the foundation for their present-day influence. Backed by financing from conservative enterprises and the wealthy, he is said to be a valuable broker for conservative think tanks in Washington. Incidentally, one of the leading sponsors of the PNAC and the publisher of the *Weekly Standard* is media tycoon Rupert Murdoch, who emigrated from Australia and became a U.S. citizen in 1985. Murdoch owns the conservative cable television network Fox News, which prominently displays its neoconservative colors in its competition with CNN.

Kristol's wife, Professor Gertrude Himmelfarb, is a prominent scholar of Victorian literature. It has been said that the social gatherings hosted by the couple became places where the Jewish intelligentsia could reaffirm their distance from the liberals.

At this point a description of the special role played by Moynihan, who died in 2003 at the age of seventy-six, is warranted.

In a series of speeches in 1967, Moynihan declared that liberal optimism was causing America to spend money in dangerous efforts to extend the U.S. system abroad. He maintained that liberalism had plunged society into a state of confusion, that social stability is of the utmost importance, and that liberals should not protect black rioters. Statements such as these were later called the starting point of the liberal conversion to the neoconservative camp.

Thus, resistance to the counterculture movement had come to the forefront. In foreign policy, Moynihan's statements—as exemplified by his skepticism of further intervention in Vietnam—were surprisingly isolationist compared to the rhetoric of today's neoconservatives. Having had the opportunity to cover the counterculture movement on location in the late 1960s, I can understand perfectly well the circumstances that spawned this neoconservative.

Moynihan was also influential in the conversion of left-wing student named David Stockman who happened to be lodging at Moynihan's home in 1968 when the latter was a professor of government at Harvard. This is of no small consequence as Stockman went on to serve in the House of Representatives and in 1981, during Reagan's first term, was appointed director of the White House Office of Management and Budget. At the youthful age of thirty-four he implemented a bold program of supply-side economics (later dubbed "Reaganomics"). The key features of this program were deregulation, large tax cuts, a balanced budget, and private-enterprise activity. These were meant to expand investments, supply, and consumption, while deterring inflation and achieving economic growth.

Stockman earned a place in American history by transforming economic policies that had been followed since the time of the New Deal. The reason these achievements are still considered highlights of the Reagan era were presented in a sharp analysis by the late Takemoto Iinuma of the *Yomiuri Shimbun* in a book titled *Amerika: Shinhoshushugi no Jidai* [America: The Age of Neoconservatism].[8] Iinuma's book described the irony of the conversion of the Moynihan-Stockman duo. Incidentally, in my work as a journalist I shared assignments with Iinuma in both Bangkok and Washington.

The Shadow of Manifest Destiny

It must not be forgotten, of course, that the anti-Communist, anti-left, and anti-liberal Moynihan staunchly opposed the liberalization of his former Democratic colleagues with the same passionate rebellion against leftism first expressed by Irving Kristol when he abandoned Trotskyism. I believe the statements and actions of the neoconservatives on foreign and defense policy since the PNAC's formation in 1997 are precisely understood as an extension of such anti-Communism.

Therefore, it seems to me that the root of the neoconservative's strong, energetic commitment to America's responsibilities as the empire of liberty can be found in their frustration over a sense of diplomatic drift following the U.S. victory in the Cold War. This is evidenced in the statements of Perle, Wolfowitz, the younger Kristol, and others who left the liberal wing of the Democratic Party and shared Henry Jackson's intense anti-Soviet, anti-Communist, and anti-détente viewpoints while assembling under Kristol senior. They finally found a cause where they could release their accumulated frustrations and a sense of mission in the post-9/11 world.

Dissatisfied with George H.W. Bush's hesitation to occupy Baghdad, the neoconservatives took explosive advantage of the 9/11 attack on post–Cold War America. With the nation's perception of itself as the superpower shaken, the younger Bush plunged into the Iraq War.

Against that backdrop, just as the best and the brightest of the Vietnam era declared that they "understood the historic link-up between our traditions and those in the underdeveloped world," the neoconservatives are repeating history with their intense passion for accelerating armed intervention in the War on Terror.

Still further in the background, the concept of Manifest Destiny asserts itself. Recall the statement, "We are the nation of human progress, and who will, what can, set limits to our onward march? Providence is with us, and no earthly power can . . ." from chapter 5.

In a 1976 article titled "Adam Smith and the Spirit of Capitalism," Irving Kristol noted:

> We certainly do not perceive George Washington as a proto-
> typical revolutionary hero. Earlier generations of Americans
> were able to do so—but that was before the intellectual currents
> of modernity washed over our traditional American pieties. In
> comparison to the French Revolution, the American Revolution
> has come to seem a parochial and rather dull event. This, despite
> the fact that the American Revolution was successful—realizing
> the purposes of the revolutionaries and establishing a durable
> political regime—while the French Revolution was a resounding
> failure, devouring its own children and leading to an imperial
> despotism, followed by an eventual restoration of the monarchy.

In this fashion, the sentiment that "we are number one," of continual reverence for the American Revolution has calmed down considerably.[9]

It would thus seem that a confrontation is impending between two groups that at one time had cooperated with one another, the paleoconservative isolationists (to use Boot's term)—represented by Patrick Buchanan's *American Conservatism* magazine—and the libertarian groups of the Reagan and Bush Senior years. The latter tend to center around the Cato Institute, which advocates small government and is named for the ancient Roman Senator Cato who trumpeted republicanism. Reportedly there were voices within the Cato group who supported the Democratic candidate Howard Dean in the 2004 presidential primaries.

It appears that such conservatives—who shun a tough foreign intervention posture while opposing the Bush administration's increasing budget deficit from the war in Iraq, Medicare, and other costs—feel very strongly that the neocon groups must not be allowed to stand by Irving Kristol's passive observation that nothing can be done about the deficit for the time being.

Accordingly, while the neoconservative groups are anti-liberal and anti-counterculture, they are clearly differentiated from the traditional conservatives who subscribe to small government in domestic politics and limited isolationism and noninterference in foreign policy. I suggest that they are best thought of as naive adherents to the path of Manifest Destiny.

On this point, however, I must also report the fact that Irving Kristol himself made some significant remarks in an article titled "The Neoconservative Persuasion" in the August 25, 2003 edition of the *Weekly Standard,* in which he declared that neoconservatism is not a movement.

In this context he emphasized that America's growing military power was not intentional:

> During the fifty years after World War II, while Europe was at peace and the Soviet Union largely relied on surrogates to do its fighting, the United States was involved in a whole series of wars: the Korean War, the Vietnam War, the Gulf War, the Kosovo conflict, the Afghan War, and the Iraq War. The result was that our military spending expanded more or less in line with our economic growth, while Europe's democracies cut back their military spending in favor of social welfare programs. The Soviet Union spent profusely but wastefully, so that its military collapsed along with its economy. Suddenly, after two decades during which "imperial decline" and "imperial overstretch" were the academic and journalistic watchwords, the United States emerged as uniquely powerful. The "magic" of compound interest over half a century had its effect on our military budget, as did the cumulative scientific and technological research of our armed forces.

Following this, he coolly analyzes the current neoconservative outlook by sarcastically adding:

> With power come responsibilities, whether sought or not, whether welcome or not. And it is a fact that if you have the kind of power we now have, either you will find opportunities to use it, or the world will discover them for you. The older, tra-

ditional elements in the Republican Party have difficulty coming to terms with this new reality in foreign affairs, just as they cannot reconcile economic conservatism with social and cultural conservatism. But by one of those accidents historians ponder, our current president and his administration turn out to be quite at home in this new political environment, although it is clear they did not anticipate this role any more than their party as a whole did. As a result, neoconservatism began enjoying a second life, at a time when its obituaries were still being published.

In other words, the senior Kristol finds commitment to foreign action to be interesting as a kind of inescapable destiny while the young second-generation neoconservatives loudly proclaim it as a responsibility of the empire of liberty. I believe this is not a convincing principle of foreign interference but rather a logic that leaves open the possibility of a return to Moynihan-style isolationism when circumstances change.

I believe we should remember that during the 2000 campaign and until the events of 9/11, President Bush himself recited the unilateralist rhetoric of noninterference overseas. I think this is an important sign that predicts the direction of America's troublesome nation-building. It is a sign that the neoconservative groups themselves are riding on the fatalism of the senior Kristol and have already begun to explore exits.

TEN

Counterattack and Exit

The President's Tug of War

The new "best and brightest" are not omnipotent, of course. Although the basic essence of this "non-movement" has materialized, the workings of internal division and confrontation can be seen. Still, shades of their power are evident in the nation-building currently under way in Iraq, even though that effort hasn't gone particularly well. I believe their influence can be seen in the beginnings of a groping for an exit as learned from the Vietnam experience.

When his administration came to power, President Bush encouraged a tug of war regarding foreign policy between the traditional Republican internationalists typified by Brent Scowcroft, national security advisor to the senior Bush and the neoconservative groups led by Richard Perle.

Standing with Scowcroft are such notables as George H.W. Bush; former Secretaries of State Kissinger, Baker, and Powell; former State Department Policy Planning Director Richard Haass; former Deputy Secretary of State Richard Armitage; career diplomat and former Under Secretary of State Mark Grossman; former CIA Director and Clinton administration holdover George Tenet; and former U.S. Ambassador to the United Nations John Negroponte.

Secretary of State Condoleezza Rice, noted for her close working relationship with President Bush, began her foreign-policy career as a protégé of her former boss Scowcroft, and with his recommendation took her first White House post at the start of the senior Bush's administration. As with Stephen Hadley, assistant to the president for national security affairs, however, she occasionally wavers between the neoconservatives and the Scowcroft-Powell camp. As a true symbol of America's multiracial power, she was appointed by President Bush to a high position of trust and served as a moderator in both speech and conduct in the facilitation of compromise between the hardline Rumsfeld and the more liberal Powell. This was an indicator of the tug of war within the Bush administration.

Rice was born in 1954 in Birmingham, Alabama, a city which was enormously prominent in Dr. Martin Luther King, Jr.'s battles against segregation and discrimination. After receiving her doctorate at the University of Denver and serving as professor of political science at Stanford, she entered the White House as director of Soviet and East European Affairs—a star student and an example of multiracial achievement who climbed the ladder of the power elite. A heavy responsibility rests on her shoulders.

Behind her and the president stands White House Deputy Chief of Staff Karl Rove, President Bush's political mentor since his days as Governor of Texas, who was granted the authority to poke his nose into everything in order to preserve, buoy, and reelect Bush. Rove's influence has been as strong as Rice's in the tug of war between the neoconservatives and the Scowcroft camp, mainly because so much foreign policy has passed through his hands, including the Iraq War.

In 2004, Rove reportedly drew up the blueprints for the complete Republican sweep, not only reelecting Bush but also maintaining Republican control of both houses of Congress, maintaining a majority of the fifty state governors and gaining majorities in most state legislatures.

When watching how the Bush administration deals with foreign policy, particularly the nation-building of Iraq, the double influences of Rice and Rove must not be forgotten.

Early to Bed, Early to Rise

This is a good time to talk about President Bush's personal character. As a successor in the Bush dynasty, he received his education at Phillips Academy, Yale, and Harvard Business School. On campus, however, he never lost his Texas ways. It is said that he was frank and popular. A C-student, he regarded himself as not intellectual. Others knew him as someone with a keen memory who remembered the names of those he had met only once.

He was a nonpolitical student uninvolved with the anti–Vietnam War movement that had blanketed the campuses during that period, nor did he take part in elitist studies. Rather, he spent most of his time organizing parties and playing sports.

In 2002 in the midst of the nationwide panic immediately following 9/11, his Texas-cowboy style of speech, with its track-meet organizer optimism, easy-to-understand language, and short sentences, invested him with a sense of reliability that got across to voters. His reception among the general population was said to be very warm and supportive. For this second-generation president—who had had his share of troubles in the 2000 election and until 9/11 had been called the 50 percent president—this connection with the public became the chance to gather and exploit popular opinion. The fact that 75 percent of the black population supported him after his post-9/11 speeches, when he had only managed to garner 8 percent of their vote during the 2000 election, is proof of his ability to speak a language reassuring to Americans.

As for Bush's personality as a leader who employed his one chance efficiently, domestic public opinion is widely divided. However, I must report that long-time Washington political pros who transcend partisan politics appreciate the leadership abilities he demonstrated in his successful post-9/11 turnabout, regardless of their positions on Bush's domestic and foreign policies, including the Iraq War.

He goes to bed by ten at night at the latest and wakes up at five. He keeps in shape through jogging and other exercise, and since conquering alcoholism at the age of forty-two with the help of his wife, Laura, he has refrained from all alcohol. With Laura, who prefers conservative clothing and has a distaste for elaborate accessories, he limits his participation in social functions to the bare minimum. Upon marriage he converted from the Bush family's traditional Episcopal Church to his wife's Methodist Church. He is a pious believer who has not missed a Sunday worship service. It is said that every morning he reads aloud a prayer by the World War I–era Scottish Reverend Oswald Chambers.

It is difficult to find a historical precedent for such a president who was reliable and steady enough to unite the people in his administration. The discipline of the Bush White House in controlling leaks offers a powerful contrast to that of former President Clinton. A former senior Reagan administration official told me that there is no comparison even to the Reagan era, during which three factions, including one centered on Nancy Reagan, continuously and half openly fought with each other.

While starting the Iraq War after 9/11—and thus siding with neoconservative allies Cheney and Rumsfeld who had also signed the PNAC declaration—Bush also used Secretary of State Powell to the maximum. He did this even though the former general, who as the deputy commander of an infantry battalion in Vietnam, had differing opinions regarding the need for an exit strategy when using force. Bush maneuvered Powell to defend the invasion at the United Nations. The likes of this were seen in neither the Reagan nor the senior Bush administrations. Clearly, George W. Bush's ability to balance individual confidences is extraordinary.

On the other hand, there are also voices in Washington that express worry about the rigidness often found in those who have conquered alcoholism, suggesting that actions and decisions of such people may become dogmatic. This, of course, comes from the Democrats who oppose him.

Yet while the miscalculations regarding nation-building in Iraq have become clear as of the end of 2003, there is no sign of a rebellion within the Republican Party similar to Senator McCarthy's opposition to Johnson during the Vietnam War. To the contrary, reelection campaign donations on an unprecedented scale, exceeding $1 billion, were collected by supporters nationwide a year prior to the 2004 election. When forecasting the direction of the tug of war between the neoconservative groups and the Scowcroft camp, it is necessary to grasp precisely the ability of this early-to-bed, early-to-rise president.

Comparison with the Berlin Airlift

President Bush delivered an important speech on November 9, 2003. In his address commemorating the twentieth anniversary of Washington's National Endowment for Democracy, he stated, "The establishment of a free Iraq at the heart of the Middle East will be a watershed event in the global democratic revolution."

He compared nation-building in Iraq, exposed to attacks by former

Saddam loyalists and terrorists, to the trials of the Berlin Airlift and Greek Civil War immediately following World War II. On top of this, he declared that "the strength and will of free peoples are now being tested before a watching world. And we will meet this test."

To me, the speech was so thoroughly colored by neoconservative ideas that I thought it could have been drafted by Max Boot.

Bush went on to praise a June 1982 speech by then-President Reagan denouncing the evil empire of the former Soviet Union. Reagan delivered this highly lauded speech, in which he predicted the fall of communism, before the British Parliament. Bush declared his determination to extend the worldwide democratization that Reagan had initiated based on the efforts of more than two hundred years of U.S. democracy. Beginning with an explanation of how nobody had believed that Japan and Nazi Germany would be reborn as democratic nations following World War II, he appealed for a showdown on what he called the front line in the fight against oppression in Cuba, Burma, North Korea, and Zimbabwe. And in a warning to China, he added "We must be staunch in our conviction that freedom is not the sole prerogative of a lucky few, but the inalienable and universal right of all human beings."

Bush's speech reflected the neoconservatives' insistence that failure to democratize Iraq will extinguish the hope of millions in the Middle East for democracy and their view that such a democratic breakthrough is compatible with Islamic traditions. In those respects, the speech also served as a warning signal to Iran and Syria.

Bush asked Americans for patience in understanding the increasing casualties and costs associated with nation-building in Iraq, and declared his intention to fight for an "uncompromising breakthrough" while running for reelection in 2004.

In this way will President Bush march along with the powerful new "best and brightest" to a tragic second Vietnam in Iraq? Will he suffer the same fate as fellow Texan Lyndon Johnson? It is not beyond the realm of possibility.

It is my position, however, that a simple analogy with Vietnam must be avoided. This uncompromising breakthrough strategy has been appropriately calculated, and it cannot be said that its achievement is impossible. The chances that U.S. public opinion would allow that are by no means low.

The Bush administration or the neoconservatives themselves, cannot deny that they are learning from the failure in Vietnam, because the self-interests inherent in Nixon's exit strategy, which achieved "exit with honor" through "Vietnamization," are not coming into view in Iraq.

The fact that Iraq and Vietnam cannot be directly compared has already been discussed in chapter 9. There are, in addition, three further points illustrating that they are more unlike than alike.

First, certain conditions in which Johnson found himself have changed. The United States had to fight a guerilla war in the jungles of Vietnam while being constrained by the need for nuclear coexistence with the Soviet Union. With the U.S. victory in the Cold War, the overwhelming predominance of American military has been established. Moreover, the projection of America's sole-victor power in the Afghan and Iraq Wars is centered in its economics and society.

In addition, both Russia and China are cooperating in the War on Terror. Even Vietnam is asking for port calls by the U.S. Seventh Fleet. Hussein's remaining loyalists have no assistance available to them such as the North Vietnamese once received from the Soviet Union or China to compensate for the damage caused by American bombing. The Special Forces who were utilized as a last resort on the battlefields of Vietnam have played an active and crucial part in Afghanistan and Hussein's seizure. It is a historical irony that America's former enemies are now cooperating with it, and that formerly last-resort special forces are now used openly and actively.

The Existence of the Liberal Hawks

A second important fact is that, while the Iraq war has not been without its share of vocal protests, powerful antiwar demonstrations such as those that characterized the Vietnam War have not erupted in the United States. In September 2002, when I was visiting Washington, a protest occurred in front of Vice President Cheney's official residence. For me, who covered the intense antiwar demonstrations at the end of the 1960s, it was a disappointing demonstration that lacked any real force. It felt as though the usual anti-globalization demonstrations against the International Monetary Foundation/World Bank summit, which had opened in Washington at exactly that same time, had just moved on to a different battlefield.

Around the same time, three liberal Democratic congressmen who arrived in Baghdad appeared on television and said that President Bush was exaggerating the threat posed by Iraq. Earlier, during the Vietnam War,

Hanoi had invited American journalists to locations in North Vietnam that had been bombed by the United States and asked them to report on the meaningless degree of damage. By using this same tactic, it was readily apparent that Hussein had studied the former North Vietnamese leaders who had succeeded in creating a second front in the form of antiwar movements at home in the United States.

Hussein's expectations, however, were to be frustrated, because the coverage in the next day's morning newspapers was very light, and Richard Gephardt, a Democrat and then House minority leader, issued a statement of sharp disagreement with the three congressmen. Additionally, nothing comparable to the black-power movement, which helped give the protests of the 1960s their militant edge, could now be found in the anti-Bush protests. In fact, there were many blacks on the police forces controlling the demonstrations. At the same time there was no draft system to hasten young men into the war as there had been in the past.

A December 8, 2002 *New York Times Magazine* article titled "The Liberal Quandary Over Iraq" by liberal author George Packer explained these factors clearly. In his discussion, Packer reports that while liberal Democratic groups had constituted the leadership of the Vietnam-era antiwar movement, today "liberal hawks," advocating the use of force against Iraq, now exist on the fringes of the left-wing camps themselves.[1]

This so-called liberal hawk camp distinguishes itself from Noam Chomsky and others who are still opposed to any use of force by the United States, and recognizes the humane employment of American military might to protect human rights and prevent genocide.

In 1992 the so-called Bosnia intervention by NATO military force relieved the oppression of Bosnian Muslims by the Serbs. This was the beginning of a continuing protection of ethnic minorities and abolition of discrimination against women in Haiti, East Timor, Kosovo, and Afghanistan. Advocates of these actions express appreciation for the use of military force to preserve human rights.

In other words, the military intervention in Iraq is judged to be of the same kind that toppled the militarism of the Nazis and Japan, as opposed to Vietnam where the military was used to prop up a puppet regime. Even an official of Human Rights Watch, originally a liberally oriented group active at the United Nations, said around the same time that, as in Bosnia and Kosovo, U.S. military force is necessary in order to truly preserve human rights.

According to Max Boot, whom we met in a previous chapter, the deployment of USAF-led NATO forces without the approval of the U.N. Security Council to preserve human rights was the only commendable achievement of the Clinton administration, and it is his view the approximately 5,500 American servicemen now stationed as the core of the NATO force are the solution to the Kosovo crisis. I believe this illustrates the connection between the "liberal hawks" and the neocons.

The Deep Psychology of Counterattack

A third important fact is that, after the deep shock of 9/11, strong support for Bush took root in the United States. In short, the public would not dare abandon its support of preemptive strikes and the Bush Doctrine to eliminate the threat of Hussein deploying weapons of mass destruction. In September 2003, both houses of Congress also granted President Bush the authority to make the final decision on the use of force, a United Nations resolution notwithstanding. All the congressional members battling for the Democratic Party presidential nomination, with the exception of former Vermont Governor Howard Dean, who had no seat in Congress, approved the resolution. Those included rumored 2004 presidential candidate Senator Hillary Clinton and Richard Gephardt, the liberal House minority leader.

I was contemplating the question of why the Bush alternative, which appeared so self-righteous, was enjoying so much domestic support in the United States as I toured the country. For three weeks starting in mid-September 2002 I traveled from Southern California, where I visited Los Angeles and the Nixon Library, to New York, Washington, and Boston, making special stops at the Mayflower landing site at Plymouth and Harvard University in Cambridge.

In encountering the variety of people planted across this vast expanse and in keeping up with newspapers and television every day, I noticed that President Bush's logic in explaining that America had no choice but to live in the midst of fear, and his argument that preemptive strikes would be indispensable in ensuring the safety of the United States, was strangely persuasive.

Indeed, his argument, that ensuring one's own safety is one's own responsibility, reaches to the core feelings of many Americans. Police stations do not stand on every corner, and police cars are often not there to respond immediately. The sense of fear that I felt when wondering if just purchasing a cell phone in Los Angeles at the start of a trip would afford ample protection is still fresh in my mind. I was also aware that gun control is hardly practiced in this country. I felt that I was able to see the reason why the Second Amendment was so revered. My impression grew that the United States was a country born with the DNA of the use of force which encouraged the possession of arms.

One day later I was in suburban Washington, D.C., which was at that moment in a state of panic. Just a day after it happened, I stood not far from the spot where a sniper shooting had proven to be the first of a series that terrified the nation's capital for weeks. I was waiting for a friend to come pick me up in the parking lot of a Metro station in order to go to the new National Archives building near the University of Maryland. Thinking that I, too, might perhaps be targeted, I realized how great a shock it must be for Americans—unlike me, a visitor—to constantly feel the stress of having to preserve their own safety since 9/11.

In hearing the accounts of that incident directly from Americans in different walks of life, I understood the shocking scale on which the economic and political centers of New York and Washington were attacked simultaneously. This was, in fact, the first attack on the U.S. mainland since the British Marines landed in Washington and burned the White House in the War of 1812. There were many who had truly felt that death was on their doorstep, especially when they had heard that the fourth hijacked jet was still flying. In Washington and Boston people feared they might come under nuclear attack. It is said that almost everyone talked with relatives or best friends over the telephone.

Conversely, the terror of 9/11 tore asunder the order and rules of a gun society that had become accustomed to protecting itself. At the outset of the still-unsolved anthrax incident and the serial sniper killings, people at first wondered if these were acts of terrorism, and I could sense the cycle of fear continuing to drag the nation on silently and deeply.

The hard line taken by President Bush in quickly wanting to remove the danger of the use of weapons of mass destruction by the Hussein regime was supported by the majority of ordinary citizens who had experienced 9/11. My friend told me he wanted me to understand precisely the sense of retaliation against this fear, which he himself had experienced, and the deep psychology of Americans who wish to prevent a recurrence. Considering this point, I believe that 9/11 had provoked America as a democracy with a gun, and caused it to launch a counterattack. Fear had lit the fuse of counterattack existing in the DNA of the use of force

As for the weapons of mass destruction—which the Bush administration had used as its justification for going to war and even though none were found—a Democratic strategist stated in November 2003 that the issue could not be used as a criticism of Bush in the election since a poll indicated that public opinion was still deeply entrenched. Moreover Bush's assertion that Hussein was now gone could not be disputed. It would be better to think that the deep psychology of this counterattack won't waver even if the nation-building gets bogged down. The uncompromising breakthrough strategy of the Bush administration is built on just such a premise and was an important highlight of the 2004 presidential election.

During the middle of my trip, I came across a joint *USA Today*/CNN/Gallup Poll reporting that 58 percent of women polled supported the introduction of U.S. ground troops to overthrow Hussein. Support among men was 56 percent, a reversal from the Gulf War of 1991, when 45 percent of women and 67 percent of men supported the attack.

The reasons for these "surprising results," according to *USA Today*, were the great uneasiness about homeland security since 9/11, a desire to protect children from terrorism by biological and chemical weapons, and the belief from the experience in Afghanistan that there would be few U.S. casualties. On top of this, the paper explained that President Bush had gained the trust of women by explaining that the effort was being undertaken to protect America's children. In addition, the public liked Bush for his consistent and sincere statements.

In a November 2003 public opinion survey conducted by the conservative Fox News, 44 percent of respondents said that the military's response to the ongoing violence in Iraq had "not been aggressive enough," 35 percent said it was "about right," and 11 percent responded that it was "too aggressive."

The political significance of this cannot be overstated. It is the reason the Democratic Party stooped to passing a congressional resolution in 2002 supporting the use of force and that antiwar demonstrations never really took off. I presume that the psychological makeup of the support for this counterattack won't waver, and it remains to be seen if a tug of war will result from casualties and increased costs.

A Matter of Expediency or Theology?

> We are ready. We're prepared ... should we be forced to
> act ... you will be fighting not to conquer anybody, but to liber-
> ate people.

President Bush opened the New Year on January 3, 2003, with these words before an audience of soldiers at Fort Hood in his home state of Texas.

Had the neoconservatives pulled him along this far? Surrounded by such deep emotions, that same month I once again met with my neoconservative friends in Washington and New York.

Naturally, they were bullish. They didn't need the support of the United Nations. On the contrary, they took the attitude that the participation of the United Nations wasn't needed in the democratization of Iraq after the regime change. They also felt the need to keep the option of using force against the remaining "axis of evil" countries, Iran and North Korea.

However, in July 2003 following the onset of the Iraq War, when I revisited them in order to collect material for this book, their remarks had changed subtly, and they did not seem so confident. Those same people with whom I had earlier spoken told me frankly that although Rumsfeld's War had brought about regime change by making maximum utilization of high-tech weapons, they were having a hard time dealing with the subsequent nation-building. The protracted stationing of the 140,000 U.S. troops could no longer be avoided, and nine National Guard brigades (about forty-four thousand people) had been called up to provide replacements and maintain morale. One person told me honestly, "I fully understand now that the occupation of Japan was a special case."

They had changed their tune, saying that for the time being, even though the military might actually be readied to use against North Korea, it would be theoretically impossible. At that point the only actions possible would be the maritime interception of North Korean missiles and/or drug exports.

And wouldn't you know it: immediately after I returned to Japan, Boot contributed a piece titled "America and the U.N.: Together Again?" to the opinion page of the *New York Times* on August 3, 2003, in which he wrote, "If another United Nations resolution could reduce the strain on American forces and wallets, why not seek it?"[2]

I think that the logic Boot shows in this contribution is important when reading the developments of the future. It is a logic that cannot be overlooked by Japan in its decision to deploy its Self-Defense Forces. Allow me to explain in more detail.

Boot develops the following assertions:

The rebuilding of Iraq is exposing an interesting rift on the political right: is "unilateralism" a matter of expediency or theology?

The United States is finding itself short of soldiers and money as it tries to bring democracy and stability to Iraq. It has deployed nearly 150,000 soldiers, many of whom have been there since last year, and some are openly grumbling that they want to go home. But given the demands of deployments in Afghanistan, Kosovo, Bosnia, South Korea and elsewhere, there are few if any replacement units available.

There is also not much money available to cover reconstruction efforts that will most likely cost more than $100 billion. With the United States spending almost $4 billion a month on its Iraqi military operations, and with this year's budget deficit ballooning to more than $450 billion, neither the Bush administration nor Congress is eager to tap the Treasury for more reconstruction aid.

The White House would love to get more help, financial and military, from our allies, but so far they are coming up with only a pittance. There are just thirteen thousand non-American soldiers in Iraq, most of them British. A Polish-led polyglot division of nine thousand more is set to arrive in September. But potential major contributors like Egypt, Germany, India, Pakistan, Russia and Turkey—to say nothing of France—have hinted they would help only if the occupation carried more of a United Nations imprimatur.

Are they serious? Who knows? They may not want to get involved at any price as long as a nasty guerrilla war is going on. But there's no harm in testing their sincerity. If another United Nations resolution could reduce the strain on American forces and wallets, why not seek it? We have worked well with the

United Nations in Bosnia, Kosovo, Afghanistan and many other places. Why not in Iraq?

The only serious argument against the idea is that the occupation would be hindered by having to deal with tangled lines of authority and conflicting agendas. This is a legitimate worry, but it's hard to believe that administrative efficiency is such an overwhelming consideration when you consider that the Polish-led division will field troops from more than a dozen countries.... A United Nations presence might even help if it delivered more Arabic speakers and experts familiar with nation-building efforts. Yes, it might entail some loss of American control ... (but) the vast bulk of military forces would still be from America—at the end of the day, it would still call the shots. Another Security Council resolution would change the perception of American dominance more than the reality.

There was nothing wrong with President Bush's decision to invade Iraq without United Nations blessing. President Bill Clinton and NATO did the same thing in Kosovo in 1999. The issue of whether to involve the United Nations in a particular problem should be based on pragmatic considerations: does it help or hurt in achieving America's foreign policy objectives?

Unfortunately, an excess of emotion in our politics has long made it hard to think rationally about this issue. Many on the left automatically assume that the United Nations is always the solution, while many on the right make the equally knee-jerk assumption that it is always the problem.

The reality is that the United Nations, while hardly a panacea, has its uses, especially in a place like Liberia where America has no intention of taking on the long-term task of nation-building. It's too soon to know whether Iraq falls into this category. Much will depend on negotiations over what form an additional Security Council resolution might take. But conservatives shouldn't try to short-circuit this process by ruling out United Nations involvement no matter what. The primary objective should be to help Iraq and help America, not to hurt the United Nations.

The quotation is long, but the frank logic developed by this young neo-conservative is important in understanding how the neoconservatives will try to overcome this current situation, which increasingly resembles the quagmire of nation-building in Vietnam.

It was immediately after the appearance of this Boot article that President Bush began his approach to the United Nation in quest of a new resolution in response to the advice of Secretary of State Powell.

Expedient Unilateralism

Boot provided a clear-cut solution to the problem of simultaneously defending unilateralism and resorting to the United Nations. We have to pay attention to the logic making clear that the United States had rushed into regime change, bypassing the United Nations not as a matter of "theology" but of "expediency." The logic of expediency would allow going back to the United Nations again, since U.S. troops and finances are insufficient for Iraqi reconstruction. I think the suggestion of consideration of a Liberia-type solution, leaving everything in the hands of the United Nations as one of the long-term options, is important.

There is also a conspicuous lack of optimism in this article, which includes references to cracks within the conservative camp about the nature of unilateralism. The reduced brashness was clear between my two meetings with Boot in May and October 2002.

When I debated the definition of unilateralism with him during our first meeting in May 2002, he adhered strongly to this expedient unilateralist principle. It involved a deft resourcefulness.

That is to say, before this he had highly valued Nixon's achievement of an honorable withdrawal from Vietnam that was justified by a dramatic reconciliation with China. Further, he described his adherence to unilateralism by explaining that even if neoconservatives oppose isolationists like Pat Buchanan, they need not reject unilateralism. The transformation of U.S. foreign policy during the Nixon era was correct in the sense of having departed from the dreamy multilateralism of the liberals. Boot also believed in the same way that the costs associated with attacking Iraq were important. He added that the United States had made a mistake in its unilateralism by hesitating to use force, and the terrorist attacks of 9/11 were a direct result of this.

In other words, he had properly developed his two-pronged logic. He sometimes stressed the egoism displayed in Nixon's motto of "No more American blood" and commitment to the idea that the number one national interest of the United States was to win the multilateral competition. At other times he stressed the responsibilities of the empire of liberty. Sometimes he even used these phrases together.

In fact, since 9/11 the unilateralism the Bush administration pushed after its inauguration quickly evolved into an exuberant embrace of the responsibilities of the empire of liberty.

In the fiscal year 2001, the United States suddenly paid the United Nations $582 million in late dues, which had been long shelved. It also appointed an ambassador to its vacant seat and ceased to question Pakistani and Indian nuclear developments, lifting its sanctions against those countries. Similarly the United States reversed its positions on Taiwan and China, reducing its criticism of China on human rights and achieving cooperation with Chinese intelligence services in sharing counterterrorism information. In 2002 former Chinese President Jiang Zemin was invited to Bush's Texas ranch. At this meeting Bush committed himself to opposition to Taiwanese independence, and the two nations since seem to have entered a honeymoon period.

However, the Bush administration's policies for protecting U.S. national interests and preserving U.S. freedom of action shows an unchanging indifference toward multilateralism. This is demonstrated by its secession from the Kyoto Protocol, withdrawal of support for the Clinton-signed treaty establishing the International Criminal Court, its unilateral withdrawal from the antiballistic missile treaty, the imposition and lifting of steel import restrictions based on local electoral campaign strategies, and the signing of an agricultural protection program that surprised even the Democrats. The neoconservatives cannot reject this expedient unilateralism.

A Look at Self-Centeredness

Accordingly, it seems to me that the type of unilateralism actually espoused by the neoconservatives can be seen in the stance once taken by Nixon toward localizing the Vietnam War. As a correspondent, I happened to observe a place where such egoism goes unchallenged.

Following my first assignment to the United States, I covered the Indochina War from my base in Bangkok for three years from 1972 until the fall of Saigon in April 1975. On March 29, 1973, I covered the U.S. military withdrawal ceremony at Tan Son Nhut airfield near the former South Vietnamese capital of Saigon, now called Ho Chi Minh City.

I listened to the American national anthem flowing from a frequently skipping tape and could see the lonely American flag as it fluttered. On that day I sent a story documenting my observations to the head office of Kyodo News in Tokyo. It was eleven years after the U.S. Military Assistance Command was established.

A Dreary Deactivation Ceremony in Saigon

Here is my record of that day when the U.S. began to abandon the pro–American Saigon regime in the name of Vietnamization, even as it took one more step toward defeat in the longest war in U.S. history.

> SAIGON—March 29, 1793. Fumio Matsuo, Kyodo News Special Correspondent
>
> The U.S. military departed abruptly. What remained behind was a sense of liberation and the right to self-determination tempered by tension among the still-quarreling Vietnamese people.
>
> What was seen at Tan Son Nhut Airfield on the outskirts of Saigon was a nervousness strangely interwoven with the certain arrival of a different kind of change in South Vietnam.
>
> Before departing for Hawaii, General Weyand, the last commander of the Military Assistance Command Vietnam (MACV), delivered a farewell speech in Vietnamese to Army Chief of Staff Cao Van Vien and other senior South Vietnamese government officials. Although he emphasized the completion of the U.S. mission and an expectation for a continuation of honorable peace, his speech was met by only moderate applause and the polite but unemotional smiles typical of the Vietnamese. Further adorning the ceremony were a red carpet and a glittering army band and honor guard. Slogans of gratitude to the American servicemen were written on various-colored banners waving beautifully under the blue sky.
>
> Compared to the preceding lively deactivation ceremony for the MACV, this send-off ceremony displayed neither the joy nor excitement of a victorious return home.

The eyes of eight Vietnamese officers from North Vietnam and the Provisional Revolutionary Government (PRG) monitoring the departure of the U.S. forces gazed sharply at the American servicemen. Lieutenant Colonel Bui Tin, spokesman for the North Vietnamese delegation, said quietly, "A year ago we would never have believed that the U.S. military would be leaving. Now that has become a reality. This is the first time in a hundred years that foreigners have departed our land."

U.S. soldiers boarding the last C-141 that took off just before 8:00 p.m. for Travis Air Force Base were asked insensitively by American reporters:

"What do you think was the meaning of the Vietnam War?"

"Do you think South Vietnam can carry on with the withdrawal of U.S. forces?"

"Will you stay in the military after going home?" They would hear questions such as these about the escape from Vietnam throughout American society upon their return.

One red-faced sergeant roared, "We'll be back to fight again!" but the others simply disappeared back into the plane. Finally, before reaching the crew entry ladder, Colonel David O'Dell, commander of the 333rd Air Base Group, victoriously raised a bottle of champagne. That lifted spirits, but it was the only sense of exuberance visible in the American servicemen on that day.

Lieutenant Colonel Nguyen Sinh of the PRG delegation emotionally remarked, "This is a new beginning for our people. Although there will be many difficulties, we have to build a true reconciliation among our race from this point forward."

The North Vietnamese and the PRG wore smiles in all directions and even turned on the charm toward the American servicemen with comments like, "Let's stop fighting. Now is the time for friendship." The last U.S. soldiers to leave were presented picture postcards of President Ho Chi Minh and some rattan handicrafts.

By contrast, the attitudes of the South Vietnamese Army officers present were stiff. Suddenly, they gathered together a group of cameramen and pointed to the end of the airfield, saying, "There's the ceasefire over there!" In that spot—only 1,500 feet from the final group of U.S. servicemen boarding their aircraft—lay the bodies of dead government soldiers that had just arrived and several families standing and weeping.

This was the stark scene before the Vietnamese people illustrating the steepness of the road to self-determination and reconciliation ahead of them—this and the deep scars left by the U.S. military intervention. (End)

The Abandoned South Vietnamese Regime

Three days after I sent this report, on April 1, 1973, four hundred U.S. military prisoners of war detained in Hanoi—mostly pilots—were released, and the last group departed for home. The withdrawal of U.S. forces was one of the bargaining chips employed for the release of these POWs.

Despite the strong objections of South Vietnamese President Nguyen Van Thieu, this was part of the deal signed by Kissinger and North Vietnamese Special Advisor Le Doc Tho at the so-called Paris Peace Talks in January of that year. For Nixon, already beset with the intense and unexpected calamity of Watergate, the success of a deal with North Vietnam, encompassing an exchange of POWs, a ceasefire, and the withdrawal of U.S. forces with honor under the name of Vietnamization—but which was in fact far from any mutual withdrawal—had domestically become the top priority. Constructing an exit was the first order of business. In order to force the leadership in Hanoi into accepting a deal, Nixon also executed large scale bombings of Hanoi and Haiphong for eleven days at the end of 1972.

The dull faces of the South Vietnamese soldiers at Tan Son Nhut airfield were to be expected. The North-South Vietnamese self-determination and reconciliation of which I wrote in the article would not come to pass. Instead, two years later the U.S. government would cruelly abandon the pro-American regime in Saigon, which would then be absorbed by North Vietnam. After covering the event at Tan Son Nhut, I traveled along the coastal Highway One from Saigon to the Quang Tri River in the Demilitarized Zone to cover the exchange of prisoners between North and South. The flag of the National Front for the Liberation of South Vietnam was already flying in some villages along the way.

From this time, the U.S. Congress set limits on military spending in Indochina, restricted assistance to South Vietnam to $1 billion, and approved a series of resolutions that cut back on military action and support for South Vietnam. In the process Congress overrode presidential vetoes. On August 9, 1974, President Nixon signed the bill limiting spending on Vietnam to $1 billion. It was one of the last bills he signed before being driven to resignation. It was a historic irony. This $1 billion, however, was reduced to $700 million just a few days following Nixon's resignation. The B-52 bombings of the Ho Chi Minh Trail in Cambodia that Nixon implemented in secrecy were also terminated by congressional resolution.

In this way, in early 1975 the North Vietnamese Army completed its infiltration into the South. Then they began their subjection of the entire country. The ancient cities of Hue and Da Nang collapsed like dominoes with the quick the surrender of Thieu's pro-American regime. The pitiful television images of six thousand people carried by seventy U.S. military helicopters from the roof of the American Embassy in Saigon to an aircraft carrier were broadcast throughout the entire world. Democracy with a gun had bitten the dust thirteen years after President Kennedy established the MACV.

On April 23, one week before the fall of Saigon, Nixon's successor, President Ford, stated:

> Today America can again regain the sense of pride that existed before Vietnam. But it cannot be achieved by refighting a war that is finished.... But these events, tragic as they are, portend neither the end of the world nor of America's leadership in the world.

The Defense Secretary versus the Neoconservatives

I have spent these last pages describing the process of Vietnamization, which happened over a quarter century ago, because following Boot's comments, Secretary of Defense Rumsfeld began to reveal his intentions of reducing the number of U.S. occupation forces in Iraq and exploring an eventual exit through a nation-building process of "Iraqi-ization." In short, Rumsfeld was following Boot's prescription.

On this very point, on November 6, 2003, Secretary Rumsfeld announced a plan to reduce the approximately 130,000 U.S. troops stationed in Iraq to about 105,000 between January and May 2004.

He emphatically stated:

Today there are some 118,000 Iraqi security forces of various types. Iraq clearly is now the second-largest contributor of personnel to the coalition forces, after the U.S., and soon Iraqi forces will outnumber U.S. forces, and soon thereafter, they will outnumber U.S. plus coalition forces in the country . . . I have not been told of a single military commander in CENTCOM, in Iraq, who is recommending additional U.S. military forces; not one. . . . And there are a lot of good reasons why they don't. They believe that it is important to have Iraqis take increasing responsibility . . . the task is to see how, at what pace, we're able to see the Iraqi people take over responsibilities for their essential services, take over responsibility for the governance of the country and take over responsibilities for the security of the country. And that should be done at as rapid a rate as is possible.

There is a similarity in Rumsfeld's pronouncement to the first time the word Vietnamization was used in 1970 by then Defense Secretary Melvin Laird, who became a powerful advocate of that policy. More precisely, I see the lessons learned from Secretary Laird.

Also, Rumsfeld has run into some intense disputes with his supposed allies among the neoconservatives concerning the design of this Iraqi-ization.

In a piece published on the *Wall Street Journal* opinion page on September 29, 2003, Rumsfeld admitted that U.S., British, and other forces were faced with a dangerous situation, yet he also spelled out the following six points as accomplishments that the newspapers and television had seldom reported in the five months since the start of the Iraqi occupation.[3]

1. More than forty thousand Iraqi police were conducting joint patrols with coalition forces.

2. A new Iraqi Army was being trained.

3. All major hospitals and universities had reopened.

4. An independent Iraqi Central Bank had been established and a new currency announced.

5. The Iraqi Governing Council had been formed and had appointed a cabinet of ministers.

6. Municipal councils had been formed in major cities and most towns and villages.

Moreover, Rumsfeld maintained, the results of maintaining the peace with respect to the revival of the private sector were attained at a speed easily exceeding that of the start of the German occupation following World War II. He declared that a reinforcement of U.S. troops was unnecessary.

He further took his critics to task by stating:

> In Baghdad, I met with members of the Governing Council. One message came through loud and clear: They are grateful for what Coalition forces are doing for their country. But they do not want more American troops—they want to take on more responsibility for security and governance of the country. The goal is to help them do so. Those advocating sending more Americans forces—against the expressed wishes of both our military commanders and Iraq's interim leaders—need to consider whether doing so would truly advance our objective of transferring governing responsibility to the Iraqi people.

A Glimpse of the "Exit" Strategy

Who are those whom Secretary Rumsfeld refers to as advocating sending more American forces? They are the neoconservative exponents that have been opposed to this Rumsfeld thesis from its very start.

More precisely, Rumsfeld's *Wall Street Journal* contribution itself was a counterattack to the harsh criticisms carried in the *Weekly Standard* by William Kristol, Robert Kagan, Tom Donnelly, and others, and their argument for a reinforcement of American troops in Iraq. This was evidence that the neoconservative groups, which are "not a movement" as the senior Kristol says, are also not a monolith.

The primary assertions on the part of the neoconservatives are as follows:

1. U.S. military strength is insufficient, and American troops are unable to defend the borders and highways. The United States rushes with requests to the United Nations to deploy multi-national forces and turn duties over to Iraqi security forces, but lacks the capability to back up such requests. The United States is abandoning its responsibility to build a strong democracy in Iraq, which would serve as a milestone in the democratization of the Middle East.

2. Secretary Rumsfeld may have been successful in waging his war with fewer soldiers and dependence on high-tech weapons up to the time of occupation, but high-tech weapons aren't very useful in maintaining peace or fighting gueril-las. Further administration by the traditional deployment of adequate military forces is indispensable at this point. The commanders on the ground agree with the neoconservatives on this point. The reconstruction plan by U.S. forces being rationalized and advocated by Rumsfeld should be secondary to the achievement of victory in the Iraq War.

There is a considerable discrepancy between the positions of Rumsfeld and the neoconservatives. As Mr. Boot would say, these opinions define the theology of unilateralism.

Two days later on October 1, in a counterargument to Rumsfeld, Francis Fukuyama, Johns Hopkins University professor and influential neoconserva-tive theorist known for his book *The End of History?* contributed a piece titled "Nation-Building 'Lite'" to the opinion page of the *Wall Street Journal*.[4]

In this piece Fukuyama vehemently asserts:

It is very important to understand that nation-building involves a lot more than training indigenous police and military forces to take over their coercive roles from the occupying power. Unless such forces are embedded in a broader structure of political par-ties, civilian administration, respect for individual rights, and rule of law more generally, they are subject to being hijacked or abused in the internal struggle for power. . . . No one is today explicitly calling for a "decent interval" strategy by which we

stand up a weak Iraqi government and use it as cover for a pre-
mature exit. But as costs of the occupation mount, there will be a
strong temptation to use nation-building "lite" as an intellectual
justification for what ultimately becomes a simple exit strategy,
regardless of the risks it poses for the future of a democratic
Iraq. . . . Important as it is to turn over functions to the Iraqis
quickly, it is important also to recognize that nation-building
is an extraordinarily complex and time-consuming process. . . .
Failure to pay the necessary costs now will be a false economy
that will jeopardize all that we have invested up to now.

Rumsfeld had drawn a line between himself and then Secretary of
State Colin Powell, who was requesting U.N. cooperation in providing a
deployment of multinational forces and reinforcements. However, Powell had repeatedly stated that U.S. forces should remain in Iraq until power
could be transferred responsibly to the Iraqi people. I believe that perhaps he
unexpectedly shared Rumsfeld's position to seek an exit from Iraq by accepting the nation-building lite resisted by the neoconservatives. I also believe
that, in the end, they might perhaps have even agreed to accept a settlement
whereby U.S. forces operated as a part of the Iraqi-ized security force and as a
part of a multinational force under the umbrella of the United Nations.

This exposes the fact that President Bush could ride along with this
one-sided American exit approach similar to the Vietnam policy of the past.
At the same time, establishing security in Iraq is also a top Rumsfeld objective of the U.S. presence there, and he warns that Iraqi-ization will not occur
solely for the purpose of providing an exit.

However, taken together with Boot's expedient unilateralism, the rift
between Rumsfeld's exit strategy and the neoconservatives is a sign that this
democracy with a gun is retreating from the counterattack mentality born
from the shock of 9/11. I think the true character of these neoconservative
groups should be understood.

The Reagan Sense of Security

There is one last point I'd like to clarify, the influence of Ronald Reagan. In
its 1997 "statement of principles," the PNAC declared:

We seem to have forgotten the essential elements of the Reagan Administration's success: a military that is strong and ready to meet both present and future challenges; a foreign policy that boldly and purposefully promotes American principles abroad; and national leadership that accepts the United States' global responsibilities.

As this statement indicates, the path that Reagan took, and its influence on the present Bush administration, cannot be overemphasized as the model for the neoconservatives.

In his speech to the National Endowment for Democracy, we saw President Bush praise Reagan and express his determination to follow in his footsteps. Ronald Reagan, who called the former Soviet Union an evil empire, is unquestionably Bush's hero because he took the policy of peaceful coexistence one step further and, despite his earlier confrontational stance toward the USSR, opened the door to bringing an end to the Cold War and led America to its emergence as the sole superpower. However, as I understand the Reagan era, contrary to the hawkish and belligerent pronouncements and images, Reagan provided the nation with an extraordinary sense of calm and security. In the summer of 1984, when I returned to Japan following my second assignment to Washington, many people asked me why Reagan was so popular with Americans. I explained that the major reason was the sense of security that Reagan provided. Though this brought many looks of puzzlement, I could confirm that the answer lay in the American people's view of Reagan as the father of the country's revival.

The one who taught me how to understand President Reagan by using the word "secure" was the late Paul Warnke, whom I met in 1982. Warnke had been assistant secretary of defense for National Security Affairs in the Johnson administration, director of the Arms Control and Disarmament Agency under Carter, and a central figure in the so-called Washington establishment of liberal Democrats. At that time he was also one of the leaders of the nuclear freeze movement opposed to the Reagan administration.

The man who introduced me to Warnke was the late Francis Valeo, a friend from my Washington correspondent days in the late 1960s. At that time he was working as executive assistant to Democratic Senator Mike Mansfield who later became the Secretary of the Senate. Valeo was one of

Japan's hidden benefactors. In response to a request from Mansfield, he conducted a survey of the administrative government on Okinawa in 1957 and recommended the early return of Okinawa to Japan. In 1968, immediately after McCarthy had almost caught up with Johnson in the New Hampshire primaries, he was the one who first predicted Nixon's victory to me. Right up to the time he passed away, he still was teaching me many things.

Mr. Warnke told me, "I don't support hardly any of Reagan's policies, but as president and the nation's leader, he does bring a sense of security. We can't avoid recognizing this point. He pulls no punches when he talks about anti-Communism and conservatism. But his actions are quite down-to-earth, and I feel I can live in peace after all."

Though puzzled by this unexpected commentary on Reagan by a leader of the Democratic Party, his comments are still fresh in my mind.

Warnke further told me:

This is probably the first time we've felt this secure under any president since Eisenhower. All the presidents from Kennedy to Carter had their virtues, but none could maintain a skillful balance between principles and intentions like President Reagan, and as a result that sense of security was missing. The Democrats have no more formidable opponent than Reagan.

Incidentally, he also mentioned that then Secretary of State Alexander Haig, while very bright, lacked a sense of security just as former General MacArthur had. For me, who had lived through MacArthur's occupation, his sharp analysis hit home.

Alert Blue Eyes

Certainly, if Reagan's foreign and domestic policies are analyzed on this scale, what emerges is a shrewd, measurable realism that can be assessed as security.

For example, while Reagan boasted of achieving a revitalization of the U.S. economy through large tax cuts, taxes were in fact increased substantially twice, in 1982 and 1983, in order to reduce the serious budget deficit. At first Reagan's loudly advertised restrictions on exports of oil and natural gas equipment to the Soviet Union brought strong protests from domestic and allied industries. Nevertheless, before anyone knew it, he had quietly returned to standard commercial practice.

In 1984 Reagan touted the noble cause of protecting Lebanese sovereignty and sent the U.S. Marines to Lebanon in their first deployment overseas since the Vietnam War. Yet when 241 died in a terrorist attack on their barracks, the United States quickly implemented a full withdrawal.

Despite the strong, hawkish image he projected in continuing to challenge the evil empire of the Soviet Union, Reagan took care in his diplomacy not to repeat the mistakes of Vietnam that had, more or less in vain, cost the lives of fifty-eight thousand American soldiers.

At the same time, he knew how to instill a sense of euphoria in the public. He called for a strong America without shedding American blood unnecessarily. For example, in the 1983 invasion of Grenada combat casualties were limited to just eighteen. The starting point of Reagan's sense of diplomacy may be called a kind of patriotic realism. The "Reagan détente" that proclaimed negotiations with the Soviet Union possible—as a result of having regained military deterrence capability—also saw its beginnings here.

President Reagan proudly boasted in a 1984 campaign speech, "In the four years before we took office, country after country fell under the Soviet yoke. Since January 20, 1981, not one inch of soil has fallen to the Communists. . . . Today, our combat troops have come home. . . ."

During his reelection campaign, Reagan's handshake with Soviet Foreign Minister Gromyko at the White House quietly cemented his reelection because it signaled that the Soviet Union had stepped into the ring of Reagan diplomacy. A sense of security was preeminent in his China policy as well, which included a formal state visit to China even as he maintained friendly relations with Taiwan, including the continuation of arms exports. He was a president who indeed provided the American public with a considerably high sense of security. I remember that those in Japan who constantly described Reagan as a "Hollywood B-movie actor" were concerned about a gap between the Japanese and American perceptions of Reagan.

After returning to Japan in 1984, when I was asked to describe the key to Reagan's successful post-Hollywood career in my lectures about America, I always emphasized that I thought the title "former president of the Screen Actors' Guild" exactly summed it up.

Reagan served as president of the Screen Actors' Guild for five years beginning in 1947—a time when many actors and directors were reeling from the McCarthy communist witch-hunts. *Washington Post* journalist and Reagan biographer Lou Cannon wrote that President Reagan (who at the time had been a Democrat) protected the organization from attacks on both sides by a skillful sense of balance and took his first step forward as a practical politician before he realized where his ambitions would lead him.

Reagan, who began to succumb to Alzheimer's disease in 1994, first began to court his wife Nancy when the troubled young actress went to his office to ask for advice after a left-wing paper labeled her as a comrade.

During my second assignment to Washington, I had the good fortune to shake Reagan's hand on three occasions, once in the Oval Office during a special interview with selected reporters from participating Summit nations, and twice at receptions. I was blessed with these opportunities because then Press Secretary Larry Speakes recognized me from my unwavering attendance at all of the daily 9 a.m. press briefings, which he held in his small West Wing office in the White House. Furthermore, Mr. Speakes kindly arranged for me to have a private audience with President Reagan in the Oval Office just before my return to Japan, and later sent me a photograph, autographed by Reagan himself, of the president shaking my hand at that meeting. When I stood to face Reagan and shook his hand, I was impressed by his soft, large hands and the alert sparkling blue eyes, behind his smiling face.

Encounters with Cheney and Rumsfeld

There was, by the way, one other person in Washington who spoke about Reagan's sense of security, then Wyoming Congressman and current Vice President Richard Cheney.

The story starts thirty-five years ago in September 1969 in the Japanese town of Shimoda south of Tokyo, where Townsend Harris, first U.S. Consul General to Japan, opened his office in 1856. Having returned to Japan after witnessing the birth of the Nixon administration in Washington, I met Donald Rumsfeld at the Second Japanese American Assembly Shimoda Conference organized by Tadashi Yamamoto, now president of the Japan Center for International Exchange. Rumsfeld had just been appointed chief of the Office of Economic Opportunity under the new Nixon administration after serving his fourth term as a congressional representative from Illinois. After the conference, Rumsfeld, Yamamoto, others, and I took a cab to a sushi restaurant. We enjoyed a nice conversation about Nixon and the future of

U.S.-Japan relations. He was thirty-seven years old at the time, a graduate of Princeton University, and a former navy pilot. A navy wrestling champion, Rumsfeld was filled with confidence and ambition as a member of the power elite.

After leaving Shimoda and serving in several positions in the Nixon White House, Rumsfeld served as U.S. ambassador to NATO in 1973. Fortunately, he did not get caught up in the Watergate scandal, and one year later, he was appointed the Ford administration's chief of staff and later the youngest secretary of defense in the history of the United States. After Ford lost the presidential election of 1976 to Carter, he took the position of CEO at the pharmaceutical firm G. D. Searle.

The next time I met him was twelve years later in May 1981, in his corporate office in the Chicago suburbs. On my way to Washington for my second assignment as Kyodo News Bureau chief, I had made it a special point to drop in and ask if he could introduce me to someone in Washington who could give me a comprehensive overview of the new Reagan administration.

Cordially responding to my request, he immediately asked his secretary to call the office of then Congressman Cheney. Politely introducing me as "the man who wrote about Nixon and translated Nixon's memoirs," he wrote down for me Cheney's office telephone number in the House of Representatives and even the name of Cheney's secretary. I thought that he was a kind and steady person who did not cut corners. I still remember to this day that when I asked him if he would ever return to Washington, he just winked and said, "Someday."

Congressman Cheney saw me right away. Forty-one years old at the time, his reputation as a quick study came through clearly, and I understood at once that he was a serious man of great ability. Frank from the very beginning, he joked, "Rumsfeld's my mentor. I listen to everything he says. Fire away."

After graduating from the University of Wyoming, he got his first job as an intern in the Nixon White House as special assistant to Rumsfeld in a kind of senior-junior relationship, as we say in Japan. It must not be forgotten that this relationship continues to exist to this day, even though their roles have been reversed and Cheney is now vice president and Rumsfeld secretary of defense.

The Ford administration promoted Cheney to chief of staff following

Rumsfeld. After Ford's defeat, Cheney returned to Congress to serve a second term as a representative, and throughout the duration of my assignment until 1984 I met him four times. He was always kind and provided relevant answers to my questions.

"Don't Underestimate Reagan"

I most remember that Cheney kept telling me over and over again:

> Don't underestimate Reagan. He's faithful to his anti-
> Communist and conservative roots and challenges the Soviet
> Union with strong language like "evil empire," but in the end his
> actions are realistic and reassuring. Because of the United States'
> recouping of its military deterrence against the Soviet Union,
> negotiations with the Soviets are possible. Reagan's objective is
> not to escalate the Cold War, but to end it.

It is easy to imagine how valuable these comments were to me at the time.

Cheney served as secretary of defense in the senior Bush administration and cooperated with Powell (then chairman of the Joint Chiefs of Staff) in waging the Gulf War. Now he has again returned to his mentor-pupil relationship with Rumsfeld in the current Bush administration, which is trying to repeat the successes of Reagan's strong America. Their association with the neoconservatives is well known.

However, we must not lose sight of the fact that the two are politicians with experience in the House of Representatives. They are a completely different breed from Irving Kristol. They are not movement neoconservative theorists, and, as I think they would tell you, they were able to compromise in their differences of opinion with Colin Powell out of their respect for President Bush. Their common ground with Boot's expedient unilateralism is deeply interesting.

Although I consider myself to be especially privileged to have had the opportunity to meet Rumsfeld and Cheney, whom Rumsfeld introduced to me, I regret that I was never able to meet these two gentlemen again as a result of the completion of my tour in Washington in 1984 and because of Cheney's health.

Both of them, but especially Cheney, appear to have grown considerably grim when I see them on television, and the heavy responsibilities that they bear are evident. Their eyes, now deeper set, evoke the weight of their burdens. But the sharpness of their tongues is the same as always. Like Reagan, I hope that they, too, will always offer a sense of security to the very end.

Can There Be Another "Dresden Reconciliation"?

Faces from Fifty-Four Nations

In August 2003, as I was writing the second half of this book, I spent about a week traveling through England. The purpose of my trip was to lend encouragement to my third daughter, who was studying in London, and to visit Scrooby, the town from which the separatist Puritans had set out. And while I was deeply impressed with the maturity of this nation that officially calls itself the United Kingdom of Great Britain and Northern Ireland, I also found myself experiencing complex feelings when thinking about the British-descended United States from the other side of the Atlantic.

This was not my first visit to England. The first time was in June 1968, when I dropped by London on my way back to Washington after finishing up my coverage of the Vietnam Peace Talks and the May Revolution in Paris. In addition, I have visited there five or six more times since. When I was there in 1998, a Japanese banker friend living in London took me to the modern glass-front restaurant "Bank" located in the center of the city near the Royal Courts of Justice. At that time an independent investigating committee was holding hearings into Prime Minister Tony Blair's suspect intelligence operations on Iraq.

I remember thinking that the fish and chips tasted exquisite and, indeed, seemed quite different from another such meal, wrapped in newspaper, that I munched on thirty years earlier. I also traveled to Paris via the Channel Tunnel, which had just opened for traffic in 1994. As I rode, I could feel the shadow of the European Union hovering over a new London and a new England.

What struck my eye on my most recent visit, however, were all the different shades of skin color to be seen in the multiracial London that has emerged in recent decades. For a moment, I thought I was in New York. Each of the fifty-four countries in the worldwide British Commonwealth of Nations seemed to be represented in the accents and demeanor of those passing by. It was a remarkable feeling. It is worth noting that Queen Elizabeth is still monarch of sixteen nations, including, of course, the United Kingdom. Here they are, listed in alphabetical order: Antigua and Barbuda; Australia; Bahamas; Barbados; Belize; Canada; England (United Kingdom); Grenada; Jamaica; New Zealand; Papua New Guinea; Saint Christopher and Nevis; Saint Lucia; Saint Vincent and Grenadine; Solomon Islands; Tuvalu.

This visit brought home to me the fact that the United Kingdom itself now is also a great multiracial nation, and I was able to gain a fresh look at these former colonies, especially the small island nations, that were once ruled as vassals of the seven seas by the military force of the "new-style empire" of the British Commonwealth.

I also took a tour of Buckingham Palace, which had been opened to the public during the summer vacation period. As I walked from room to opulent room, I felt deeply impressed with all the different articles of wealth collected from around the world. As I listened to the welcoming voice of Prince Charles in my headphones, I thought of something the late Dr. Shigeharu Matsumoto, my mentor, had written.

In his essay *Amerika Minshushugishiso no Genkei* [The Prototype of American Democratic Thought] published in 1970, Dr. Matsumoto wrote:

When seen by later generations, Britain's policies toward the American colonies, which drove them to independence, revolution, and the founding of the United States, were clearly a huge blunder. Had Britain, which took pride in its shrewd diplomacy, at the time correctly evaluated the colonies' strengths, nationalism, and anti-European-tyranny sentiments, the history for future generations would have been drastically different. The present conditions that Canada, Australia, New Zealand, and even the independent India enjoy today in the Great British Commonwealth of Nations are a result of the lessons learned by Britain from its policy failures toward America in those days.[1]

As I stood this time on British soil and thought of the United States far to the west, I finally began to understand why Dr. Matsumoto, who studied at universities in both the United States and Europe, had always and repeatedly raised this point in my conversations with him.

According to the *Buckingham Palace Handbook* sold to visitors, the palace was purchased by the royal family in 1761 for George III, who used it as a private residence and who was responsible for the loss of America. The day after I thumbed through this guide, the evening papers carried articles reporting that a nineteen-year-old black woman from Barbados had been selected as a member of the queen's Royal Horse Guards, the first of her race and gender to assume this position.

A Visit to Scrooby

Scrooby is located an hour and a half by train due north of London. In the seventeenth century it was a small village in the agricultural region spread out along the northeastern part of Sherwood Forest, made famous by the Robin Hood legend. The village faced the old Great Northern Road extending to Edinburgh in Scotland, and the Manor House estate, where the king and archbishop had visited since around the tenth century, still stood. It is said that Henry VIII held Privy Council meetings there. There was also a station for horse-drawn carriages.

The name of Scrooby's Manor House has remained throughout history, however, as the place where Brewster inherited the position of caretaker from his father and became the most influential leader of the Pilgrim Fathers. The story of these events appears in chapter 4.

Scrooby's present-day population is about three hundred. There is one combination pub/restaurant in town, which is called the Pilgrim Fathers Inn. Nevertheless, the village has not become a tourist attraction, and there are only three historical markers. Malcolm Dolby, a local historian who himself lives in Scrooby and the museum director for the Basset Law District, was kind enough to show me around.

Scrooby Manor House—where Brewster and others discussed Puritan doctrine of God and direct faith through an independent church, even as they were being persecuted by the king and the Church of England—is a private residence today. I would never have realized the historical significance of this building if Dolby had not shown me the citations from the Plymouth Association attached to the old brick wall. In the front yard laundry danced in the wind. In the facing pasture several horses were munching on grass.

As if noticing my slight bewilderment at so much quiet and the ordinary scenery, Dolby said, "They were a pure but radically heretical group for that time. Whereas the Puritans tried to reform the rot and authoritarianism from within the Church of England, the Separatist Puritans attempted to separate from the Church and its order brought severe persecution upon themselves. Escaping to Holland and then to the New World—where most Britons couldn't comprehend such an existence—were desperate and extreme acts for that time. About forty years later, religious hostility had reached the point where Charles I was executed, smearing his blood on the Puritan revolution."

Now, after its single-handed victory in the Cold War and the shock of 9/11, the American democracy that was born from the radical elements of the former British Empire about four centuries ago is still radical in its sense of mission as the empire of liberty. Breathing the air of England, I could at last see this still young and green United States. Isn't the practice of democracy with a gun in Iraq perhaps one part of this story?

Considering all of this while standing in front of Manor House, I started to wonder about the role played in England by Article Seven of the Bill of Rights, which was enacted after the Glorious Revolution of 1688. I also wondered what the British today think about the continued existence of the Second Amendment of the U.S. Constitution.

As discussed in chapter 2, Article Seven of the Bill of Rights gave general citizens, known as freemen, the right to bear arms for self-defense against the king, institutionalized the militia to put a stop to the tyranny of the king and his standing army, and supported the institution of a constitutional monarchy.

Very radical for its time, this regulation crossed the Atlantic, served as the foundation of the American colonial militia system, and engrained the

DNA of use of force into that democracy. It is the origin of democracy with a gun. The independence of the United States was the result of the militia's victory over the king's standing army. Moreover, the DNA of use of force born from Article Seven was applied to the Second Amendment in the U.S. Constitution, which accepts the bearing of arms as a civil right and is set into the infrastructure of American democracy.

Later, this democracy with a gun continued to expand westward along with the belief in Manifest Destiny, dragging the shadow of Indian exclusion and black discrimination along with it. Soon the militia changed its name to the National Guard, fought in the Civil War, and became a powerful component of the standing army that evolved into the United States Armed Forces. In the aftermath of World War I, World War II, the Cold War, the Korean War stalemate, and the experience of defeat in Vietnam, the United States now stands as the sole superpower in the world. It also stands in a position of overwhelming dominance with nuclear weapons since their first use at Hiroshima and Nagasaki.

Against this backdrop of overwhelming power, I look at the extreme unilateralism put into practice in the Iraq War and how the Bush administration ignored the United Nations in the aftermath of 9/11. And I have to ask myself, where now does that Article Seven of the Bill of Rights exist—that Article Seven which the United States inherited from the British Empire now matured and known as the British Commonwealth of Nations? Where is the spirit of that article?

England—A Country with No Second Amendment

The answer provided by my long-time British friend when I saw him was simple, "Nobody knows about Article Seven. Even the concept of a militia is long gone. First of all, Britain is a country without a single constitution, but has accumulated customary law over the years, and the people wouldn't even think about caring so much for a Second Amendment that's over two hundred years old like the United States does."

Regular British police do not carry pistols, and gun-related crime in London is reportedly one-tenth that of New York. First of all, unlike the situation in the United States, citizens who wish to purchase guns and ammunition must undergo a strict investigation by the local residential area chief of police. In addition, owners must provide a storage place for, and always lock up, the weapon. Licenses can be easily annulled, and the number of actual owners is extremely limited. Gun manufacturers and sellers are registered, and they must record to whom weapons are sold or transferred.

Such regulations are based on legislation such as the Gun Licenses Act of 1870, the Pistols Act of 1903, the Firearms Act of 1920, the Firearms Act of 1937, and the Air Guns and Shotguns Act that was strengthened in 1989. Such strictness is unthinkable in the United States, and, incidentally, there are no gun lobbies like the NRA. The largest gun organization is the British Association for Shooting and Conservation, a society straight out of the world of Sherlock Holmes, whose purpose is to protect the rights of gun possession for hunting and shooting game.

From a historical perspective, the confrontation between the citizen militia and the king's standing army after the Bill of Rights did not continue for very long. In its great wars with France and Spain and its skirmishes with its foreign colonies, England repeatedly and increasingly used the militia to augment its standing army when deploying troops overseas. Fighting the American colonial militia was a part of their job, and ironically by 1815, after wars with the U.S. colonies and Napoleonic France, the militia system in England disappeared.

In the United States the gun became a domestic commodity with the intense use of violent force in the exclusion of the Indians and the Civil War. In contrast, the last war fought on British soil was the Battle of Culloden in Scotland where the rebellious army of Charles Edward Stuart, also know as Bonnie Prince Charlie, was defeated in 1746. British society's dependence on the militia has decreased sharply ever since.

Then there was the "desperate and extreme act," in Dolby's words, of the Pilgrim Fathers' settlement at Plymouth. The Bill of Rights and its Article Seven were the products of the most radical movement of the time, the establishment of the constitutional monarchy. The American continent absorbed the extreme acts taking place in England, and even now this excessiveness still continues in the democracy to which it gave birth. The DNA of use of force has become a part of daily life, and the democracy with a gun has continued to hold sway.

I thought of this as I gazed out of the train at the boundless beauty of Britain's countryside on my way back to London and absorbed its truth. And now I feel a certain sympathy for the United States, which has stumbled into a one-man show in Iraq as a result of this excessiveness.

When I had returned to London from Scrooby, I found that the *Sunday Times* had reported that many requests were arriving unexpectedly from U.S. universities for lectures by scholars on the history of the British Empire. This appeared to stem from a desire by the U.S. to learn more from the United Kingdom about how to maintain an empire amidst the deeply troubled nation-building in Iraq.

In this context, Professor Linda Colley of the London School of Economics summarized a lecture soon to be delivered at Princeton University. The lecturer was to tell Americans that erecting an empire is not an easy task. It not only extracts costs in economic terms, but time and human life as well.

President Rice?

The United States must now ask itself whether it is willing to sacrifice the time and human life required of an empire, as Professor Colley puts it, and to accept the task of nation-building in Iraq. Has the shock of 9/11 been tamed with the mere banishment and capture of Saddam Hussein? Or, as the neoconservatives who have dragged the Bush administration thus far would say, should the United States do its best to bear the responsibility and sacrifices of the empire of liberty until the day that democratization in Iraq is achieved? Or should it once again use the United Nations and seek multinationalization and an "honorable" exit through Iraqi-ization as Nixon did with Vietnamization? In their 1999 book, *A World Transformed*, coauthors Brent Scowcroft and the senior George Bush confess that the trials now faced by the United States as the sole superpower are infinite.[2]

Comfort can be found, however, in the United States' unique presidential election system, a stabilizing factor that has existed since the nation's founding. The people had their chance to use this system in 2004. The 2004 presidential election was a narrow vote of confidence in President Bush, who unquestionably started the Iraq War.

During the Constitutional Convention held in Philadelphia in 1787, the term of office for president was originally proposed as seven years. One of the Founding Fathers, Alexander Hamilton, explained why the term was changed to four years in the the *Federalist* No. 71: "The personal firmness of the executive magistrate, in the employment of his constitutional powers; and . . . [for] the stability of the system of administration which may have been adopted under his auspices."

The system whereby the people choose their president once every four years together with congressional elections every two years is the product of the wisdom of the Founding Fathers, who took pains to produce an American democracy unlike anything in England or France. Their handiwork is called a masterpiece resulting from their originality and determination.

In November 2003, on my final trip for researching this book, I once again met and had dinner with former Secretary of the Senate Francis Valeo. Valeo, who had recently lost his wife, was living with his rare French Bulldog, Buddy, and seemed spry for his eighty-six years. The sharpness of his political analysis had not dulled at all since predicting Nixon's successful election to me in February 1968. On this occasion he told me:

> The United States will probably someday have a woman presi-
> dent. A lot of people say it will be Senator Hillary Clinton.
> I'm a faithful Democrat, so that's fine with me. But if Bush
> gets reelected in 2004, I think Condoleezza Rice is going to be
> appointed secretary of state or to some other important position.
> If that happens, it's quite possible that Rice could become the
> first woman and the first black to run for president in 2008 or
> later after going through the baptism of fire of serving in Con
> gress like Hillary or as state governor. I'm a second-generation
> Italian immigrant from Brooklyn. My father was a shoemaker
> who couldn't speak English very well. This country has come
> a long way with all the different races we've got here. It's the
> "American dream." President Rice would not be a bad thing. I
> don't know if I'll see it in my lifetime, though.

I firmly believe that the United States is still a radical young country. When I first started writing this epilogue, Arnold Schwarzenegger was inaugurated Governor of California, America's most populous state, following the radical recall of a governor elected only a year before. In 1969, the same year I completed my first assignment as special correspondent to the U.S., Schwarzenegger emigrated from Austria. He was only seventeen with no money and very little English ability, but he succeeded in Hollywood.

This was only the second such time a gubernatorial recall had taken place in the history of the United States, the first being the recall of the governor of North Dakota in 1921. This is the same California that had been successfully acquired by military force from Mexico by President Polk in the 1840s. It was George Washington who observed in 1783 that the United States would become an "actor on a most conspicuous theatre" watched by the entire world.

When I think of these episodes of history, I as a Japanese always take newly to heart the radical and pluralistic energy of America. That energy is the origin of democracy with a gun.

A Return to Herzog's Speech

Finally, I have to return again to my reflections on the disparity with Dresden that I discussed in chapter 1.

I wrote there about the differences between Japan and Germany in light of the reconciliation ceremony between Germany and the former Allies held on February 13, 1995, the fiftieth anniversary of the indiscriminate bombings of the city of Dresden. These bombings occurred about one month before General LeMay, who orchestrated the B-29 indiscriminate incendiary bombings on the cities of Japan, commenced his air raids on Tokyo. Later, I acquired the official English translation of President Roman Herzog's speech at the ceremony, which appeared in the *Washington Post* at the time. Since the entire speech is too lengthy to provide in its entirety, I shall recount only the main points here. This speech was barely reported in Japan and elsewhere, but I hope that many Japanese readers will someday read it.

Herzog was born in 1934. An alumnus of the Christian Democratic Union (CDU), he was the former chief justice of the Federal Supreme Court of the former West Germany, and was the second German president following reunification. After ceding the office to Johannes Rau in 1999, he served as president of the European Union's Charter Convention of Fundamental Rights until 2000.

Herzog took one step further the famous 1985 "Forty Years of Wilderness" speech by his predecessor, fellow CDU alumni and President Richard von Weizsäcker, by stating that, in addition to learning from history, he could not "offset" the dead. He pressed the former Allies into accepting responsibility for the bombings of noncombatants, and appealed to both his former enemies and allies with the moral logic of learning to live with one another peacefully and in a spirit of trust. Following is text from that speech:

- During the night of February 13–14, 1945, the city of Dresden was destroyed by bombs within just a few hours. Tens of thousands of people perished in the fire storm The suffering of the survivors was beyond imagination. Irreplaceable values of European culture were lost forever, values that were also part of the human soul.

- As we recall this event today, as so often before, clarification is needed. No one present in this room intends to indict anyone or expects anyone to show remorse or indulge in self-accusation. No one wants to offset the wrongs committed by the Germans in the Nazi state against anything else. If that had been the intention, the people of Dresden would not, once again, have extended such a warm welcome to our British and American guests.

- We are here first and foremost to mourn, to lament the dead—an expression of human emotion dating back to the beginnings of civilization . . . we mourn the German victims of our history, the countless people who lost their lives or whose health was ruined in the war or in camps, during flight, through expulsion or deportation, in houses and on the streets, in ditches and cellars. One cannot come to terms with the past, one cannot find peace or reconciliation unless one faces up to history in its entirety. We object to our mourning being seen as an attempt to square the suffering of the victims of crimes committed by Germans against people of other nations, and against fellow countrymen, with the suffering of German victims of war and expulsion.

- Anyone who, like the Germans of today, wants to break the vicious circle of injustice and violence, of war and inhumanity, anyone who seeks peace, friendship and reconciliation among the nations, cannot simply strike a balance between the dead, the injured and those who suffered distress in the various nations. One cannot offset life against life, pain against pain, fear of death against fear of death, expulsion against expulsion, horror against horror, degradation against degradation.

Human suffering defies accounting. We can only overcome it together, through compassion, reflection and learning.

- By letting democracy take firm root in our country and committing ourselves to the cause of European integration, we have drawn the right consequences from our history. We are able to face up to the past. That is why we are not trying to lighten our own burdens by comparing them with those of others. It is our own history that concerns us here, not the history of others. One's own history teaches one the best lesson.

- If one looks at history merely in terms of states and nations, the settlement of accounts seems simple: the Germans started the war, and just punishment was meted out to them for doing so. But this is too simplistic a view. Only if one imagines all those different people who must have died in that night of destruction does the human tragedy of modern warfare become fully apparent. There were dyed-in-the-wool Nazis. There were Gestapo officers who drew up the lists for the deportation of Jews. There were the Jews on these lists. There were people who had rejoiced when the war broke out, but also those who had cried and could do nothing only because they had not resisted at the outset, in 1933, or had not found sufficient support for their resistance. There were silent enemies of the Nazi regime, there were the fellow travelers and those who turned a blind eye. There were resistance fighters, those still busy secretly distributing leaflets to protest against the madness or those already behind bars for having done so.

- We must use every means at our disposal to prevent war, not only through pacts and alliances, but first of all by ensuring that the nations learn to live with one another peacefully and in a spirit of trust. Many European peoples have learnt this lesson over the past decades. And there is tangible proof of this today—beyond the politics of these decades. How else could former enemies meet on May 8 this year to mark the end of the war by jointly contemplating the future? And how else could our British and American friends, led by His Royal Highness the Duke of Kent and the Ambassador of the United States of America, be with us here today?

- It is with particular pleasure that we welcome them and their delegations not as representatives of former adversaries, but of today's friends. Nothing could better manifest this change than the American institution "Friends of Dresden" and the British "Dresden Trust," whose donations will help us rebuild the Frauenkirche.[3]

- When this former symbol of the destruction of Dresden soars over the reconstructed city, its spire will bear a cross that we owe to British donations. It will be a symbol more powerful than words. Standing high above the city, this cross will forever remind us that, half a century after Dresden's destruction, we have found peace with each other. That is the right course. We Germans will do our utmost to ensure that we continue along this path.

Differences with Germany

Among those in attendance, who were welcomed in President Herzog's speech "not as the representatives of our enemies of the past and but of our friends of today," were not only the Duke of Kent, but also Peter Inge, former Chief of the Defence Staff of the United Kingdom, and John Shalikashvili, chairman of the Joint Chiefs of Staff, America's top uniformed official.

As far as my research could determine, neither of these men said anything during this ceremony. Wasn't it enough, however, for them just to be there on that occasion and listen to Herzog's speech? It is unknown whether Germany or the United States came up with the idea of assembling such attendants for this ceremony. Yet, wasn't this the product of the highest level of diplomatic efforts to close the "wounds" between Germany, the United States, and Britain?

Could not Japan's Prime Minister deliver a speech similar to Herzog's before representatives from the United States on March 10 in Tokyo, August

6 in Hiroshima, or August 9 in Nagasaki? Standing on the logic of "not offsetting the dead," can't we also hold a ceremony to mourn Japan's noncombatant victims and, like Germany, close the wounds between Japan and the United States? In 2004, Japan and the United States celebrated the 150th anniversary of the Peace and Amity Treaty of 1854. Wouldn't this be an appropriate time for concluding such a Dresden-like ceremony and for Japan to develop an even deeper relationship with the United States? Isn't this the opportunity to take that first step? Isn't Japan able to do with the United States what Germany was able to do? It's not too late. Shouldn't the opportunity come to full fruition?

These were my thoughts as I began to pen this book.

However, during the year and a half in which I made a total of five trips to the United States for my research, I came to the realization that this proposal is rather difficult to accomplish. I concluded that relations between Japan and the United States have not yet reached the stage at which we could do the same thing that Germany did. Furthermore, as I was finishing up this book, the Japanese Cabinet was making its policy decision to deploy Japan's Self-Defense Forces to Iraq. So I was disturbed even more about the fact that the Self-Defense Forces would depart without achieving Japan's version of the Dresden Reconciliation.

I think the most important thing right now is to keep these differences between Japan and Germany in mind when considering Japan's relationship with the United States. From this perspective, U.S.-Japanese relations can be seen clearly.

Public support in the United States is now being solicited by comparing the nation-building in Iraq to the Berlin Airlift. In addition, leading figures in the current administration, beginning with President Bush, when speaking of the future of Iraq, refer to the democratization and economic prosperity of Germany and Japan, two nations that few expected to adopt long-lasting democracies after World War II. The use of such verbiage is nothing new; however, it has been used in abundance since the beginning of the Iraq War. President Bush used these phrases as key parts of two speeches in November 2003 in a public relations attempt to put the best spin possible on the U.S. occupation.

Such jarring logic is certainly good for Japan, which was once an Axis ally with Germany and Italy.

Nevertheless, in their relations with the United States, Japan and Germany have different histories. As we have already seen, German American citizens first appeared as indentured servants prior to independence. During the War of Independence, about thirty thousand German mercenaries were dispatched to the new continent to reinforce the British Army. A substantial number of these settled permanently in America afterward. They became part of America's founding.

There is no comparison to America's relations with Japan, which began when Commodore Perry—brimming with the chosen-people attitude of the Anglo-Saxons—arrived to open the country on the path of Manifest Destiny. Also, during World War II, only Japanese Americans were interred in concentration camps, not German Americans.

In the years since the war there has been no end to the differences between Germany and Japan, which was described as having "embraced defeat."[4] Japan and Germany were Axis allies. Both were defeated and their leaders tried in international courts. Here the similarities end, however. German history is marked by the existence of the Nazi Party; the prosecution of the Holocaust; Hitler's suicide; the occupation by the United States, Britain, France, and the former Soviet Union; the division of Germany into East and West for forty-one years; the Berlin Wall; the adoption of federal republicanism in West Germany; the establishment of the Federal Army under the Basic Law (Constitution) from the institution of the draft for men eighteen years of age and older; and participation with NATO forces beginning in 1994.

There are also differences in how each country has taken its "war responsibilities." Still, I am not going to delve into the theories of how Japan and Germany are different at this point. That is not the purpose of this book, and I have not studied enough about Germany.

The "Historical Issue" Is Now

But there is one thing that I do understand. In the middle of Washington, on a corner not so far from Potomac Park famous for its cherry trees, the Washington Monument, the Smithsonian, and the White House, stands the Holocaust Museum. There, the Nazi crimes continue to be revealed and silently indicted to throngs of citizens and tourists for the purchase of a daily ticket. Weren't the Dresden Reconciliation and Herzog's rejection of offsets made possible by this thorough coming to terms with the past?

The Holocaust Museum is known formally as the "United States Holocaust Memorial Museum." In order to perpetually teach the lessons of the Holocaust, the construction of the Holocaust Museum on federal property in central Washington resulted from a proposal by the President's Commission on the Holocaust commissioned by President Carter in 1978. The project received about $194 million in private donations, and the facility was completed and opened to the general public in April 1993. In 1980 Congress unanimously approved the U.S. Holocaust Memorial Council Authorization, establishing the U.S. Holocaust Memorial Council with an annual budget of $23 million. The museum attracts about two million visitors each year. It attracts more visitors than any other museum in Washington next to the Smithsonian's National Air and Space Museum.

It turns out that Herzog was able to make his 1995 speech after seeing this process of closing the wounds of the Holocaust domestically in the United States.

And I believe that although Germany, like Japan, is still the same "ally" it has been since World War II, the actions that it took that differed from Japan's in the recent Iraq War were possible only as a result of the achievement of closing those wounds.

In addition, unlike Germany, Japan has not been able to settle the past with its neighboring countries. Japan's "historical issues" with the neighboring Korean Peninsula and China is a stark reality. Japan must face up to the fact that it started World War II and conducted the same kind of indiscriminate bombing campaigns against China as LeMay prosecuted against Japan. It is a reality, for better or worse. I believe this kind of historical issue no longer exists in Germany.

Since 2002, whenever I have met my American friends, I have asked them whether they thought a ceremony like the Dresden Reconciliation could not be held in Japan to close the wounds of the atomic bomb victims. Without exception, they always say, "Yes, that would be great. Perhaps the time has come." Most will stop there, but there was one who went further. This man, who spent many years as a diplomat in Japan and Asia, observed, "It's okay for the United States to have a Dresden Reconciliation in Japan. But how would Japan explain this to its neighbors? Would Japan do the same thing for them? Has it already done so?" I could find no answers to his questions.

Japan's historical issues remain not only with its neighbors, but with the United States as well. In 2003 two bills were submitted in the Senate and seven in the House of Representatives to "preserve" the rights of former U.S. servicemen captured by the Japanese Imperial Army during World War II by demanding compensation from some Japanese corporations.

Still, Japan is in a position to ask this same America for assistance in resolving the issue of the kidnapping of Japanese nationals by North Korea. In this same America, Syracuse University in northern New York State tendered invitations and sponsored IT training in the field of system assurance for six IT researchers from an industrial university in Pyongyang over a period of about one month in April 2003. This was undeniably a private sector exchange. The program also included goodwill visits to Niagara Falls and the New York Stock Exchange. The State Department matter-of-factly issued visas, and a leading think tank which was well known for its anti-Communist position in the past offered funding. It's safe to think that the official and non-official channels existing between New York and Washington and Pyongyang are far deeper than those between Tokyo and Pyongyang. Compared to the channel that existed between Washington and Beijing prior to Nixon's visit to China, aren't the inroads into North Korea considerably more varied, not only via its mission at the U.N., which China did not have at the time, but also through a large number of civilian cultural and educational exchanges? This is a point that we Japanese cannot ignore.

Ignoring the Dead of Hiroshima and Nagasaki

One more answer came to me in my conviction to pursue a Dresden Reconciliation for Japan.

In November 2003, during the final stage of my research in Washington for this book, I heard that the fully restored *Enola Gay* was to be put on display at the Smithsonian's National Air and Space Museum Annex near Dulles International Airport in the Washington suburbs, and I wanted to try to cover the event if possible.

At the time Dr. Martin Harwit, the museum's director, an astrophysicist and former head of Cornell University's astronomy department made the purely scientific proposal that "We should explain the reality of 140,000 casualties at Hiroshima and 70,000 at Nagasaki, and make a place for it in our national history education." However, he was silenced by powerful conservatives. The American Legion and the Air Force Association were opposed to any mention of the number of deaths, and the explanatory placards in the exhibit hall contained only a description of the body of the aircraft itself.[5] At the time these actions were quite controversial within the Japanese community in Washington. In addition, as mentioned in chapter 1, the cancellation of the exhibition placard had also saddened a former Reagan White House senior official, who lamented that "the best chance to remove the atomic-bomb thorn from U.S.-Japanese relations has disappeared."

With this in mind, I applied to the Smithsonian Annex to cover this event, stating that I wanted to see what had become of the display placards for the fully restored aircraft in the eight years since I had last visited in 1995 (also the year of the Dresden Reconciliation). The answer was "no," with an explanation that the press briefing had already taken place. Instead, I received a package postmarked November 7 from the Air and Space Museum containing an announcement and a sheet of frequently asked questions (FAQ) and answers.

In addition to an explanation that the museum had considered a petition from the Committee for a National Discussion of Nuclear History and Current Policy signed by over 150 people from both the U.S. and Japan, including Hiroshima Mayor Tadatoshi Akiba, the package announced that the exhibition placards would remain unchanged from the previous eight years; that is, there would be no mention of the numbers of casualties at Hiroshima and Nagasaki. The museum explained coolly that its mission was to document "the history of developments in American aviation and space flight" and to offer "accurate data," allowing visitors to evaluate all exhibitions for themselves. I could only naturally conclude that the influence of the conservatives in Washington was much stronger than it was eight years earlier under President Clinton.

The FAQ sheet stated that the legacy of the superior B-29 was that dropping the atomic bomb contributed to the unconditional surrender of Japan, and that the aircraft served as a mainstay of nuclear deterrence in the early stages of the Cold War. It seemed to me that I could see traces of the philosophy of the LeMay bombings.

Placing the use of atomic bombs in the same category as the nighttime indiscriminate incendiary bombings, its establishment as a pillar of deterrence after the war, and General LeMay's logic of preemptive nuclear strikes against the former Soviet Union have all clearly endured. In other words, the position of the United States has remained consistent throughout its history and to the present day.

Therefore, I was again touched to the core by the differences between Japan and Germany. As I wrote in chapter 1, in 1992 German Prime Minister Kohl had issued a statement of protest when a statue of Royal Air Force Commander-in-Chief General Harris, who pressed for the Dresden bombings, was erected before the British Ministry of Defence in London. By contrast, Japan had presented General LeMay with its highest honor.

The Dresden Reconciliation clearly revealed Japan's disparities with Germany. I recognize these disparities in U.S.-Japanese relations and, in facing this reality, believe we have to bury the hatchet and start over once again from the beginning. Considering the difficult first step of the current Self-Defense Force deployment in Iraq, I believe we must not give up, no matter how long it takes.

I've come to believe anew that the Self-Defense Force deployment should have taken place after the achievement of a Dresden-like reconciliation. I think this must be done at some time in order to strengthen our alliance with the United States. And furthermore, we have to solve our historical issue with our neighbors, not by following in America's footsteps, but by our own power and initiative.

Shock at Chiran

In June 2003 with the help of a friend from Kagoshima I was finally able to obtain a visit to the former Chiran Special Attack Forces ("kamikaze") Air Base on the Satsuma Peninsula. The streets of the beautiful town of Chiran were lined with Japanese yew trees. Embraced in the gentle bosom of this beauty is the Chiran Special Attack Peace Hall that enshrines the final resting place of the 1,036 young souls, 439 from Chiran alone, who carried out kamikaze operations against U.S. ships near Okinawa. These were launched from twenty-two Special Attack Bases from Kyushu, Yamaguchi, and Taiwan. The park was carefully hand-kept by the people of Chiran Town. I thought the museum had assembled a good collection, with four thousand items from the period, including photographs of the deceased, last wills and testaments, final writings, articles left behind by the departed, and restored Nakajima Ki-84 Hayate, Kawasaki Ki-61 Hien, and Mitsubishi Zero fighters used by the Special Attack Forces.

I entered the triangular-roofed soldiers' barracks that had been restored to their original form. The interiors of the rooms where the Special Attack troops spent the nights prior to their missions were low, narrow, and dark, and for a moment I once again felt the helplessness of being driven into the corners of Japan's desperate past. The days when I had been frightened and attacked by LeMay's B-29s, and yet survived, came back to me. The youngest member of the Special Attack Forces was seventeen years and one month old, a difference of only five years from my age at that time. This was a moving moment for me, and I unexpectedly became shaken as I thought of the closeness of our ages.

According to the explanation given by Morihiko Orita, director of the Chiran Special Attack Peace Hall, the rate of ingress into the area occupied by the U.S. fleet in Okinawan waters was only 21 to 22 percent for the entire operation. There are no data beyond that point.

I began to think deeply that we lost the war as a result of our complete lack of knowledge about the United States.

Five months later, I closed this book at last and remembered again the shock I felt at Chiran on that day.

I am of the opinion that an alliance with the United States is in Japan's national interest. The problem is in the specifics. The alliance should not consist of the mere sharing of Ichiro, Matsui, and Little Matsui with the major leagues or of Tokyo Disneyland, where 58 percent of repeat visitors have attended more than ten times.[6]

Hasn't our alliance to this point been merely a virtual one? Hasn't our friendship been imaginary? With the Iraqi deployment of the Self-Defense Forces now underway, I think the feelings of tension throughout Japan have proved the existence of the gap between our two nations. In other words, the roots of the feeling that we are passing each other in the night lie very deep.

First of all, wasn't MacArthur's occupation of Japan an American occupation? Didn't this unique occupation by a one-of-a-kind general differ completely from that of Germany? Hadn't the U.S. and Japan passed each other by once again at that time? Perhaps this can be traced back to the Meiji Period when, despite Commodore Perry's arrival and the modernization of our country, we passed each other by for the first time by modeling our new nation after Europe, especially the newly unified German Empire under Bismarck, instead of the United States, and this contributed to a war seventy-three years later. In the end, I return with General LeMay to the self-reflection in the prologue, "An Encounter as 'Enemies.'" My never-ending internal struggle continues.

In any event, I believe we must use the Self-Defense Force deployment to Iraq as a new opportunity to ponder U.S.-Japanese relations from their roots. To that end, I believe we must once again try to understand correctly this country called America and its democracy with a gun. I will be pleased if my awkward book becomes a springboard for this understanding.

Postscript

In my continuing preoccupation with my experiences with the B-29 bombings, I took up an immense challenge with this book. Now that I have finished grappling with the United States over the course of five trips in my year and a half of research, I am filled with the impression that I still have a long way to go.

This is because I do not seem to have answered my own question, What kind of country is the United States? What is the United States to Japan? Aren't we continuing to pass each other by? And then there are other questions I haven't even touched on. Are not U.S.-Chinese relations deeper than U.S.-Japanese relations? I have not been able to answer many of the questions that have absorbed me for many years. There is still much more to learn; I must continue the challenge. I keep in mind the greatness of the spirits of the distinguished teachers who guided me.

In 1952 I advanced from Gakushuin High School (formerly a school for mainly the Imperial Family and aristocracy) to Gakushuin University, which had been newly founded as a private university just four years earlier under Yoshishige Abe during the U.S. occupation. I was blessed with the opportunity to meet wonderful professors on that campus, which was awhirl with a vibrancy born of a mixture of old traditions and new ideas.

Beginning in my freshman year, I sneaked into the late professor of sociology Ikutaro Shimizu's senior classes, where he repeatedly taught me to arm myself with mental fangs and sent me out onto the road of journalism. He always taught me, "Don't avoid confrontations with logic when you write." I feel that, in writing this book, I heeded my teacher's instruction for the first time.

During the course of my American studies, I heard a lecture on U.S. political history by the late Professor Yasaka Takagi, truly a pioneer of American studies in Japan, and was blessed with the good fortune of having received individual instruction from him. In August 2003 as I stood before manor house in Scrooby—the place of origin of the separatist Puritans and Pilgrim Fathers—what came to mind was the handsome face of this teacher who told me quietly as I was about to be dispatched to New York for the first time as a correspondent, "The Americans' attitude toward life is simple from the beginning, and the Puritan work ethic, thrift, and self-control is still alive. Do well to watch for that."

After I graduated, Professor Takagi introduced me to two of his most accomplished students. The first was the late Dr. Shigeharu Matsumoto, a well-respected scholar-turned-senior-journalist at Domei News Agency, the predecessor of Kyodo News. As Shanghai bureau chief, Dr. Matsumoto had an international scoop with the Xian Incident, in which Zhang Xueliang, the leader of the Manchurian army, arrested Chinese leader Chiang Kai-shek on December 12, 1936. This incident led to the formation of the united front against Japanese invasion between the Kuomintang and the Chinese Communist Party in September 1937.

From him I was able to draw upon the knowledge of an international journalist, and he introduced me to many prominent Americans. "You must do what you can to get on your feet and meet all kinds of people in order to learn from others in addition to academicians and form your own opinions. You can't write a good report without developing a give-and-take relationship with your sources." I now wonder how far I was able to live up to my teacher's lesson in the years before he passed away in 1989. When I returned to active journalism in 2002, I wished I could approach his level of passion in my pursuit of American studies and in maintaining friendships with Americans. I would like to dedicate this book to my three late teachers of the days long past.

The second top student to whom Professor Takagi introduced me was Professor Makoto Saito at Tokyo University, under whom I studied American History as an "off-campus journalist" and today as a member of the Japanese Association of Early Americanists. I was able to tackle the theme of democracy with a gun only through Professor Saito's multifaceted lessons in American Studies, starting with Plymouth. For this book, I drew upon his translations in *Sekai Kenposhu, Daiyonpan* [Constitutions of the World, fourth edition],

(Iwanami Bunko, 1983) in discussing the Articles of the U.S. Constitution. I acknowledge this man's contributions from the bottom of my heart.

In writing this book, I obtained the cooperation of many friends in both Japan and the United States, and I regret that I cannot mention each one of them by name. But among them I would like to mention the kind cooperation of Mr. Robert Nedelkoff at the National Archives and everybody at the libraries of the Foreign Correspondents' Club of Japan and the International House of Japan. I also benefited greatly from the valuable cooperation and advice provided by Mr. Katsuhiko Tanabe, who translated German-language materials from Dresden for me, and by Mr. Nobuyuki Sato, who created chronologies for me in support of this effort. And, of course, all my friends from my days at the Kyodo News Foreign News Department, I deeply appreciate everything they have done.

At Shogakukan, I'd like to express my deepest gratitude to the late Mr. Hiroshi Araki, whom I have never forgotten since his passing many years ago. He was responsible for editing and publishing *Nixon's Memoirs* in 1978, which I had translated together with Mr. Ichiro Saita, my colleague also at the Kyodo News Foreign News Department. Mr. Araki's keen insight made possible the publication of that work, which has value even today, during a time when Nixon was severely criticized. Mr. Araki, who contributed to the publication of well-known Japanese weekly news magazines in their infancy, died in July 1985. I pray again that he shall rest in peace.

Mr. Kunimasa Endo, recently retired from Shogakukan, gave me the opportunity for this publication. I still live as one of the analog generation, but the very patient Mr. Ken Shiomi, who managed this project, warmly accepted my handwritten draft manuscript. I deeply appreciate him and his staff.

Lastly, I dedicate this book to my wife Naoko, who fell victim to misfortune and illness and who has been bedridden for more than ten years. Naoko has always supported and helped me with her excellent Sacred Heart–educated English in my unending work as a journalist over the years, including eleven hard years abroad as a foreign correspondent. After her hospitalization, our three daughters have taken her place in allowing me to pursue my work. I also dedicate this book to them.

Fumio Matsuo
December 2003

Notes

ONE   A Decoration for General LeMay

1. Thomas M. Coffey, *Iron Eagle: The Turbulent Life of General Curtis LeMay* (New York: Crown Publishers, Inc., 1988).

2. The term "precision bombing" is used to connote quite a different concept than it does today. In the context of World War II, it refers to the high-altitude daytime bombing using the powerful Norden bombsight. There was no intention to confuse this with the Global Positioning System (GPS) precision bombing used abundantly in the Iraq War. However, unlike nighttime indiscriminate incendiary bombing, the two have in common the primary objective of restricting attacks to military targets.

3. Regarding Generals LeMay and Arnold, other references used in addition to U.S. sources include numerous papers by National Defense Academy Professor Colonel Takashi Genda published in the JASDF research magazine, *Hoyu*. Colonel Genda has produced valuable information through his studies of the strategies of the U.S. Army Air Corps during World War II and the postwar U.S. Air Force.

4. Ronald Schaffer, *Wings of Judgment: American Bombing in World War II* (Oxford: Oxford University Press, 1988).

5. Richard Rhodes, "Annals of the Cold War: The General and World War III," *New Yorker*, June 19, 1995.

6. Albert Atkins, *Air Marshall Sir Arthur Harris and General Curtis E. LeMay: A Comparative Analytical Biography* (Writers Club Press, 2000).

7. According to reports in the *Washington Post*, May 22, 2003; the *Los Angeles Times*, May 23, 2003; and the *New York Observer*, September 29th, 2003. The movie *The Fog of War* debuted in the United States in February 2004.

8. David Halberstam, *The Best and the Brightest* (New York: Random House, 1969).

9. According to Doshisha University Professor Cary Otis, Henry Stimson was deeply impressed with the ancient city of Kyoto after having spent some time

with his wife sightseeing there and staying at the Miyako Hotel at the rate of 30 yen per night in October 1926. Cary Otis, "Mr. Stimson's 'Pet City': The Sparing of Kyoto," *Japan Quarterly*, October/December 1975, and "Atomic Bomb Target—Myths and Realities," *Japan Quarterly*, October/December 1979. The same issues with Kyoto are presented by Leon V. Sigal in *Fighting to a Finish: The Politics of War Termination in the United States and Japan, 1945* (New York: Cornell University Press, 1988). Both documents are laborious works covering the Japanese surrender following the atomic bomb through the Okinawa occupation period, and the resulting secret struggles of the military authorities in both the governments of Japan and the United States. Sigal is a graduate of Yale University, taught as a professor at Wesleyan University, and is currently serving as Director of the Northeast Asia Cooperative Security Project at the Social Science Research Council in New York.

10. Robert S. Norris, *Racing for the Bomb: General Leslie R. Groves, the Manhattan Project's Indispensable Man* (Hanover, NH: Steerforth Press, 2002).

11. General Curtis E. LeMay with MacKinlay Kantor, *Mission with LeMay: My Story* (New York: Doubleday, 1965). LeMay's statement about the number of victims at Hiroshima and Nagasaki is at odds with the facts. He was probably referring to the number who had died on the spot. According to the broadcast *Kaku no Jidai ni Ikiru Ningen no Kiroku* [Record of Survivors of the Nuclear Age] broadcast by the Japan Broadcasting Corporation (NHK) in August 2003, the number of atomic bomb casualties had reached 140,000 in Hiroshima and 70,000 in Nagasaki by the end of December 1945.

12. Rhodes, "Annals of the Cold War" (see note 5).

13. Ibid.

14. Ibid.

TWO The DNA of the Use of Force

1. Professor Tsuyoshi Shimamura of the Takushoku University Overseas State of Affairs Research Institute compiled detailed reports about the Timothy McVeigh–Terry Nichols terrorist bombing and paramilitary group organizations for the July, August, and October 1995 issues of the institute's periodical *Kaigai Jijo* [Foreign Affairs]. These were used as reference materials for this book.

2. Yukio Tomii, *Republicanism, Militias, and Gun Control: How to Read the Second Amendment* (Kyoto: Showado, 2002). I have learned much from Mr. Tomii's very comprehensive research and have pulled information from chap. 3.

3. The National Firearms Act of 1934 holds great significance as the first gun-control act in the history of the United States. Although it was enacted as part of the revenue code as a means of exacting tax from small arms sales, it had the effect of an anti-gang measure during the Prohibition era. Nevertheless, it was far from

Japanese-style gun control. At first the program was administered by the Internal Revenue Service (IRS) under the Department of the Treasury, but in 1972 management was transferred to the Bureau of Alcohol, Tobacco and Firearms (ATF), also under the Treasury Department. The ATF exercises gun control through the management of monopoly enterprises, and the equal footing of firearms with alcohol and tobacco is interesting. The ATF has been understaffed since the reductions in federal government personnel during the Reagan administration, and that weakening has contributed to the problem of school shootings. The Secret Service, famous for providing protection to VIPs such as the president, incidentally also belongs to the ATF. Subsequent gun-control legislation consisted of the Gun Control Act enacted in 1968 which regulated the possession of firearms according to age, criminal history, and other factors, and by which gun transactions in states fell under the federal licensing system; the Arms Export Control Act of 1976; and the Brady Bill enacted in 1993 and named for Press Secretary Brady who was wounded during the attempted assassination of President Reagan in 1981. The centerpiece of the Brady Bill is the NICS, an FBI-run system that conducts computer checks of the criminal histories of potential gun buyers for five days prior to gun purchases. In 1994, the Assault Weapons Ban was enacted with tougher restrictions on assault weapons like the AK 47 with their greater killing and wounding ability compared to handguns.

4. The state of America's gun society, which is 180 degrees different from Japan, is explained in a comprehensive and useful article titled "Beikoku no Juki Kanri Seisaku" [U.S. Firearms Management Policy], by Yoshiyuki Tsuji, in the February 2003 issue of *Keisatsugaku Ronshu* [The Journal of Police Science] 56, no. 2. This paper, which sums up the conditions and limits of gun control in the United States as seen through the eyes of Tsuji, a Japanese police officer who studied at Harvard University for two years after 2001. The work also presents in full detail a summary explanation of the differing firearms regulations.

5. John R. Lott, Jr., *More Guns, Less Crime: Understanding Crime and Gun-Control Laws* (Chicago: University of Chicago Press, 1998. Reprinted by the University of Chicago Press, 2000).

6. David B. Kopel, *The Samurai, the Mountie, and the Cowboy: Should America Adopt the Gun Controls of Other Democracies?* (Amherst, NY: Prometheus Books, 1992).

7. Regarding the relationship between U.S. gun crimes and regulatory laws, Professor Hiraku Tanaka of Hosei University advised me to continue comprehensive research in this area. Professor Tanaka's contributions to the periodicals *Horitsu no Hiroba* and *Jurist*, and his 1998 paper "Shogaikoku ni okeru Juki Josei ni kansuru Chosa Kenkyu" [Investigative Research on the Firearm Situation in Various Foreign Countries"], written for Japan's Public Policy Research Association, were used as references. Incidentally, the table of guns and small arms used in this book is common, and the noted weapons are classified as handguns, rifles, shotguns, and others, according to the FBI's Annual Report on Crime. Handguns account for a

little less than 60 percent of all weapons used.

8. Richard Poe, *The Seven Myths of Gun Control: Reclaiming the Truth About Guns, Crime, and the Second Amendment* (New York: Random House, 2001).

9. Laurence H. Tribe, *American Constitutional Law, First Edition* (Foundation Press, 1978), p. 226.

10. Laurence H. Tribe, *American Constitutional Law: Volume One, Third Edition* (Foundation Press, 2000), preface, p. vi.

11. Ibid, pp. 895–96, 903.

12. Katsumi Hiragi and Tim Talley, *Freeze! Peairs wa Naze Hattori-kun o Utta no ka?* [Freeze! Why Did Peairs Shoot Hattori?] (Tokyo: Shueisha, 1993).

THREE   Birth From "Disorder"

1. Leonard W. Levy, *Origins of the Bill of Rights* (New Haven: Yale University Press, 1999).

2. David E. Young, ed., *The Origin of the Second Amendment: A Documentary History of the Bill of Rights, 1787–1792* (Golden Oak Books, 1991).

3. In 1786, farmers in western Massachusetts suffering from debt resulting from an overproduction of agricultural goods after the War of Independence staged an armed uprising, led by Daniel Shays, and were put down by the state militia. This incident became the basis for the Federalist theory of the need for a federal central government.

4. Norio Akashi, *Tomasu Jeffaason to Jiyu no Teikoku no Rinen* [Thomas Jefferson and His Ideas for the Empire of Liberty] (Kyoto: Minerva Shobo, 1999).

5. Samuel Elliot Morrison, *Oxford History of the American People* (Oxford: Oxford University Press, 1965).

6. Irving Kristol, *Neoconservatism: The Autobiography of an Idea/Selected Essays, 1949–1995* (New York: Free Press, 1995).

7. Adam Smith, *An Inquiry into the Nature and Causes of the Wealth of Nations*, 1776.

FOUR   Of the *Mayflower's* Origin

1. Shigeharu Matsumoto, *Amerika Minshushugi Shiso no Genkei* (Sekai no Meicho 33) [The Prototype of American Democratic Thought (World Masterpieces 33)] (Tokyo: Chuo Koronsha, 1970).

2. C. Vann Woodword, ed., *The Comparative Approach to American History*, translated by Shoichi Oshita, Sadao Asada, and others, vol. 1, chap. 4, Robert R. Palmer's "Revolution," translated by Shoichi Oshita.

3. Morrison, *Oxford History of the American People* (see chap. 3, note 5).

4. Akashi, *Tomasu Jeffaason to Jiyu no Teikoku no Rinen* (see chap. 3, note 4).

5. Levy, *Origins of the Bill of Rights* (see chap 3, note 1).

6. Ibid, p. 149.

7. Makoto Saito, *Amerika Kakumeishi Kenkyu—Jiyu to Togo* [Studies in the History of the American Revolution: Liberty and Integration] (Tokyo: Tokyo University Press, 2001).

8. Makoto Saito, "Amerika Shakai Rikai no Shiteki Genten—Purimasu Shokumin-chi Keisei o Megutte" [A Historical Starting Point for Understanding American Society: The Establishment of Plymouth Plantation], *Kokusai Kisokyo Daigaku Gakuho, Shakai Kagaku Journal,* no. 29 (3), Professor Saito's Seventieth Birthday Edition, 1991, chap. 3.

9. David Beale, *The Mayflower Pilgrims: Roots of Puritan, Presbyterian, Congregationalist, and Baptist Heritage* (Greenville, SC: Ambassador-Emerald International, 2002).

10. Yasaka Takagi, *Beikoku Seijishi Josetsu* [An Introduction to American Political History], collection by Yasaka Takagi, vol. 1, *Amerikashi 1* [American History 1] (Tokyo: Tokyo University Press, 1931).

11. William Bradford, *Of Plymouth Plantation: 1620–1647,* introduction by Francis Murphy, Modern Library College Editions (New York: Random House, 1981).

12. Makoto Saito, "Minhei Seido to Kakumei Senso (1)—Amerika Dokuritsu Senso o Megutte" [The Militia System and the Revolutionary War (1):—The American War for Independence], *Kokka Gakkai Magazine* 104, nos. 3 and 4, March 1991. I learned much from these papers.

13. Harold L. Peterson, *Arms and Armament of the Pilgrims: 1620–1692* (Plymouth Plantation, Inc. and The Pilgrim Society, 1957).

14. *Mourt's Relation: A Journal of the Pilgrims at Plymouth,* with an introduction by Dwight B. Heath, from the original text of 1622 (Carlisle, MA: Applewood Books, 1963).

15. Morrison, *Oxford History of the American People* (see chap. 3, note 5).

16. Morrison Sharp, "Leadership and Democracy in the Early New England System of Defense," *American Historical Review,* 1944/45.

17. Makoto Saito, "Amerika Kakumei no Haikei toshite no Daikakusei" [The Great Awakening Against the Backdrop of the American Revolution], *Nippon Gakushiin Kiyo* [Proceedings of the Japan Academy] 51, no. 2, Special Edition, 1997.

18. Charles II declared war on the Netherlands in 1664 over the Dutch territorial colonies. He then presented them to his younger brother, the Duke of York, and thus gave rise to the present-day city of New York.

FIVE Belief in Manifest Destiny

1. Naoki Onishi, *Pirugurimu Faazaazu to iu Shinwa: Tsukurareta "Amerika Kenkoku"* [The Myth of the Pilgrim Fathers: The Manufactured "Founding of America"] (Tokyo: Kodansha Sensho Metier, 1998).

2. Alexis de Tocqueville, *Democracy in America*, vol. II, sec. 3, chap. 16, 1840.

3. Akashi, *Tomasu Jeffaason to Jiyu no Teikoku no Rinen* (see chap. 3, note 4).

4. Takeshi Igarashi, *Amerika no Kenkoku: Sono Koei to Shiren* [The Founding of America: Its Honor and Trials] (Tokyo: Tokyo University Press, 1984).

5. Foster Rhea Dulles, *China and America: The Story of their Relations Since 1784* (Princeton: Princeton University Press, 1946).

6. A.T. Steele, *The American People and China* (New York: McGraw-Hill Book Company, 1966).

7. Thomas R. Hietala, *Manifest Design: American Exceptionalism and Empire* (Ithaca, NY: Cornell University Press, 2003 edition).

8. James M. MacPherson, *Battle Cry of Freedom: The Civil War Era* (Oxford: Oxford University Press, Inc., 1988).

9. Townsend Harris, *The Complete Journals of Townsend Harris: First American Consul and Minister to Japan* (Tokyo: Charles E. Tuttle, 1930).

10. Michael A. Bellesiles, *Arming America: The Origins of a National Gun Culture* (New York: Random House, 2001).

SIX Discrimination and Exclusion

1. MacPherson, *Battle Cry of Freedom* (see chap. 5, note 8).

2. Based on the Missouri Compromise, Congress prohibited slavery in the territories north of lat. 36°30' N.

3. MacPherson, *Battle Cry of Freedom* (see chap. 5, note 8).

4. There has also been much research in Japan about slavery and the southern philosophical thinkers such as Jefferson and Mason, who were both Virginia slave owners and landowners instrumental in the development of American democracy. In his book *Amerika Kakumeishi Kenkyu– Jiyu to Togo* [Studies in the History of the American Revolution—Liberty and Integration] (Tokyo: Tokyo University Press, 1991), Makoto Saito maintained that both men disliked slavery and felt the anxiety of negative morality toward slave owners. Their slavery policies stopped at prohibition of the slave trade. Saito wrote that Jefferson reasoned in his draft Declaration of Independence that the British Crown and government had forced black slaves into the North American market against the will of the colonies. Under this position, Britain had the theoretical obligation for slavery and the colonists were psychologically exempt from responsibility.

5. In writing about the wars with the Native Americans, including this episode, I referred to all papers collected in the book *Amerika no Sensou: Dokuritsu kara Sekai Teikoku e* [America's Wars: From Independence to Global Empire] (Tokyo: Kodansha, 1985), edited by Kaname Sarutani, especially Torao Tomita's "Indian Seifuku Senso" [The Wars of Indian Conquest]. According to this work, the Cherokee tribe later responded to "civilization" by composing the Constitution of the Cherokee Nation in 1827, developing a Cherokee written language, publishing an English-language newspaper, and pursuing the dream of national independence. However, they were never recognized by the State of Georgia or the Supreme Court, and were eventually forced to relocate to the Oklahoma Territory.

6. See note 5.

7. Yasaka Takagi, *Beikoku Seijishi ni Okeru Tochi no Igi* [The Significance of Land in American Political History], vol. 1 (Tokyo: Tokyo University Press, 1970).

8. Michael A. Bellesiles, *Arming America: The Origins of a National Guard Culture* (New York: Random House, 2000).

9. Jack T. Levy, "Loaded Dice," *New Republic*, October 15, 2003.

SEVEN   The Standing Army and Multiracial Power

1. James Madison, "The Influence of the State and Federal Governments Compared," *Federalist* no. 46, 1788.

2. Levy, *Origins of the Bill of Rights* (see chap 3, note 1).

3. Torao Tomita, "Indian Seifuku Senso" ["The Indian Conquest Wars"], chap. 2 of *Amerika no Senso: Dokuritsu kara Sekai Teikoku e* [America's Wars: From Independence to Global Empire], edited by Kaname Sarutani.

4. During World War I, the number of conscripts totaled 2,810,296; in World War II, 10,110,104; in the Korean War, 1,529,539; and in the Vietnam War, 1,857,304. Incidentally, President Franklin Roosevelt signed the Selective Training and Service Act in November 1940, which became the first conscription law in peacetime, about one year before the Japanese attack on Pearl Harbor.

5. According to the national census of 2000, the U.S. population was 75.1 percent Caucasian, 12.3 percent black, 12.5 percent Hispanic, 3.7 percent Asian-Pacific Islander, and 0.9 percent Native American. The percentages of blacks, Asian-Pacific Islanders, and Native Americans in the active-duty military far exceeded the national average.

6. William Safire, *Safire's New Political Dictionary: The Definitive Guide to the New Language of Politics* (New York: Random House, 1993).

7. *Rikujo Kyogi Magajin* [Track and Field Magazine], special Mexico Olympics edition, 1968.

EIGHT The 1968 Watershed

1. Robert S. McNamara, *In Retrospect: The Tragedy and Lessons of Vietnam* (New York: Vintage, 1996).

2. Halberstam, *The Best and the Brightest* (see chap. 1, note 8).

3. Don Oberdorfer, *Tet!: The Turning Point in the Vietnam War* (Baltimore: John Hopkins University Press, 2001).

4. Theodore C. Sorensen, *Let the Word Go Forth: The Speeches, Statements, and Writings of John F. Kennedy 1947 to 1963* (New York: Delacorte Press, 1988).

5. Stanley Karnow, *Vietnam: A History: The First Complete Account of Vietnam at War* (New York: The Viking Press, 1983).

6. Robert L. Bartley, "Kennedy's Vietnam," *Wall Street Journal*, June 16, 2003.

7. Richard M. Nixon, *RN: The Memoirs of Richard M. Nixon* (New York: Grosset and Dunlap, 1978).

NINE The Real Neoconservatives

1. James Dobbins, John G. McGinn, Keith Crane, Seth G. Jones, Rollie Lal, Andrew Rathmell, Rachel M. Swanger, Anga Timilsina, "America's Role in Nation-Building—From Germany to Iraq" (RAND, 2003).

2. Irving Kristol, "The Neoconservative Persuasion," *Weekly Standard*, August 25, 2003.

3. The twenty-five signers of the PNAC's March 1997 "Statement of Principles" are as follows: Elliott Abrams, Gary Bauer, William J. Bennett, Jeb Bush, Dick Cheney, Eliot A. Cohen, Midge Decter, Paula Dobriansky, Steve Forbes, Aaron Friedberg, Francis Fukuyama, Frank Gaffney, Fred C. Ikle, Donald Kagan, Zalmay Khalilzad, I. Lewis Libby, Norman Podhoretz, Dan Quayle, Peter W. Rodman, Stephen P. Rosen, Henry S. Rowen, Donald Rumsfeld, Vin Weber, George Weigel, Paul Wolfowitz.

4. Max Boot, *The Savage Wars of Peace: Small Wars and the Rise of American Power* (New York: Basic Books, 2002).

5. Bill Keller, "How Paul Wolfowitz's Agenda Became the Bush Agenda," *New York Times Magazine*, September 22, 2002.

6. Safire, *Safire's New Political Dictionary* (see chap. 7, note 6).

7. The laborious book *Amerika no Hoshu to Riberaru* [America's Conservatives and Liberals] by Takeshi Sasaki studies the actions of Irving Kristol as the godfather of the neoconservatives as well as those of former Vice President Gore and other liberals of the Democratic Party.

8. Takemoto Iinuma, *Amerika: Shinhoshushugi no Jidai* [America: The Age of Neoconservatism] (Tokyo: Sanseido, 1983).

9. Kristol, *Neoconservatism: The Autobiography of an Idea* (see chap. 3, note 6).

TEN Counterattack and Exit

1. George Packer, "The Liberal Quandary Over Iraq," *New York Times Magazine*, December 8, 2002.

2. Max Boot, "America and the U.N.: Together Again?" *New York Times*, August 3, 2003.

3. Donald H. Rumsfeld, "Help Iraq to Help Itself," *Wall Street Journal*, September 29, 2003.

4. Francis Fukuyama, "Nation-Building 'Lite,'" *Wall Street Journal*, October 1, 2003.

EPILOGUE Can There Be Another "Dresden Reconciliation"?

1. Matsumoto, *Amerika Minshushugi Shiso no Genkei* (see chap. 4, note 1).

2. George Bush and Brent Scowcroft, *A World Transformed* (New York: Random House, 1998).

3. *Der Frauenkirche* was an ornate baroque cathedral that was preserved in its ruined state after the bombings. It was restored in July 2004 with funds that included contributions from the United States and Great Britain.

4. John W. Dower, *Embracing Defeat: Japan in the Wake of World War II* (New York: W. W. Norton, 1999).

5. Regarding the scene revolving around the *Enola Gay* exhibit in 1995, the account of museum director Mr. Martin Harwit, who resigned over the matter, has been translated precisely into Japanese. Martin Harwit, *An Exhibit Denied: Lobbying the History of the Enola Gay* (New York: Springer Verlag, 1996).

6. The year 2000 repeat-visitor rate for Tokyo Disneyland is fairly outdated. However, according to the *Nihon Keizai Shimbun*, statistics in 2003 compiled over the previous fourteen years showed that, while Tokyo Disneyland once ranked first in the world among theme parks for the number of visitors, it had fallen to second place. Even so, its 13 million visitors differed from the 14 million at first-place Magic Kingdom by only one million people, and exceeded the 12.7 million visitors at the original Disneyland in the United States. When combined with the 12 million visitors to the adjacent Tokyo Disney Sea, it unquestionably remains in first place.

Index

About the Author

FUMIO MATSUO is one of Japan's well-known international journalists, recognized as an expert on U.S. political affairs. Born in 1933, he joined Kyodo News in 1956 and served in the U.S. as a foreign correspondent from 1964 to 1969, covering the massive upheavals in U.S. society. In 1971, three months prior to Henry Kissinger's secret visit to China, Mr. Matsuo wrote an article titled "Nixon's America: Its Skillful Approach to China" in anticipation of the historic reconciliation between the U.S. and China. When his predictions proved correct, Mr. Matsuo became renowned for his keen insight on the American political arena. He published the book *Nixon's America* in 1972 and translated *The Memoirs of Richard Nixon* into Japanese in 1980. From 1972 to 1975 Mr. Matsuo was Kyodo's Bangkok Bureau Chief, where he witnessed the final phase of the Indochina War. From 1981 to 1984 he was Washington Bureau Chief, covering the first term of the Reagan administration. During the late '80s and '90s he was an executive at Kyodo News, and in 2002 he returned to active journalism as a specialist on the United States. "Tokyo Needs Its Dresden Moment," his editorial in the *Wall Street Journal* on August 16, 2005, generated significant discussion on the nature of reconciliation.

Mr. Matsuo majored in Political Science at Gakushuin University. He has lectured at the University of Tokyo's Institute of Journalism and Communication Studies, and is a trustee of the AFS (American Field Service) Japan Association. He is regularly invited to speak at Japanese and American universities. *Democracy with a Gun* was first published in Japanese in 2004 and won the 52nd Annual Award of the Japan Essayist Club.

About the Translator

DAVID REESE is a retired U.S. Air Force linguist now working as the Director of the U.S. Army Asian Studies Detachment at Camp Zama near Tokyo, Japan. He has lived and worked in Japan for a total of twenty-four years beginning in 1979. He holds an Associate of Applied Science degree in Interpreting and Translating from the Community College of the Air Force and a Bachelor of Arts degree in Business and Management from the University of Maryland with a secondary concentration in Asian Studies. Since 1991 he has worked as a Japanese-to-English translator for several U.S. Department of Defense agencies, and today operates his own successful freelance translation service in Japan. He is a member of the American Translators Association (ATA) and the Japan Association of Translators (JAT). *Democracy with a Gun* is his first commercially published book translation.